Bloom's Modern Critical Interpretations

Bloom's Modern Critical Interpretations

William Shakespeare's
Hamlet
New Edition

Edited and with an introduction by
Harold Bloom
Sterling Professor of the Humanities

Yale University

BLOOM'S
LITERARY CRITICISM
An imprint of Infobase Publishing

Bloom's Modern Critical Interpretations:
William Shakespeare's *Hamlet*—New Edition
Copyright © 2009 by Infobase Publishing

Introduction © 2009 by Harold Bloom

Bloom's Literary Criticism
An imprint of Infobase Publishing
132 West 31st Street
New York NY 10001

Library of Congress Cataloging-in-Publication Data

William Shakespeare's *Hamlet* / edited and with an introduction by Harold Bloom.
—New ed.
        p. cm.—(Bloom's modern critical interpretations)
Includes bibliographical references and index.
ISBN 978-1-60413-632-6 (acid-free paper)
1. Shakespeare, William, 1564–1616. *Hamlet*. 2. Hamlet (Legendary character)
I. Bloom, Harold. II. Title: *Hamlet*.

PR2807.W456 2009
822.3'3—dc22
                                2009018234

Bloom's Literary Criticism books are available at special discounts when purchased in
bulk quantities for businesses, associations, institutions, or sales promotions. Please call
our Special Sales Department in New York at (212) 967-8800 or (800) 322-8755.

You can find Bloom's Literary Criticism on the World Wide Web at
http://www.chelseahouse.com.

Cover design by Alicia Post

Printed in the United States of America
MP BCL 10 9 8 7 6 5 4 3 2 1

This book is printed on acid-free paper.

All links and Web addresses were checked and verified to be correct at the time of
publication. Because of the dynamic nature of the Web, some addresses and links
may have changed since publication and may no longer be valid.

Contents

Editor's Note

My introduction suggests "family romances," catastrophe-creation, and transference as three paradigms for studying *Hamlet*.

Daryl W. Palmer begins with a discussion of Hamlet's origins. Carolyn Sale rightly sees *Hamlet* as embodying a theory of performance, while Amy Cook and Lingui Yang apply cognitive science to interpreting the play.

The "City of London," commercial core of the capital, may have housed performances of *Hamlet*, if the argument of Paul Menzer proves correct.

T. S. Eliot's absurd declaration that *Hamlet* is an "aesthetic failure" is fully contextualized by Bradley Greenburg.

Ophelia's madness and suicide are clarified by Maria Del Sapio Garbero, after which Sayre N. Greenfield catalogs the copious quotations from *Hamlet* in the early seventeenth century.

Richard Levin concludes this volume with a wryly wise account of poor Gertrude's permanent bad press, vilified as she may have been by the Ghost and Hamlet, two males with one common grudge against her.

HAROLD BLOOM

Introduction

I

The last we see of Hamlet at the court in Act IV is his exit for England:

> HAMLET: For England?
> CLAUDIUS: Ay, Hamlet.
> HAMLET: Good.
> CLAUDIUS: So is it, if thou knew'st our purposes.
> HAMLET: I see a cherub that sees them. But come, for England!
>   Farewell, dear mother.
> CLAUDIUS: Thy loving father, Hamlet.
> HAMLET: My mother: father and mother is man and wife, man
>   and wife is one flesh—so my mother. Come, for England!
>   Exit

It is a critical commonplace to assert that the Hamlet of Act V is a changed man: mature rather than youthful, certainly quieter, if not quietistic, and some-how more attuned to divinity. Perhaps the truth is that he is at last himself, no longer afflicted by mourning and melancholia, by murderous jealousy and incessant rage. Certainly he is no longer haunted by his father's ghost. It may be that the desire for revenge is fading in him. In all of Act V he does not speak once of his dead father directly. There is a single reference to "my father's signet" which serves to seal up the doom of those poor schoolfellows, Rosencrantz and Guildenstern, and there is the curious

1

phrasing of "my king" rather than "my father" in the halfhearted rhetorical
question the prince addresses to Horatio:

> Does it not, think thee, stand me now upon—
> He that hath kill'd my king and whor'd my mother,
> Popp'd in between th'election and my hopes,
> Thrown out his angle for my proper life
> And with such coz'nage—is't not perfect conscience
> To quit him with this arm?

When Horatio responds that Claudius will hear shortly from England,
presumably that Rosencrantz and Guildenstern have been executed, Hamlet
rather ambiguously makes what might be read as a final vow of revenge:

> It will be short. The interim is mine.
> And a man's life's no more than to say "one."

However this is to be interpreted, Hamlet forms no plot, and is content
with a wise passivity, knowing that Claudius must act. Except for the scheme
of Claudius and Laertes, we and the prince might be confronted by a kind of
endless standoff. What seems clear is that the urgency of the earlier Hamlet
has gone. Instead, a mysterious and beautiful disinterestedness dominates this
truer Hamlet, who compels a universal love precisely because he is beyond
it, except for its exemplification by Horatio. What we overhear is an ethos so
original that we still cannot assimilate it:

> Sir, in my heart there was a kind of fighting
> That would not let me sleep. Methought I lay
> Worse than the routines in the bilboes. Rashly—
> And prais'd be rashness for it: let us know
> Our indiscretion sometimes serves us well
> When our deep plots do pall; and that should learn us
> There's a divinity that shapes our ends,
> Rough-hew them how we will—

Weakly read, that divinity is Jehovah, but more strongly "ends" here are
not our intentions but rather our fates, and the contrast is between a force
that can *shape* stone, and our wills that only hew roughly against implacable
substance. Nor would a strong reading find Calvin in the echoes of the Gospel
of Matthew as Hamlet sets aside his own: "Thou wouldst not think how ill
all's here about my heart." In his heart, there is again a kind of fighting, but
the readiness, rather than the ripeness, is now all:

Not a whit. We defy augury. There is special providence in the fall of a sparrow. If it be now, 'tis not to come; if it be not to come, it will be now; if it be not now, yet it will come. The readiness is all. Since no man, of aught he leaves, knows aught, what is't to leave betimes? Let be.

The apparent nihilism more than negates the text cited from Matthew, yet the epistemological despair does not present itself as despair, but as an achieved serenity. Above all else, these are not the accents of an avenger, or even of someone who still mourns, or who continues to suffer the selfish virtues of the natural heart. Not nihilism but authentic disinterestedness, and yet what is that? No Elizabethan lore, no reading in Aristotle, or even in Montaigne, can help to answer that question. We know the ethos of disinterestedness only because we know Hamlet. Nor can we hope to know Hamlet any better by knowing Freud. The dead father indeed was, during four acts, more powerful than even the living one could be, but by Act V the dead father is not even a numinous shadow. He is a merely a precursor, Hamlet the Dane before this one, and this one matters much more. The tragic hero in Shakespeare, at his most universally moving, is a representation so original that conceptually *he contains us*, and fashions our psychology of motives permanently. Our map or general theory of the mind may be Freud's, but Freud, like all the rest of us, inherits the representation of mind, at its most subtle and excellent, from Shakespeare. Freud could say that the aim of all life was death, but not that readiness is all.

II

Originality in regard to Shakespeare is a bewildering notion, because we have no rival to set him against. "The originals are not original," Emerson liked to remark, but he withdrew that observation in respect to Shakespeare. If Shakespeare had a direct precursor it had to be Marlowe, who was scarcely six months older. Yet, in comparison to Shakespeare, Marlowe represents persons only by caricature. The Chaucer who could give us the Pardoner or the Wife of Bath appears to be Shakespeare's only authentic English precursor, if we forget the English renderings of the Bible. Yet we do not take our psychology from Chaucer or even from the Bible. Like Freud himself, we owe our psychology to Shakespeare. Before Shakespeare, representations in literature may change *as* they speak, but they do not change *because* of what they say. Shakespearean representation turns upon his persons listening to themselves simultaneously with our listening, and learning and changing even as we learn and change. Falstaff delights himself as much as he delights us, and Hamlet modifies himself by studying his own modifications. Ever since, Falstaff has been the inescapable model for nearly all wit, and

Hamlet the paradigm for all introspection. When Yorick's skull replaces the helmeted ghost, then the mature Hamlet has replaced the self-chastising revenger, and a different sense of death's power over life has been created, and in more than a play or a dramatic poem:

> HAMLET: To what base uses we may return, Horatio! Why may not imagination trace the noble dust of Alexander, till it find it, stopping a bunghole?
> HORATIO: 'Twere to consider too curiously to consider so.
> HAMLET: No, faith, not a jot, but to follow him thither with modesty enough, and likelihood to lead it.

Probability leads possibility, likelihood beckons imagination on, and Alexander is essentially a surrogate for the dead father, the Danish Alexander. Passionately reductive, Hamlet would consign his own dust to the same likelihood, but there we part from him, with Horatio as our own surrogate. Hamlet's unique praise of Horatio sets forever the paradigm of the Shakespearean reader or playgoer in relation to the Shakespearean tragic hero:

> Dost thou hear?
> Since my dear soul was mistress of her choice,
> And could of men distinguish her election,
> Sh'ath seal'd thee for herself, for thou hast been
> As one, in suff'ring all, that suffers nothing . . .

Which means, not that Horatio and the reader do not suffer with Hamlet, but rather that truly they suffer nothing precisely because they learn from Hamlet the disinterestedness they themselves cannot exemplify, though in possibility somehow share. And they survive, to tell Hamlet's story "of accidental judgments" not so accidental and perhaps not judgments, since disinterestedness does not judge, and there are no accidents.

Only Hamlet, at the last, is disinterested, since the hero we see in Act V, despite his protestations, is now beyond love, which is not to say that he never loved Gertrude, or Ophelia, or the dead father, or poor Yorick for that matter. Hamlet is an actor? Yes, earlier, but not in Act V, where he has ceased also to be a play director, and finally even abandons the profession of poet. Language, so dominant as such in the earlier Hamlet, gives almost the illusion of transparency in his last speech, if only because he verges upon saying what cannot be said:

> You that look pale and tremble at this chance,
> That are but mutes or audience to this act,

Had I but time—as this fell sergeant, Death,
Is strict in his arrest—O, I could tell you—
But let it be.

Evidently he does know something of what he leaves, and we ache to
know what he could tell us, since it is Shakespeare's power to persuade us that
Hamlet has gained a crucial knowledge. One clue is the abiding theatrical
trope of "but mutes or audience," which suggests that the knowledge is itself
"of" illusion. But the trope is framed by two announcements to Horatio and
so to us—"I am dead"—and no other figure in Shakespeare seems to stand
so authoritatively on the threshold between the worlds of life and death.
When the hero's last speech moves between "O, I die, Horatio" and "the
rest is silence," there is a clear sense again that much more might be said,
concerning our world and not the "undiscovered country" of death. The hint
is that Hamlet could tell us something he has learned about the nature of
representation, because he has learned what it is that he himself represents.

Shakespeare gives Fortinbras the last word on this, but that word is
irony, since Fortinbras represents only the formula of repetition: like father,
like son. "The soldier's music and the rite of war" speak loudly for the dead
father, but not for this dead son, who had watched the army of Fortinbras
march past to gain its little patch of ground and had mused that: "Rightly to
be great / Is not to stir without great argument." The reader's last word has to
be Horatio's, who more truly than Fortinbras has Hamlet's dying voice: "and
from his mouth whose voice will draw on more," which only in a minor key
means draw more supporters to the election of Fortinbras. Horatio represents
the audience, while Fortinbras represents all the dead fathers.

III

We love Hamlet, then, for whatever reasons Horatio loves him. Of Horatio we
know best that what distinguishes him from Rosencrantz and Guildenstern,
and indeed from Polonius, Ophelia, Laertes, and Gertrude, is that Claudius
cannot use him. Critics have remarked upon Horatio's ambiguously shifting
status at the court of Denmark, and the late William Empson confessed a
certain irritation at Hamlet's discovery of virtues in Horatio that the prince
could not find in himself. Yet Shakespeare gives us a Hamlet we must love
while knowing our inferiority, since he has the qualities we lack, and so he
also gives us Horatio, our representative, who loves so stoically for the rest
of us. Horatio is loyal, and limited; skeptical as befits a fellow student of the
profoundly skeptical Hamlet, yet never skeptical about Hamlet. Take Horatio
out of the play, and you take us out of the play. The plot could be rearranged
to spare the wretched Rosencrantz and Guildenstern, even to spare Laertes,
let alone Fortinbras, but remove Horatio, and Hamlet becomes so estranged

from us that we scarcely can hope to account for that universality of appeal which is his, and the play's, most original characteristic.

Horatio, then, represents by way of our positive association with him; it is a commonplace, but not less true for that, to say that Hamlet represents by negation. I think this negation is Biblical in origin, which is why it seems so Freudian to us, because Freudian negation is Biblical and not Hegelian, as it were. Hamlet is Biblical rather than Homeric or Sophoclean. Like the Hebrew hero confronting Yahweh, Hamlet needs to be everything in himself yet knows the sense in which he is nothing in himself. What Hamlet takes back from repression is returned only cognitively, never affectively, so that in him thought is liberated from its sexual past, but at the high expense of a continued and augmenting sense of sexual disgust. And what Hamlet at first loves is what Biblical and Freudian man loves: the image of authority, the dead father, and the object of the dead father's love, who is also the object of Claudius' love. When Hamlet matures, or returns fully to himself, he transcends the love of authority, and ceases to love at all, and perhaps he can be said to be dying throughout all of Act V, and not just in the scene of the duel.

In Freud, we love authority, but authority does not love us in return. Nowhere in the play are we told, by Hamlet or by anyone else, of the love of the dead king for his son, but only for Gertrude. That Hamlet hovers always beyond our comprehension must be granted, yet he is not so far beyond as to cause us to see him with the vision of Fortinbras, rather than the vision of Horatio. We think of him not necessarily as royal, but more as noble, in the archaic sense of "noble" which is to be a seeing soul. It is surely no accident that Horatio is made to emphasize the word "noble" in his elegy for Hamlet, which contrasts angelic song to "the soldier's music" of Fortinbras. As a noble or seeing heart, Hamlet indeed sees feelingly. Short of T. S. Eliot's judgment that the play is an aesthetic failure, the oddest opinion in the *Hamlet* criticism of our time was that of W. H. Auden in his Ibsen essay, "Genius and Apostle," which contrasts Hamlet as a mere actor to Don Quixote as the antithesis of an actor:

> Hamlet lacks faith in God and in himself. Consequently he must define his existence in terms of others, e.g., I am the man whose mother married his uncle who murdered his father. He would like to become what the Greek tragic hero is, a creature of situation. Hence his inability to act, for he can only "act," i.e., play at possibilities.

Harold Goddard, whose *The Meaning of Shakespeare* (1951) seems to me still the most illuminating single book on Shakespeare, remarked that,

"Hamlet is his own Falstaff." In Goddard's spirit, I might venture the formula that Brutus plus Falstaff equals Hamlet, though "equals" is hardly an accurate word here. A better formula was proposed by A. C. Bradley, when he suggested that Hamlet was the only Shakespearean character whom we could think had written Shakespeare's plays. Goddard built on this by saying of Shakespeare: "He is an unfallen Hamlet." From a scholarly or any Formalist perspective, Goddard's aphorism is not criticism, but neither historical research nor Formalist modes of criticism have us much in learning to describe the unassimilated originality that Shakespearean representation still constitutes. Because we are formed by Shakespeare, paradoxically most fully where we cannot assimilate him, we are a little blinded by what might be called the originality of this originality. Only a few critics (A. D. Nuttall among them) have seen that the central element in this originality is its cognitive power. Without Shakespeare (and the Bible as his precursor text) we would not know of a literary representation that worked so as to compel "reality" (be it Platonic or Humean, Hegelian or Freudian) to reveal aspects of itself we previously could not discern. Such a representation cannot be considered antimimetic or an effect of language alone.

IV

One way, by no means unproductive, of accounting for the force of Shakespearean representation is to see it as the supreme instance of what the late Paul de Man called a poetics of modernity, of a revisionism of older literary conventions that at once subsumed and cancelled the illusions always present in all figurative language. Howard Felperin, working in de Man's mode, adroitly reads Macbeth's "modernity" as the dilemma of a figure totally unable to take his own nature for granted: "He cannot quite rest content in an action in which his role and his nature are determined in advance, but must continuously reinvent himself in the process of acting them out." In such a view, Macbeth is a strong misreading of a figure like Herod in the old morality plays. I would go further and suggest that the drama *Macbeth* is an allusive triumph over more formidable precursors, just as *King Lear* is. The Shakespearean Sublime, too strong to find agonists in Seneca or in the native tradition (even in Marlowe), and too remote from Athenian drama to feel its force, confronts instead the Sublime of the Bible. What breaks loose in the apocalyptic cosmos of *Macbeth* or of *Lear* is an energy of the abyss or the original chaos that is ignored in the priestly first chapter of Genesis, but which wars fiercely against Jehovah in crucial passages of Job, the Psalms, and Isaiah. To subsume and supersede the Bible could not have been the conscious ambition of Shakespeare, but if we are to measure the preternatural energies of *Macbeth* or of *Lear,* then we will require Job or Isaiah or certain Psalms as the standard of measurement.

What is the advance, cognitive and figurative, that Shakespearean representation achieves over Biblical depiction? The question is absurdly difficult, yet anything but meaningless. If Shakespeare has a true Western rival, then he is either the Yahwist, the Hebrew Bible's great original, or the Homer of the *Iliad*. Can there *be* an advance over Jacob or Achilles as representations of reality, whatever that is taken to be? What the question reduces to is the unanswerable: can there be advances in reality? The arts, as Hazlitt insisted, are not progressive, and if reality is, then its progression suspiciously resembles a speeding up of what Freud called the death drive. Reality testing, like the reality principle, is Freud's only transcendentalism, his last vestige of Platonism. Freud's own originality, as he deeply sensed, tends to evaporate when brought too near either to the originality of the Yahwist or to the originality of Shakespeare. This may be the true cause of the disaster that is *Moses and Monotheism,* and of Freud's own passion for the lunatic thesis that Shakespeare's plays were written by the Earl of Oxford.

By Nietzsche's genealogical test for the memorable, which is cognitive pain, Job is no more nor less forgettable than *Macbeth* or *Lear*. The rhetorical economy of Job's wife, in her one appearance, unmatchable even out of context, is overwhelming within context, and may have set for Shakespeare one of the limits of representation:

So went Satan forth from the presence of the Lord, and smote Job with sore boils from the sole of his foot unto his crown.
And he took him a potsherd to scrape himself withal; and he sat down among the ashes.
Then said his wife unto him, Dost thou still retain thine integrity? Curse God, and die.

Lear's Queen, the mother of Goneril, Regan, and Cordelia, had she survived to accompany her husband onto the heath, hardly could have said more in less. In Shakespeare's tragedies there are moments of compressed urgency that represent uncanny yet persuasive change with Biblical economy. The dying Edmund sees the bodies of Goneril and Regan brought in, and belatedly turns his lifetime about in four words: "Yet Edmund was belov'd." The phrase is a vain attempt to countermand his own order for the murder of Cordelia. "Yet Edmund was belov'd"—though loved by two fiends, the shock of knowing he was loved, unto death, undoes "mine own nature." One thinks of Hamlet's "Let be" that concludes his "We defy augury" speech, as he goes into the trap of Claudius' last plot. "Let be" epitomizes what I have called "disinterestedness," though Horatio's word "noble" may be more apt. That laconic "Let be," repeated as "Let it be" in Hamlet's death speech, is itself a kind of catastrophe creation, even as it marks another phase in Hamlet's release from what Freud called the family romance, and even as it compels another transference for our veneration to Hamlet. Catastrophe creation, family romance, transference: these are the stigmata and consequently the paradigms for imaginative originality in the Bible and, greatly shadowed, in Freud, and I suggest now that they can be useful paradigms for the apprehension of originality in Shakespeare's tragic representations. The fantasy of rescuing the mother from degradation is palpable in Hamlet; less palpable and far more revelatory is the sense in which the prince has molded himself into a pragmatic changeling. The ghost is armed for war, and Hamlet, grappling with Laertes in the graveyard, accurately warns Laertes (being to that extent his father's son) that as the prince he has something dangerous in him. But is Hamlet psychically ever armed for war? Claudius, popping in between the election and Hamlet's hopes, could have shrewdly pled more than his nephew's youth and inexperience while properly arguing that his own nature was better qualified for the throne. Hamlet, in the graveyard, shocked back from beyond affect, accurately indicates whose true son he first became as changeling:

> Alas, poor Yorick. I knew him, Horatio, a fellow of infinite jest, of most excellent fancy. He hath bore me on his back a thousand times, and now—how abhorred in my imagination it is. My gorge rises at it. Here hung those lips that I have kissed I know not how oft . . .

Harry Levin, for whom strong misreading is not serendipity but misfortune advises us that "Hamlet without *Hamlet* has been thought about all too much." One might reply, in all mildness, that little memorable has been written about *Hamlet* that does not fall into the mode of "Hamlet without *Hamlet*." Far more even than *Lear* or *Macbeth*, the play is the figure; the question of *Hamlet* only can be Hamlet. He does not move in a Sublime cosmos, and truly has no world except himself, which would appear to be what he has learned in the interim between Acts IV and V. Changelings who move from fantasy to fact are possible only in romance, and alas Shakespeare wrote the tragedy of Hamlet, and not the romance of Hamlet instead. But the originality of Shakespearean representation in tragedy, and particularly in *Hamlet*, hardly can be overstressed. Shakespeare's version of the family romance always compounds it with two other paradigms for his exuberant originality: with a catastrophe that creates and with a carrying across from earlier ambivalences within the audience to an ambivalence that is a kind of taboo settling in about the tragic hero like an aura. At the close of *Hamlet*, only Horatio and Fortinbras are survivors. Fortinbras presumably will be another warrior-king of Denmark. Horatio does not go home with us, but vanishes into the aura of Hamlet's afterlight, perhaps to serve as witness of Hamlet's story over and over again. The hero leaves us with a sense that finally he has fathered himself, that he was beyond our touch though not beyond our affections, and that the catastrophes he helped provoke have brought about, not a new creation, but a fresh revelation of what was latent in reality but not evident without his own disaster.

V

As a coda, I return to my earlier implication that Shakespearean originality is the consequence of diction or a will over language changing his characters, and not of language itself. More than any other writer, Shakespeare is able to exemplify how meaning gets started rather than just renewed. Auden remarked that Falstaff is free of the superego; there is no over-I or above-I for that triumph of wit. Nietzsche, attempting to represent a man without a superego, gave us Zarathustra, a mixed achievement in himself, but a very poor representation when read side by side with Falstaff. Falstaff or Zarathustra? No conceivable reader would choose the Nietzschean rather than the Shakespearean over-man. Falstaff indeed *is* how meaning gets started: by excess, overflow, emanation, contamination, the will to life. Zarathustra is a juggler of perspectives, a receptive will to interpretation. Poor Falstaff ends in tragedy; his catastrophe is his dreadfully authentic love for Hal. Zarathustra loves only a trope, the solar trajectory, and essentially is himself a trope; he is Nietzsche's metalepsis or transumption of the philosophical tradition. A Formalist critic would say that Falstaff is a trope also, a gorgeous and glowing hyperbole. Say rather that Falstaff is a representation, in himself, of how meaning gets started, of how invention is accomplished and manifested. But we remember Falstaff as we want to remember him, triumphant in the tavern, and not rejected in the street. We remember Hamlet as he wanted us to remember him, as Horatio remembers him, without having to neglect his end. Perhaps Hamlet is a representation, in himself, not just of how meaning gets started, but also of how meaning itself is invention, of how meaning refuses to be deferred or to be ended. Perhaps again that is why we can imagine Hamlet as the author of *Hamlet,* as the original we call Shakespeare.

DARYL W. PALMER

Hamlet's Northern Lineage: Masculinity, Climate, and the Mechanician in Early Modern Britain

"That all mental form being indefinite and ideal, realities must needs become cold. . . ."

—Coleridge, *Coleridge's Shakespeare Criticism*

For centuries, the study of early modern men has been troubled by Hamlet's famous declaration of grief: "But I have that within which passes show, / These but the trappings and the suits of woe."[1] In the play, Hamlet needs to justify his dull behavior before an unsympathetic audience. In critical commentaries, scholars have accepted this fact and gone on to search for what was "within," even as others have protested that the search was hollow.[2] In the essay that follows, I propose that we would be better served by focusing on the way Hamlet's rhetoric of justification evolves over the course of the play. As early modern observers would have done, I am inclined to ground this inquiry in regional and lineal terms. I will suggest that, as *Hamlet* unfolds, the prince aligns himself with the active voyagers of the frozen north by engaging with his environment and redefining himself in exoteric, or outward terms. How, I want to ask, do Hamlet's northern predecessors—real and fictional—inform the play's innovative apologia for early modern man?

Renaissance Drama, Volume 35 (2006): pp. 3–25. Copyright © 2006 Northwestern University Press.

Of course the context for such questioning is both humoral and geographical. To an extent rarely remarked, we have tended to nationalize gender in this period even though early modern observers paid more attention to what Mary Floyd-Wilson has termed "geohumoralism,"[3] the classical notion that habitat shapes human being. Writers such as Jean Bodin and Levinus Lemnius drew on Aristotle, Hippocrates, and Galen in order to elaborate this zonal vision.[4] In the hands of these commentators, classical notions of region (centered on the Mediterranean) merged with Macrobian cartography, which seemed to frame, even explain, fluidic and thermal variation in the human body. Other commentators, such as Giovanni Botero, paid scrupulous attention to the ways in which "situation" determined human being: "So we may see, that the Englishmen which inhabit a plaine and plentifull soile, have always prevailed against the Scots & Welshmen, who presuming upon the strength of their owne countrey, have divers times molested them."[5] According to these models, habitation exercised a profound and predictable influence on human behavior. In this context, Britain and its people were usually seen as "northern," an identity they shared with many other people who inhabited a region famous for its frostiness.[6] In *Famous Frosts and Frost Fairs in Great Britain*, William Andrews documents this thermal perception with a chronology of famous English winters, beginning in c.e. 134, when the Thames was frozen for two months.[7] With good reason, Macrobian cartographers located Britain in a larger territory they called "Europa Frigida." In his *Historia de gentibus septentrionalibus* (1555), Olaus Magnus describes the people of this region and celebrates their common identity:

> I have written above about the various activities of the northern peoples, looking at their violent struggles in war, their buildings, their social intercourse, and also the cheerful processions that entertain this race, who live under the influence of the harsher planets, and how they celebrate their feast days in the regular yearly course, as other nations do.[8]

Having chronicled the violent animosities between Poles and Swedes and Russians, the writer looks back and declares with complete confidence that his great work deals with a single "race" of people. It is no coincidence, I suggest, that the most discussed character in English literature is a Dane.

And how did such theorizing matter to notions of northern masculinity? As Mark Breitenberg has pointed out, "Masculinity is inherently anxious...."[9] Men fumbled about in the cold, searching for a way to justify their own versions of masculine identity. Climate only complicated this search. According to humoral theory, the steady dose of northern cold could either seal in a man's natural heat or undermine his masculinity. Floyd-Wilson describes

another layer of permutation: "The logic of inversion fixed the white northerner and the black southerner in an interdependent relationship: if the
southerner is hot and dry, then the northerner must be cold and moist; if the
southerner is weak and wise, the northerner must be strong and witless."[10] To
be sure, early modern Britons could find little comfort in this sort of identification. Floyd-Wilson writes, "to be white and British in the early modern
period was not a badge of superiority but cast one instead on the margins as
uncivil, slow-witted, and more bodily determined than those people living in
more temperate zones."[11] The author of *Batman uppon Bartholome* declares,
"in the bodies that colde hath the masterie over, the coulour is white, the haire
soft and straight, the wit hard and forgetful, little appetite, much sleep, heavie
in going and slow. . . ."[12] In this spirit, Lemnius points to northern "Dolts
and Asseheads."[13] Bodin simply declares that people of the north tend to be
beastly and cruel.[14]

Of course Britons resisted such verdicts, but the complexity of this
opposition has only begun to be studied. Floyd-Wilson explains, "In
both imaginative and non-imaginative literature, late sixteenth- and early
seventeenth-century English writers struggle to stabilize and rehabilitate
their northern identity."[15] We can mark the heterogeneity of this rhetoric in
the writings of two men, Raphael Holinshed and Robert Burton. Holinshed
recounts the year of Shakespeare's birth:

> The one and twentith of December began a frost, which continued
> so extremlie, that on Newyeares even, people went over and alongst
> the Thames on the ise from London bridge to Westminster. Some
> plaied at the football as boldlie there, as if it had been on the drie
> land: diverse of the court being then at Westminster, shot dailie at
> pricks set upon the Thames: and the people both men and women
> went on the Thames in greater numbers, than in anie street of the
> citie of London.[16]

In these and similar humoral histories, the chronicler records winter behavior alongside accessions and depositions. In fact, Holinshed savors the
winter cold, relishing the way it continues "so extremlie," transforming their
known world into a place of wonder. Thermal extremity inspires masculine
activity as Holinshed celebrates people (men?) who play "boldlie" and shoot
"at pricks." Unlike a number of his partisan colleagues, he makes no attempt
to celebrate the masculine mind. Perhaps bold football will compensate for
dull wits? Another version of this response can be found in Robert Burton's
Anatomy of Melancholy. As leaf after leaf charts the fluidic instabilities of
the masculine body, Burton arrives at a solution. Breitenberg explains,
"How can such potent internal pressure be released? By writing about it,

externalizing it, and especially by assigning it to someone other than one-self."[17] Of course Burton's efforts both underwrite and unsettle those of Holinshed. One man values thought, the other physical exertion. Both value writing, and the conversation proceeds in this manner. What stands out in the growing argument, as I hope to show, is a rather consistent attempt to emphasize the external.

Shakespeare, for his part, seems to have found this conversation irresist-ible. Cold permeates the plays. The word appears some 217 times, but more often—and with greater complexity—in the tragedies, histories, and roman-ces. As a backdrop to these more complex invocations, Shakespeare invokes winter to sound an old seasonal note of lack, as when Cleopatra recollects Antony: "For his bounty, / There was no winter in't" (5.2.86–87). Or the play-wright conjures up a chill when he wants to talk in traditional terms about justice and mortality. At the end of *Titus Andronicus*, Lucius addresses his dead father: "O, take this warm kiss on thy pale cold lips" (5.3.153). Likewise, Cleopatra gestures toward Antony's corpse: "This case of that huge spirit now is cold" (4.15.89). Quite suggestively, Shakespeare's characters use the same terms to talk about modesty. In this vein, Ferdinand tries to impress his purity upon his future father-in-law in *The Tempest:* "I warrant you, sir / The white cold virgin snow upon my heart / Abates the ardor of my liver" (4.1.54–56). On the other hand, Shakespeare's women often seem cold. Isabella in *Mea-sure for Measure* and Marina in *Pericles* come to mind (2.2.45; 4.6.139). In *Much Ado About Nothing*, Beatrice takes pride in her "cold blood" (1.1.130). But, as Paster points out, the codes of humoral temperature always seem to work against women, who are figured as inherently imperfect.[18]

In the comedies, men feel nipped and pinched by brumal experience that usually has much to do with failed romance and usually, via the discourse of humors, intimates a moist masculinity. When the King of Navarre and his cohorts don Muscovite costumes in order to woo the visiting ladies, the Princess sends them off in this spirit: "Twenty adieus, my frozen Muscovites" (5.2.265). Shakespeare carries the theme forward in *The Merchant of Venice*. Once the Moor discovers he has chosen the wrong casket and lost his chance for Portia's hand, he says, "Cold indeed, and labor lost: / Then farewell heat, and welcome frost!" (2.7.74–75).[19] Frost describes the suitor's penalty, for he has promised, if wrong, "Never to speak to lady afterward / In way of mar-riage" (2.1.41–42). In *All's Well That Ends Well*, the sage Lafew knows that the lords who prance before Helena will fail: "These boys are boys of ice, they'll none have [her]" (2.3.93–94). In *The Merry Wives of Windsor*, Falstaff cries, "Come, let me pour in some sack to the Thames water, for my belly's as cold as if I had swallow'd snowballs for pills to cool the reins" (3.5.21–24).

In his tragedies, Shakespeare leaves little doubt that inner cold cripples a man's capacity for violent action. In *Richard III*, the main character instructs

Buckingham how to speak with Hastings: "If he be leaden, icy, cold, unwilling, / Be thou so too, and so break off the talk" (3.1.176–177). At the end of the play, Richard describes his own weakness to himself in the same evolving language: "Cold fearful drops stand on my trembling flesh. / What do I fear? Myself? There's none else by" (5.3.181–182). For Richard, the cold that seeps into a man makes him tremulous. When Mowbray confronts Bullingbrook at the beginning of *Richard II,* he shows in his public address that he understands the implications of this sensibility. He wants to speak less than his adversary, but he must excuse himself: "Let not my cold words here accuse my zeal" (1.1.47). A heroic version of this condition emerges when Richard declares his sudden judgment against Bullingbrook:

> K. RICH: Six frozen winters spent
>   Return with welcome home from banishment.
> BULL: How long a time lies in one little word!
>   Four lagging winters and four wanton springs
>   End in a word: such is the breath of kings. (1.3.211–215)

As the play commences, Bullingbrook's sense of deprivation and dislocation is perfectly rendered by the king's seasonal sentence. The predicament has a long history in English literature. Old English lyrics such as "The Wanderer" and "The Seafarer" describe imposed exiles in this fashion. When set against these examples, Bullingbrook's situation seems like destiny. He does not choose winter, but confronts exile as so much snow and ice. What sets Bullingbrook apart is the way he chafes at his fate, eventually returning to his people as their ruler. When we hear Macbeth and Iago use the same terms, a paradigm of tragic incapacity becomes clear. On the verge of killing Duncan, Macbeth chides himself: "Words to the heat of deeds too cold breath gives" (2.1.61). In precisely the same spirit, Iago urges himself, "Ay, that's the way; / Dull not device by coldness and delay" (2.3.387–388). Cold overwhelms the willing minds of these male characters when it creeps inside them, unsought. Indeed, according to geohumoral theory, it makes these men too effeminate to carry out bloody business. Such examples suggest that Shakespeare, on many occasions, was perfectly content to follow geohumoral fashions.

When the playwright begins to figure such predicaments in terms of voyaging, a remarkable pattern of innovation begins to unfold. The plight of Sir Andrew in *Twelfth Night* signals the change. Paster observes that Sir Andrew's name marks "his phallic deficiencies just as his small wit, dry hand, scanty hair, and inability to cut high-stepping capers do: they are the bodily and behavioral signifiers of his lack of manly heat."[20] In other words, traditional notions of geohumoral destiny can certainly explain the man; but

Shakespeare sets a new course when Fabian describes Andrew's failure with Olivia: "you are now sail'd into the north of my lady's opinion, where you will hang like an icicle on a Dutchman's beard, unless you do redeem it by some laudable attempt either of valor or policy" (3.2.26–29). Andrew is northern man but also a failed mariner on a northerly course that will spell his doom. The reference to "a Dutchman's beard," as I discuss below, demands that the audience consider the character's masculinity in terms of contemporary voyage narratives, an interpretive leap that puts new emphasis on a man's outward and valorous engagement with the cold.

Of course northern voyaging begins with the 1553 expedition of Sir Hugh Willoughby which, under the London-based direction of Sebastian Cabot, aimed for Cathay. As old markets like Antwerp had begun to fail, English merchants pooled their funds in order to share the risk of seeking out eastern trading partners. Willoughby commanded the venture from the *Bona Esperanza*. Richard Chancellor, a skilled navigator, served as chief pilot and captain of the *Edward Bonaventure*. The *Bona Confidentia* completed the party, which departed on May 11. Here were Britons who, instead of simply accepting their fate, chose the frosty unknown.

Remarkable for its masculine boldness, the expedition also demands attention because of the way it counters the image of the dull-witted Englishman with the new "mechanician." The fact is, Willoughby and company were able to set sail because of a veritable explosion of English learning and technology in the 1540s.[21] John Dee seems to have orchestrated this ferment, which included the labor of skilled pilots, craftsmen, and mathematicians. Men such as Leonard Digges and Robert Recorde published important manuals that clearly demonstrated the Englishman's perspicacity. Chancellor, as well as anyone, seems to have embodied this new masculinity. Well known as a gifted pilot, a man capable of sailing boldly through frosty seas, Chancellor was much more. E.G.R. Taylor explains that the man "was a mathematician of such an order that Dee worked with him on equal terms, and he had a further talent, one which always commanded Dee's respect: he was a mechanician. . . ."[22] The *Oxford English Dictionary (OED)* quotes Dee and credits him with the invention of the word: "A Mechanicien, or a Mechanicall workman is he, whose skill is, without knowledge of Mathematicall demonstration, perfectly to worke and finishe any sensible worke. . . ."[23] In everything that happened during his northern voyages, Chancellor stood for this improved Englishman, the mechanician who converted theory into action. Of course it would be whimsical to argue that northern cold inspired this intellectual transformation, but the activities of Chancellor and his contemporaries certainly proved that male Britons could transcend the negative influences of their region.

Willoughby's great enterprise went forward without incident until the 30th of July, when the *Bona Esperanza* lost touch with the other ships in a heavy fog. After five days of searching for his companions, Willoughby pressed on to the east, wandering aimlessly for more than a month. Meanwhile, the winds grew contrary. The official log of the *Bona Esperanza* narrates the finale with a poet's eye for the exoteric:

> The next day being the 18th of September, we entered into the haven, and there came to an anker at 6 fadoms. This haven runneth into the maine, about two leagues, and is in bredth halfe a league, wherein were very many seale fishes, & other great fishes, and upon the maine we saw beares, great deere, foxes, with divers strange beasts, as guloines, and such other which were to us unknowen, and also wonderfull. Thus remaining in this haven the space of a weeke, seeing the yeare farre spent, & also very evill wether, as frost, snow, and haile, as though it had been the deeps of winter, we thought best to winter there.[24]

On that brutal September day the men believe they have found a "haven," but come to the extraordinary conclusion that they have traveled into winter. Reduced to animal-like responses, they aim to hibernate for the season among the other animals that inspire their wonder. By way of conclusion, "winter" becomes both noun and verb. Because people thought of seasons as "natural," an order ordained by the God, it made sense to adduce the coming and going of winter as evidence of a divinely ruled cosmos. A man took his place in that order, and winter happened to him. By contrast, Willoughby and his company break out of the old seasonal order by discovering a "wonderfull" new winter that gives shape to their struggle for survival. In ways that later generations would imitate, they write their own failure as a winter's tale. If bold enough, a man could transcend his geohumoral origins and choose the season that would ultimately explain his behavior.

No less compelling was the experience of Chancellor, who pushed forward and found himself in the Muscovy of Ivan the Terrible. To be sure, the pilot saw much that could be called exotic, but nothing more so than the Muscovite winter. Elaborating on Chancellor's account of the voyage, Clement Adams (Master of the Queen's Henchmen) transforms the Petrarchan discourse of fire and ice:

> The north parts of the Countrey are reported to be so cold, that the very ice or water which distilleth out of the moist wood which they lay upon the fire is presently congealed and frozen: the diversitie

growing suddenly to be so great, that in one and the selfe same firebrand, a man shall see both fire and ice.[25]

The idea of winter in Russia gave the Englishman a profoundly concrete way of writing about the yoking of elemental opposites, of temperature, and finally of intensity. Indeed, one could say that Chancellor's experience gave Petrarchan psychology a local habitation and a name. But it fell to Giles Fletcher to formulate the evolving aesthetic in a way that points directly to Shakespeare's management of his masculine characters: "The whole countrie differeth very much from it selfe, by reason of the yeare: so that a man would mervaile to see the great alteration and difference betwixte the winter, and the sommer in *Russia*."[26] Expanding on Adams's description of opposites, Fletcher concentrates on the problem of identity, on the problem of "selfe." Here was a Russian world whose climate modeled the unstable psychologies of human beings who live north of familiar civilizations and so very often "differ from themselves." By choosing to sail on into winter, Chancellor became a hero, but he also brought the English face to face with a disturbing reflection of themselves. To be northern is to differ from oneself. Famous for this behavior and his attempts to compensate for it, Hamlet might just as well have been a Russian.[27]

Surely, the advent of such frosty speculation would have been enough to mark an epoch, but the north called to a new generation of mariners whose exploits showed early modern men how to rewrite their masculinity. Some years after Willoughby's disaster, Richard Willes urged his contemporaries to seek a passage to the northwest, noting that "in the Northeast that noble Knight Syr Hugh Willoughbie perished for colde."[28] With visions of frozen failure fixed firmly in his mind, Martin Frobisher set out three times to triumph over the unseasonable cold. As Samuel Eliot Morison notes, Frobisher's exploits, along with those of Sir Humphrey Gilbert, constitute "a series of glorious failures."[29] Frost, snow, and ice sang like sirens to these men, whose journals echo each other with a poetics of entrapment and ruin that powerfully augment Surrey's new lyrics of failed love. What sonneteers merely thought, Frobisher and company enact with a highly evolved theatrical sense of ruin. Pointing to the way writers of voyage narratives shape their materials in terms of tragic conventions, Philip Edwards notes that such narratives "convert their own actions into theatre," with the failed hero at the center.[30] As Arthur Marotti, Martin Elsky, and Mary Fuller have pointed out, writing in the Renaissance is often about failure.[31] Whether the matter be lost labors of love or scuttled voyages of ambition, the writer's aim was often, in Fuller's words, to recuperate failure "by rhetoric, a rhetoric which in some ways even predicted failure."[32] It would seem that Shakespeare's Sir Andrew comes from a long line of losers and apologists.

Some years after the Willoughby tragedy, William Warner took up the matter of the leader's icy end in his *Albions England*. Warner's speaker envisions Willoughby and his crew as "Actors" whose deeds challenged the labors of Jason and Ulysses.[33] Willoughby was "a Knight both wise and his stoute," and Chancellor was a kind of Arthur.[34] Willoughby and party "weare in theat Climate Frozen dead, shut up with isie Driftes. / Thus died he and all with him, if so to die be death: / But no, faith Heaven, no faith their Fame, surviving there on Earth."[35] In these lines, Warner's speaker argues forcefully that men who hazard greatly and fail in the face of ice and snow must triumph for all eternity. Crucial to this rhetoric is the writer's insistence on the exoteric engagement as the measure of the man. "Isie Drifts" clearly ennoble defeat.

As well as any of his chilled brethren, Claudio, in *Measure for Measure*, illustrates Shakespeare's investment in this discourse of northern voyaging. Having violated Vienna's laws against premarital sex, Claudio will be executed. No one can fail to appreciate the extremity of the punishment, but Escalus creates a puzzle when he puts it into words:

> Well; heaven forgive him! and forgive us all!
> Some rise by sin, and some by virtue fall;
> Some run from brakes of ice and answer none,
> And some condemned for a fault alone. (2.1.37–40)

For generations of editors, this passage has proven opaque. Why ice? Editors have not been comfortable with the explanation. When they have been unable to account for the "ice," they have emended the text, as Kittredge did and the *Norton Shakespeare* does, to "vice."[36] Why would editors be insensitive to the cold? Or perhaps they are already too sensitive to the cold? Such whimsical questioning actually hints at the larger methodological issues addressed in this essay. Literary interpretation has always thrived on its special relationship with the esoteric, with inwardness, with entities we call "soul" and "spirit." When confronted with exoteric masculinity, the conscientious editor prefers "vice" to "ice."

We return to the "Dutchman's beard." Sarah M. Nutt has given us good reason to believe that Shakespeare was thinking of ice, more particularly Dutch explorer William Barents's experience of ice during three voyages to a string of islands off the northern coast of Russia, a region known as "Nova Zemlya." On the third voyage, in 1596, the expedition found itself trapped in the thickening ice. Against incredible odds, the party survived the winter there. De Veer published his narrative in Dutch in 1598; Latin, French, and German editions followed and circulated throughout Europe. An English translation, by William Phillip, appeared in 1609. For her part, Nutt has recounted this publishing history and described the detailed resemblances between De Veer's account and eight of Shakespeare's plays.[37] She urges us to read *Measure for Measure* alongside De Veer:

> The ice came so fast towards us, that all the ice whereon we lay with our scutes and our goods brake and ran one peece upon another, whereby we were in no small feare, for at that time most of our goods fell into the water. But we . . . drew our scutes further upon the ice towards the land . . . and as we went to fetch our goods we fell into the greatest trouble that ever we had before . . . [for] as we laid hold upon one peece thereof the rest sunke downe with the ice, and many times the ice brake under our owne feet. . . . And when we thought to draw up our boates upon the ice, the ice brake under us, and we were caried away with the scute and al by the driving ice.[38]

Escalus needs to explain how a man could end up in this preposterous position, and his language certainly draws from voyaging narratives of ensnarement, particularly De Veer's breathtaking prose of Arctic peril. What really confounds Escalus, however, is the irony that some (like De Veer and company?) are able to run safely from such pervasive disaster, while Claudio (like Willoughby and Frobisher?) find their fate sealed by something less, by "a fault alone." More than anything else, the invocation of northern voyaging foregrounds choice as an essential part of masculine definition. Barents and his company choose to sail north. Claudio simply discovers himself on thick ice. So much for puzzles.

More victim than champion, Claudio owes his predicament, in part, to a cold man. Lucio tells Isabella that Angelo is "a man whose blood / Is very snow-broth" (1.4.57–58). The wintery terms of Barents's Russian voyaging serve his theme as he concludes: "it is certain that when he [Angelo] makes water his urine is congeal'd ice, that I know to be true" (3.2.109–111). The utterly fallen angel, Angelo has succumbed to what Falstaff calls the cold of the belly. Like the Russian landscape, he differs from himself, demanding moral stricture while indulging his own licentiousness.

If Claudio turns out to be "better" than Angelo, this male aura depends on the way he comes to envision his fate, a boreality to be confronted. It is worth noting here that Claudio does not know what Escalus has said about ice; he does not borrow the figurative language of northern voyaging from the critical counselor. Instead, Shakespeare seems to be going out of his way to show Claudio choosing a frame for his plight as he talks to Isabella:

> Ay, but to die, and go we know not where;
> To lie in cold obstruction, and to rot;

This sensible warm motion to become
A kneaded clod; and the delighted spirit
To bathe in fiery floods, or to reside
In thrilling region of thick-ribbed ice;
To be imprison'd in the viewless winds
And blown with restless violence round about
The pendent world: or to be worse than worst
Of those that lawless and incertain thought
Imagine howling—'tis too horrible! (3.1.117–127)

Perhaps setting the agenda for later scholars, Alexander Gerard pointed to this passage in 1774 and concluded: "tho' each of the ideas is subservient to the end in view, yet they are so incongruous that they cannot be all adopted with propriety."[39] By now it should be clear that what Gerard calls congruity is really another example of Shakespeare's ongoing exploration of the way men explain their own endurance and worth. Ice is the proper region for northern man.

Just how horrible is this distinctively male predicament? Nutt points out that De Veer uses the descriptions of ice to heighten the drama of his chronicle: "'the ice came still more and more driving in, and made high hilles by sliding one upon the other.'"[40] In point of fact, De Veer adopts these icy terms in order to conjure up a stirring marvel: "'the ice was in such a won-derfull manner risen and piled up one upon the other that it was wonderfull, in such manner as if there had bin whole townes made of ice, with towres and bulwarkes round about them.'"[41] To be "incertain" and confront "cold obstruction" as Claudio does is to tap into the "wonderfull." By appropriating the popular Dutch discourse of northern voyaging, the prisoner can shift his consternation to a benumbed region of wonder that English travelers had described in vivid detail. In fact, Claudio recovers his will when he imagines himself a second De Veer: "Sweet sister, let me live" (3.1.132). Just as it does for Hamlet's temperament, the northern cold becomes a key to the moral mind of this character; and, like the Russian winter as Fletcher describes it, Claudio comes "to differ from himself." He seems to possess an interiority through that differing, and the wonder implicit in the experience of the exotic merges with his wonder at his "life."

Whatever the character gains through this matrix of reference, Shake-speare carefully husbands it over the remainder of the play. In the scene we have just been discussing, Isabella quickly chastises him for his self-interest. Claudio reconsiders and begs to speak with his sister, but the Duke ushers him away. The character speaks a few words in 4.2, and then remains silent until he takes his place in the Duke's orchestrations at the play's conclusion. Shakespeare has recuperated Claudio, after a fashion. What matters most for our discussion is the way this rehabilitation depends on an extraordinary synthesis of the old and the new. In Claudio, the ancient concern with internal cold merges with the contemporary interest in the exoteric assay.[42]

Sometime around 1599, in a burst of creative activity that produces *Julius Caesar* and *Hamlet,* Shakespeare sets his work apart from the ancient tradition when he divides the male population into men who are cold and men who choose the cold. (Claudio epitomizes the former category, while Willoughby and Chancellor embody the latter.) Near the beginning of *Julius Caesar,* Cassius invokes the rubric Hamlet will use when the prince attempts to justify his grief: "I know that virtue to be in you, Brutus, / As well as I do know your outward favor" (1.2.90–91). A man must be valued by some comparison of the inward and the outward. Caesar's confession to Antony frames Cassius's opinion:

> I do not know the man I should avoid
> So soon as that spare Cassius. He reads much,
> He is a great observer, and he looks
> Quite through the deeds of men.
> (1.2.200–203)

Regardless of how we judge him, Cassius surely lives up to Caesar's estimation as he explains masculinity to Brutus:

> I cannot tell what you or other men
> Think of this life; but, for my single self,
> I had as lief not be as live to be
> In awe of such a thing as I myself.
> I was born free as Caesar, so were you;
> We both have fed as well, and we can both
> Endure the winter's cold as well as he . . . (1.2.93–99)

No neutral observer, Cassius is all too aware that his fortunes have failed to keep pace with Caesar's, but this self-interest does not diminish his ability to scrutinize. Internal temperature does not matter in this analysis. Seeing through the deeds of men, for Cassius, means recognizing the male capacity for enduring winter's cold, a point the speaker supports with a story about swimming. He tells how Caesar, on a "raw and gusty day," said, "'Dar'st thou, Cassius, now / Leap in with me into this angry flood'" (100, 102–103). The formula is simple: we can value men by studying how they dare to embrace the cold.[43] On that day, Caesar sank. That Cassius braved the icy waters to save this "god" is now proof (for him) that something is rotten in Rome. Indeed, invoking the language of encompassment (so prevalent in the voyaging narratives), Cassius asks, "When could they say, till now, that talk'd of Rome, / That her wide walks encompass'd but one man?" (1.2.154–155). According to Cassius, to be "incompass'd" is the fate—perhaps the birthright—of all men. He resists Caesar's claims to special status even as he inflates himself through his narrative of an icy swim.

What Cassius inaugurates, Hamlet may be said to complete. From the first moments of the play, Hamlet appears to encourage boundless speculation: "But I have that within which passes show" (1.2.85). For centuries, critics have tried to pursue this claim. In the wake of Charles Lamb and Samuel Coleridge, Edward Dowden thought the play epitomized the value of "obscurity": "Hamlet might so easily have been manufactured into an enigma or a puzzle; and then the puzzle, if sufficient pains were bestowed, could be completely taken to pieces and explained. But Shakespeare created a mystery, and therefore it is forever suggestive; forever suggestive, and ever wholly explicable."[44] Sigmund Freud gave this "modern" appreciation of uncertainty a new twist when he began to detect Hamlet's unconscious desire for his mother, gradually coming to see himself in Hamlet. Freud concludes, "Here I have translated into conscious terms what was bound to remain unconscious in Hamlet's mind. . . ."[45] As a new century dawned, Hamlet possessed a willing mind whose obscurity could nonetheless be recovered by the aggressive analyst. Indeed it would be difficult to say whether Hamlet is the subject or the source of the analysis.[46] Bradley simply declares: "How many things still remain to say of Hamlet!"[47]

I begin with a simple fact: Hamlet, like everyone else in the tragedy, is cold. Who in Denmark would not want to go inside, whether we think of the interior space in terms of the mind or the edifice? When Kenneth Branagh directed his film version of the play, he whitened the landscape and the main character, perhaps setting a record for the use of artificial snow. The vision recalls the geohumoralism of *Batman uppon Bartholome,* with its emphasis on the whiteness of northern people. Branagh's screenplay begins in terms Willoughby could appreciate: "Darkness. Uneasy silence. The deep of a Winter's Night."[48] This seems right because the playwright takes pains to stress the frigidity of the environment from the opening lines. As Francisco says somewhat cryptically at the beginning of the drama, "For this relief much thanks. 'Tis bitter cold, / And I am sick at heart" (1.1.8–9). In Denmark, the cold indicates the condition of a solitary man, whose ailment will never be adequately communicated. Indeed, Francisco departs the stage and the play as a frosty cipher.

Garbed in an inky cloak, Hamlet takes Francisco's place, answering questions with riddles, quips, and puns. Sick at heart, he does not fit the old model of northern masculinity. Floyd-Wilson sharpens this sense: "In its representation of a melancholic *Dane,* Shakespeare's play tells the story of an extraordinary northerner—extraordinary because his inward melancholy has estranged him from his native, northern complexion."[49] Hamlet acts too little and thinks too much. Claudius makes the obvious point that the prince has given in to "unmanly grief" (1.2.94). By contrast, Hamlet's father embraced his native cold. Here was the traditional northern monarch, untroubled by cogitation, who "smote the sledded [Polacks] on the ice" (1.1.63). Here was the king who "Did slay this Fortinbras" (1. 1.86) on the day of his son's birth. Hamlet, it seems, was born under the sign of his father's prowess. Measured against this example, Hamlet appears to be an extraordinary failure, a passive victim. And it is at this juncture in the play that Hamlet defends himself by claiming to "have that within which passes show." Left alone, the man reverts to the old indictment: "O that this too too sallied flesh would melt, / Thaw, and resolve itself into a dew!" (1.2.129–130). Hamlet longs to "melt" and "thaw," a desire that reveals much about the way he sees himself in the world. He is a man of ice who has nearly succumbed to the cold. As Sidney Warhaft pointed out some time ago, Hamlet's sense of his flesh as something that would melt (and here, I am inclined to favor "solid flesh") certainly suggests the character's humorous condition, namely the cold and congealed body of a melancholy man, the estranged Dane, a failed man whose only recourse is silence.[50]

In fact, Hamlet has already begun to tinker with the old rhetoric, thinking through the cold in unprecedented ways. Although an ardent spokesman for Hamlet's inwardness, Coleridge helps to explain this innovation when he remarks the way that Hamlet's "half embodyings of thoughts, that make them more than thoughts, give them an outness, a reality *sui generis,* and yet retain their correspondence and shadowy approach to the images and movements within."[51] Coleridge, I believe, has pinpointed Shakespeare's strategy of rapprochement. For example, Hamlet's decision to think about himself as snow and ice "half-embodies" his condition. In this spirit, Hamlet rattles Horatio by seeing his father. The friend looks about, but Hamlet explains, "In my mind's eye, Horatio" (1.2.185). Over the course of the play, Hamlet will justify himself, by straddling thought and action, interiority and exteriority, erecting a field of "outness" around him that has stabilized his challenged masculinity for more than four centuries. The irony, of course, is that Hamlet's cognitive innovation does nothing to lessen the chill. With his usual intuitive genius, Coleridge, as quoted above in this essay's epigraph, diagnoses an "exhaustion of bodily feeling from perpetual exertion of mind," concluding "that all mental form being indefinite and ideal, realities must needs become cold" Hamlet attempts to survive his ordeal with half-embodying thought, but his behavior only heightens the cold.

When Hamlet decides to go out into the cold to confront the Ghost, he seems to accept the challenge set forth in the voyaging narratives. How appropriate then that as Hamlet waits for the Ghost, he declares: "The air bites shrowdly, it is very cold" (1.4.1). An Elizabethan might have wondered whether there was something effeminate in this cold, in its shrewishness, but Shakespeare emphasizes what is outside the man, namely the biting northern "air." Horatio foretells a change in the wind when he calls it a "nipping and eager air" (1.4.2). In the Danish chill, the men listen to the king's wassail, and Hamlet laments the northern propensity for "heavy-headed revel" (1.4.17). The proud prince aims for a better "attribute" (1.4.22). Indeed, we can mark his transformation when Horatio and company try to prevent him from departing with the Ghost. Hamlet declares, "My fate cries out, / And makes each petty artere in this body / As hardy as the Nemean lion's nerve" (1.4.81–83). Cold actually fortifies his body. He seems ready to follow the example of his martial father as he learns of his uncle's crime: "And thy commandment all alone shall live" (1.5.102).

To be sure, Hamlet's half-embodying thoughts immediately complicate this agenda. Having promised action, Hamlet should gather his comrades. Marcellus yells, "Illo, ho, ho, my lord!" (1.5.115). Hamlet cries: "Hillo, ho, ho, boy! Come, [bird,] come" (1.5.116). The prince has not officially assumed his antic disposition, but his thinking seems already to have made it so. In his giddy mood, Hamlet half-embodies his newfound purpose. He plays the part of a falconer calling down his bird. The inspiration is aural, the application fair, the utility in question. As the group interview begins, Horatio begins to doubt: "These are but wild and whirling words" (1.5.133). Hamlet apologizes and comes to the purpose; but his survival strategy has already begun to emerge. Henceforth he will "bear" himself in a "strange or odd" fashion (1.5.170). He will, in other words, justify himself by casting his outness as madness. Claudius glosses the effect:

> Something have you heard
> Of Hamlet's transformation; so call it,
> Sith nor th' exterior nor the inward man
> Resembles that it was. (2.2.4–7)

No simple disguise, Hamlet's "transformation" unsettles Claudius because of the way he differs from himself, inside and out.

What we make of this strategy has everything to do with the way the playwright engages the discourse of northern voyaging. When Rosencrantz and Guildenstern come snooping, Hamlet clues them in with a famous line: "I am but mad north-north-west" (2.2.378). The declaration may suggest mere flippancy, but I hear Hamlet claiming his position as yet another northern male in Willoughby's line, encompassed by extremes, near mad with dejection, epitomizing the fate of heroic masculinity. We step back in awe at this transformation, but Hamlet remains unsatisfied and quite mad. It is worth noting in this context that, according to the *OED,* for centuries before the writing of *Hamlet,* "mad" referred not only to insanity but also to being "'Beside oneself' with anger, moved to uncontrollable rage; furious."[52] For Hamlet, the problem is how to translate mere (even effeminate) fury into the more masculine *wrath.*[53] His lack of success on this score finds voice as he prepares to depart Denmark for England, only to witness the army of Fortinbras and wonder "How all occasions do inform against me" (4.4.32). Like Willoughby and Frobisher, he claims our attention because he has failed. Environed by icy circumstance, he poses the obvious question: "What is a man . . . ?" (4.4.33).

Shakespeare's answer comes straight from the nexus of climate and voyaging that we have been charting. Indeed, Chancellor, the man who helped Dee invent the paradoxal compass, the man who combined action and thought in the role of the mechanician, serves as a key to Hamlet's evolving experiment. Long before he reaches the despair of 4.4, he writes to Ophelia and promises love "whilst this machine is to him" (2.2.124). Capable of half-materializing thought, of mingling the inward and the outward, Hamlet identifies his own body as a "machine." The *OED* credits Shakespeare with the invention of this notion and so calls attention to the playwright's real innovation. What is particularly remarkable about this tack is the way the word "machine" floats between the substantial and the insubstantial, referring (as the *OED* explains) to structures "of any kind, material or immaterial."[54] Confronting his native cold with a fluidic body that seems to have failed him, Hamlet reinvents the male body as a machine. Even more ambitiously, he becomes his own mechanician.

As Chancellor might have done, Shakespeare goes on to suggest that a man is a person who sets out on a voyage. Of course he does not choose the venture; but, once at sea, Hamlet performs deeds of valor. He reports to Horatio: "Finding ourselves too slow of sail, we put on a compell'd valor, and in the grapple I boarded them" (4.6.17–19). Inspired by his own swashbuckling, Hamlet now discerns his opportunity. When Shakespeare gets Hamlet out of Denmark and into the pirates' custody, he makes it possible for Hamlet to choose to return to the "bitter cold" of his homeland. Hamlet may possess a sense of his own inwardness, but his experience under sail exposes the exoteric protocols of masculinity that he needs. Back in Denmark, Hamlet writes to Claudius and signals his explicit transformation by promising to "recount the occasion of my sudden [and more strange] return" (4.7.46–47). Hamlet is now master of his own occasion, but Hamlet's penchant for outness makes him pause.

Hamlet returns to the old question with clarity: "What is a man?" No longer focused on rhetorics of self-justification and survival, Hamlet exploits his habitual outness with an eye toward more enduring questions: "Why may not imagination trace the noble dust of Alexander, till 'a find it stopping a bunghole?" (5.1.203–204). Ever the pragmatist, Horatio counsels against such musing, but Hamlet proceeds to recast the old masculine engagement with winter:

> Alexander died, Alexander was buried, Alexander returneth to
> dust, the dust is earth, of earth we make loam, and why of that loam
> whereto he was converted might they not stop a beer-barrel?
> Imperious Caesar, dead and turn'd to clay,
> Might stop a hole to keep the wind away.
> O that that earth which kept the world in awe
> Should patch a wall t' expel the [winter's] flaw! (5.1.208–216)

I quote the passage at length because Shakespeare's hand is so evidently marking the dynamic quality of this frosty speculation as a movement into lyrical resolution. Alexander is "converted" to loam, to matter for a "stop," in prose that suggests logical demonstration; but Hamlet teaches his conclusion in verse, in couplets that emphasize the utter mutability of life. Having chosen to face the cold of his native land with all the problems it holds for him, Hamlet has satisfied a certain standard of masculine behavior. Yet he has come to understand that a man may justify himself for a time and still end up a patch, a rich word, both noun and verb, that referred to both a mechanician's repair and a fool.[55] In this way, Hamlet's outness bears fruit in the shape of skeptical wisdom: Hamlet sees through the deeds of men. Botero helps us value the prince's achievement. Questioning whether a man requires courage or wisdom most, the writer opts for courage because "wise-dome is given but to fewe, and that must be gotten too by travail."[56] At the end of the play, Hamlet has demonstrated both courage and wisdom. Like the accomplished mechanician, he can finish what he cannot demonstrate.

By the time Hamlet receives Osric, he has outmaneuvered the old thermal tests, and we measure his superiority against the lesser man. Osric thinks it very hot, but Hamlet applies correction: "No, believe me, 'tis very cold, the wind is northerly" (5.2.95). It is telling that both times Hamlet indicates direction (hearkening back to 2.2.378), he does it aggressively while in the company of lesser men who irritate him. In both scenes, the direction implies his superiority. He is not the muddled prince who cannot act, but a man encompassed by northern cold that elevates him even as it afflicts him. Such subtleties escape Osric's notice, and Hamlet toys with him. When the courtier agrees with Hamlet's temperature reading, the prince tells him, "But yet methinks it is very [sultry] and hot [for] my complexion" (5.2.98–99). Having mastered the old discourse of voyaging and cold, Hamlet amuses himself with a "yes man." After Osric departs, Hamlet comes to the point: "Thus has he, and many more of the same breed that I know the drossy age dotes on, only got the tune of the time, and out of an habit of encounter, a kind of [yesty] collection" (5.2.188–191). The Folio points more precisely to Hamlet's sentiments as he complains of this breed that has only got an "outward habit of encounter." Like Rosencrantz and Guildenstern, Osric thinks he can define his masculinity with little exoteric formulas of civility, but he seriously underestimates the venture.[57] These men stand as the real failures in the tragedy because they do not rescue their prince.

For his part, Hamlet has grown into the role of mechanician as Dee defined it. Shuttling between thought and action, the material and the immaterial, Hamlet discovers how to finish his "sensible work." With no boasts of what he holds within, he walks "here in the hall," in "the breathing time of day" (5.2.173–174). As the Folio emphasizes, Hamlet's attempt at a formal reconciliation with Laertes carries with it a nod to their quite public "audience" (5.2.240). Their contest occurs before judges who "bear a wary eye" (5.2.279). When the first hit comes, it is "palpable" (5.2.281). In the aftermath of the carnage, Fortinbras, who seems never to have questioned his outward obligations, gives the exoteric order: "Take up the bodies" (5.2.401). Branagh's film version of the play surely captures the exteriority of Hamlet's end as we look down on the pearly prince at rest in an open casket suspended above the snow.

In 1598, the Thames froze solid, as it had done many times before, and people probably tried to read the event as a sign of the times. Perhaps Shakespeare was thinking about *Hamlet.* Today, we may follow scientists who talk about our playwright's epoch as "The Little Ice Age," a chilly era that engulfed the whole of Europe. Most of us will continue to think about Hamlet, the supreme representative of this age, who takes his place in a long line of men who sought to redeem themselves through engagement with the frozen north. If he manages to rehabilitate northern masculinity, we must admit that it comes with the heavy burden of skepticism. Some 325 years later, Wallace Stevens was able to fathom the heart of this discourse for a warmer world, refashioning Hamlet's early modern speculations into a modern "mind of winter," "the listener, who listens in the snow, / And, nothing himself, beholds / Nothing that is not there and the nothing that is."[58]

NOTES

1. William Shakespeare, *Hamlet* in *The Riverside Shakespeare,* ed. G. Blakemore Evans (New York: Houghton Mifflin, 1974), 1.2.85–86. Subsequent references to the plays of Shakespeare will be from this edition and appear parenthetically in the text.

2. The scholarship devoted to this question is extensive, to say the least. One might well begin with Sigmund Freud, who has seemed to underwrite the study

of inwardness in the Renaissance, particularly with his reading of *Hamlet*. In fact, Freud points in another direction when he discusses being as an ego-effect. In "The Ego and the Id," he explains, "The ego is first and foremost a bodily ego; it is not merely a surface entity, but is itself the projection of a surface" (*The Standard Edition of the Complete Psychological Works of Sigmund Freud*, 24 vols., trans. and ed. James Strachey, [London: Hogarth Press, 1961] 19:26). Katharine Eisaman Maus offers perhaps the most cogent account of the controversy by arguing persuasively that the early modern stage afforded its audiences "inwardness displayed: an inwardness, in other words, that has already ceased to exist" (*Inwardness and Theater in The English Renaissance* [Chicago: University of Chicago Press, 1996], 32). Other crucial discussions of this problem include Francis Barker, *The Tremulous Private Body* (London: Methuen, 1984); Cynthia Marshall, "Man of Steel Done Got the Blues: Melancholic Subversion of Presence in *Antony and Cleopatra*," *Shakespeare Quarterly* 44.4 (1993): 386; Mark Breitenberg, *Anxious Masculinity in Early Modern England* (Cambridge: Cambridge University Press, 1996), 15; and Michael C. Schoenfeldt, *Bodies and Selves in Early Modern England: Physiology and Inwardness in Spenser, Shakespeare, Herbert, and Milton* (Cambridge: Cambridge University Press, 1999), 2, 76.

3. Mary Floyd-Wilson, *English Ethnicity and Race in Early Modern Drama* (Cambridge: Cambridge University Press, 2003), 2. See also Mary Floyd-Wilson, "Transmigrations: Crossing Regional and Gender Boundaries in *Antony and Cleopatra*," *Enacting Gender on the English Renaissance Stage*, ed. Viviana Comensoli and Anne Russell (Urbana: University of Illinois Press, 1999), 77.

4. John Wands, "The Theory of Climate in the English Renaissance and *Mundus Alter et Idem*," *Acta Conventus Neo-Latini Sanctandreani, Medieval and Renaissance Texts and Studies*, ed. I. D. McFarlane, vol. 38 (Binghamton, N.Y.: Medieval and Renaissance Texts and Studies, 1986), 519–520. Floyd-Wilson provides a useful bibliography for this tradition (*English Ethnicity*, 3).

5. Giovanni Bolero, *Historicall Description of the Most Famous Kingdomes and Common-weales in the World* (London, 1603), 7.

6. Bolero, by contrast, seems content to include Britain in Europe, which he describes as "passing good, holsome, temperate, and the solie exceeding fertile" (*Historicall Description of the Most Famous Kingdomes*, 10).

7. William Andrews, *Famous Frosts and Frost Fairs in Great Britain* (London: George Redway, 1887).

8. Olaus Magnus, *Historia de Gentibus Septentrionalibus*, trans. Peter Fisher and Humphrey Higgens, ed. Peter Foote (London: Hakluyt Society, 1998), 3:771.

9. Breitenberg, *Anxious Masculinity*, 2. In recent years, scholars have paid increasing attention to the unstable nature of masculinity, particularly in the plays of Shakespeare. See, for example, Coppélia Kahn, *Roman Shakespeare: Warriors, Wounds, and Women* (London and New York: Routledge, 1997); Geraldo U. de Sousa, *Shakespeare's Cross-Cultural Encounters* (Houndmills and London: Macmillan, 1999), *The Image of Manhood in Early Modern Literature*, ed. Andrew P. Williams (Westport, Conn.: Greenwood Press, 1999); Bruce R. Smith, *Shakespeare and Masculinity* (Oxford: Oxford University Press, 2000); Robin Headlam Wells, *Shakespeare on Masculinity* (Cambridge: Cambridge University Press, 2000); Alexandra Shepard, *Meanings of Manhood in Early Modern England* (Oxford: Oxford University Press, 2003).

10. Floyd-Wilson, *English Ethnicity*, 3. Of course all recent studies of humoral theory in the Renaissance owe something to the work of Gail Kern Paster. See, for example, Gail Kern Paster, "The Unbearable Coldness of Female Being: Women's Imperfection and the Humoral Economy," *English Literary Renaissance* 28.3 (1998): 416.

11. Floyd-Wilson, *English Ethnicity*, 4–5. See also Floyd-Wilson, "Transmigrations," 75.

12. Stephen Batman, *Batman uppon Bartholome* (London, 1582), 26.

13. Levinus Lemnius, *The Touchstone of Complexions*, trans. Thomas Newton (London, 1633), 25.

14. Jean Bodin, *The Six Bookes of a Commonweale*, ed. Kenneth Douglas McRae (Cambridge: Harvard University Press, 1962), 99.

15. Floyd-Wilson, *English Ethnicity*, 4.

16. *Holinshed's Chronicles*, 6 vols. (London: Johnson, 1808), 4:228; qtd. in Andrews, *Frost Fairs*, 8.

17. Breitenberg, *Anxious Masculinity*, 68.

18. Paster, "The Unbearable Coldness of Female Being," 439–440.

19. For an important geohumoral revision of the usual reading of Morocco's failure, see Floyd-Wilson, *English Ethnicity*, 42–43.

20. Paster, "The Unbearable Coldness of Female Being," 435.

21. On this phenomenon in particular and English contact with Russia in general, see Daryl W. Palmer, *Writing Russia in the Age of Shakespeare* (Aldershot and Burlington, U.K.: Ashgate, 2004), 9–11, and passim.

22. E. G. R. Taylor, *Tudor Geography 1485–1583* (London: Methuen, 1930), 91.

23. *Oxford English Dictionary*, s.v. "mechanician," n. 1.

24. Hakluyt, *Principal Navigations, Voyages, Traffiques, and Discoveries of the English Nation*, 8 vols. (London: J. M. Dent, 1927), 1:253.

25. Hakluyt, *Principal Navigations*, 1:279.

26. Giles Fletcher, *The English Works of Giles Fletcher, the Elder*, ed. Lloyd E. Berry (Madison: University of Wisconsin Press, 1964), 175.

27. Moved by ethological similarities, nineteenth-century writer and artist William Morris declared to Georgiana Burne-Jones that "Hamlet . . . should have been a Russian, not a Dane" (March 17, 1888, letter 1470, *The Collected Letters of William Morris*, ed. Norman Kelvin, vol. 2, pt. b, 1885–1888 [Princeton: Princeton University Press, 1987], 755).

28. Hakluyt, *Principal Navigations*, 5:121.

29. Samuel Eliot Morison, *The Great Explorers* (New York: Oxford University Press, 1978), 277.

30. Philip Edwards, "Tragic Form and the Voyagers," *Travel and Drama in Shakespeare's Time*, ed. Jean-Pierre Maquerlot and Michele Willems (Cambridge: Cambridge University Press, 1996), 82.

31. Arthur Moroni, "'Love is not Love': Elizabethan Sonnet Sequences and the Social Order," *ELH* 49.2 (1982): 398; Martin Elsky, *Authorizing Words: Speech, Writing, and Print in the English Renaissance* (Ithaca, N.Y.: Cornell University Press, 1989), 188–189; Mary Fuller, *Voyages in Print: English Travel to America, 1576–1624* (Cambridge: Cambridge University Press, 1995), 12.

32. Fuller, *Voyages in Print*, 12.

33. William Warner, *Albions England* (London, 1597), 273–274.

34. Warner, *Albions England*, 274.

35. Warner, *Albions England*, 274.

36. *The Complete Works of Shakespeare*, ed. George Lyman Kittredge (Boston: Ginn, 1936): 2.1.39; *The Norton Shakespeare*, gen. ed. Stephen Greenblatt (New York and London: Norton, 1997), 2.1.39, n. 2.

37. Sarah M. Nutt, "The Arctic Voyages of William Barents in Probable Relation to Certain of Shakespeare's Plays," *SP* 39 (1942): 260. Perhaps the most comprehensive discussion of this sphere of exploration is found in Sir Clement R. Markham's *The Lands of Silence: A History of Arctic and Antarctic Exploration* (Cambridge: Cambridge University Press, 1921).

38. Qtd. by Nutt, "The Arctic Voyages of William Barents," 254.

39. Alexander Gerard, "An Essay on Genius," *Shakespeare, The Critical Heritage: 1774–1801*, ed. Brian Vickers, 6 vols. (London: Routledge, 1981), 6:114.

40. Qtd. by Nutt, "The Arctic Voyages of William Barents," 254.

41. Ibid.

42. It should be noted that I have chosen to treat Claudio as a kind of prologue to my discussion of Hamlet, even though *Measure for Measure* was written after the famous tragedy. I do this for the sake of clarity in my argument, but I realize that this example proves, yet again, that genealogy is rarely linear. Although I choose to see Shakespeare as an innovator in *Hamlet,* I can assume very little about the playwright's investment in that innovation.

43. Surely this credo informs Caesar's description of soldier Antony in the Alps in Shakespeare's play (1.4.66–71).

44. Dowden, *Shakespeare: A Critical Study of His Mind and Art*, 3rd ed. (New York: Harper & Brothers, n.d.), 112.

45. Sigmund Freud, *The Interpretation of Dreams: The Complete Psychological Works of Sigmund Freud*, trans. James Strachey, 24 vols. (1900; London: Hogarth Press, 1953), 4:265.

46. Marjorie Garber, *Shakespeare's Ghost Writers* (New York: Routledge, 1987), 170. See also Julia Reinhard Lupton and Kenneth Reinhard, *After Oedipus: Shakespeare in Psychoanalysis* (Ithaca, N.Y.: Cornell University Press, 1993), 2.

47. A. C. Bradley, *Shakespearean Tragedy* (1904; New York: St. Martin's Press, 1969), 118.

48. Kenneth Branagh, *Hamlet, Screenplay, and Introduction* (New York: Norton, 1996), 1. As Russell Jackson notes in "The Film Diary" from the same volume, the exterior filming at Blenheim Palace was beset by "real snow" that "sweeps in off the lake, blanking out visibility in a blizzard that covers all of us" (190). The next day, Jackson remarks, "Dry, bitter wind. Frozen snow now like brittle wedding-cake icing, and mixed with our own foam, paper, and salt" (191). In this way, cinema elaborates the dreams of exoteric man.

49. Floyd-Wilson, *English Ethnicity*, 78.

50. Sidney Warhaft, "Hamlet's Solid Flesh Resolved," *ELH* 28.1 (1961), 22.

51. Coleridge, *Coleridge's Shakespeare Criticism*, 1:38–39.

52. S.v. "mad," 6.

53. Citing Helkiah Crooke's *Description of the Body of Man*, Paster notes that "anger" was associated with women while "wrath" was reserved for men ("The Unbearable Coldness of Female Being," 429).

54. S.v. "machine."

55. In *A Midsummer Night's Dream*, Puck uses these terms to describe Bottom and company as "A crew of patches, rude mechanicals" (3.2.9).

56. Botero, *Historicall Description*, 3.

57. John Lyly provides a comic prologue to these scenes in his *Gallathea* as Rafe, Robin, and Dick attempt to become real men after their ship sinks. Their doomed labor of masculine self-definition turns on their ability to speak in northerly terms:

DICK: I'll say it. North, northeast, northeast, nor'—nor' and by nor'east—I shall never do it.

MARINER: This is but one quarter.

ROBIN: I shall never learn a quarter of it. I will try. North, north-east, is by the west side, north and by north—

DICK: Passing ill. (*Drama of the English Renaissance*, ed. Russell A. Fraser and Norman Rabkin, 2 vols. [New York and London: Macmillan, 1976], 1:2.1.63–72).

The words of Rafe at the end of the lesson aptly sum up the condition of Rosencrantz, Guildenstern, and Osric: "I will never learn this language" (2.1.78).

58. Wallace Stevens, "The Snow Man," *The Palm at the End of the Mind*, ed. Holly Stevens (New York: Knopf, 1971), 54.

CAROLYN SALE

Eating Air, Feeling Smells:
Hamlet's Theory of Performance

In Act III of *Hamlet*, just before he sits down with Claudius, Gertrude, and Ophelia to watch *The Mousetrap*, that play for which he has written sixteen lines, Hamlet says what may very well be the oddest of the many odd things that he says throughout the play: "I eat the air, promise-crammed" (3.2.92–93).[1] He later claims that he could eat a crocodile to express the depth of his feelings for the dead Ophelia, so his culinary tastes are clearly varied, but "I eat the air, promise-crammed," part retort, part self-definition, takes us to the heart of the play's interaction or transaction with its audience. In his talk of eating air, Hamlet suggests that the corporate body whose members appear to be but "mutes" in relation to the staged action may be as busy as the actor playing him. They may be feeding, as he does, "of the chameleon's dish" (3.2.92); that is, sitting down to the same table as those creatures who can change color upon command, actors, and taking in, across the course of the performance, the invisible matter that circulates between them, breath. Hamlet's odd statement would thus function as a metonym for the play's theory of performance, one that takes it beyond both mimesis and catharsis.

That this play offers its own theory of performance cannot be doubted. As Annabel Patterson noted some fifteen years ago, "this play contains more *information*, simply speaking, on the business of play-production than any

---

Renaissance Drama, Volume 35 (2006): pp. 145–168. Copyright © 2006 Northwestern University Press.

other in Shakespeare's canon, and . . . this material is already *theoretical* when it reaches us, already, if incompletely, transformed by Hamlet's critical perspective."[2] A powerful and enthusiastic consumer of theatrical fictions, Hamlet does indeed have plenty to say about the theater's functions and workings, and is confident enough in his understanding of how the theater works to dole out advice to professional players. This may constitute some cheek, but elsewhere Hamlet displays his critical powers with a little more humility, and as he does so offers an all-important context for his odd remark about eating the air. When he leaps to the defense of an "excellent play" denounced by critics as "caviar to the general" or too fine a theatrical delicacy to "please . . . the million" (2.2.377–380), he defends the play's "honest method" by employing an extended metaphor of play-as-food: "excellent plays" well prepared and property savored or spiced are palatable to and digestible by all, for their method, "as wholesome as sweet" (2.2.384–385), results in matter "well digested in the scenes" (2.2.380). Pursuing the methods by which the play aims to offer up fare that will "please the million," I seek to offer a specific sense of how, as Steven Mullaney has suggested, the Shakespearean theater operates as an "affective rather than a didactic forum" that "produce[s] new powers of identification, projection and apprehension in audiences."[3] I will do so by focusing on the promise of Hamlet's claim, or the ways in which the character's utterance speaks to idealistic conceptions of how the theater might work—or rather work upon, and perhaps ask work of, those who take a place within it as auditors and spectators.

"Promise-crammed," Hamlet may be speaking to an ideal transaction between play and playgoer, one in which something "as wholesome as sweet" may be offered up for consumption within the theatrical space. We could argue that in this play so concerned with addressing its culture's concerns about the theater, the promise is tied to the reform of theatrical practices that Hamlet urges, or rather to one aspect or another of the concerns that antitheatrical pamphleteers raised in their texts. From Stephen Gosson's 1579 *The Schoole of Abuse* onward, Elizabethan antitheatrical pamphleteers inveighed against the theater as a site of contagion, both physical and moral. In the first volley in a campaign to make potential playgoers run from the theater before they received any kind of "hurt" therein, Gosson conceived of their particular vulnerability in terms of the "winds" that might be in circulation in the theatrical space. Every other creature had been supplied, by God, with the capacity to "peyse their bodies" against these "winds":

> But wee which are so brittle, that we brake with euery fillop, so weake, that we are drawne with euery threade; so light, that wee are blowen away with euery blast; so vnsteady, that we slip in euery ground; neither peyse our bodyes against the winde, nor

stand vppon one legge, for sleeping too muche: nor close vppe our lippes for betraying our selues, nor vse any witte, to garde our owne persons, nor shewe our selues willing too shunne our owne harmes, running most greedely to those places, where we are soonest ouerthrowne.[4]

Although in this context, the winds appear to be merely figurative, the suggestion is that in the theater playgoers open themselves up to infiltration of one kind or another and a subsequent tempest that will leave them in one way or another debilitated. More moderate than his fellow pamphleteers, Gosson nevertheless held out the possibility that the theater's dangers might be mitigated, and set the players (and those who wrote for them) a challenge:

If Players can promise in wordes, and performe it in deedes, proclaime it in their Billes, and make it good in Theaters: that there is nothing there noysome too the body, nor hurtefull to the soule: and that euerye one which comes to buye their lestes, shall haue an honest neighbour, tagge and ragge, cutte and longe tayle, goe thether and spare not, otherwise I aduise you to keepe you thence, my selfe wil begine to leade the daunce.[5]

It is an assurance of this kind that *Hamlet* offers, as it employs its own culinary metaphors to respond to Gosson's rhetoric of the noxious "dyet" that playgoers purportedly dine upon in the theatrical space.[6] The play reassures them that the things offered for their consumption in the theater will not only do them no hurt, but may very well do them some good. The "participation" that takes place as a result of this may be understood, as Anthony Dawson and P. A. Skantze have argued, as a kind of "secular transubstantiation,"[7] and there can be no doubt that for some playgoers in the Globe Shakespeare's theater operated as a venue for the transmission of a spirit that was very much religiously inflected.[8] I am not, however, interested in the religious aspects of the transmission here. I wish to pursue the play's theory and practice of the transfer of breath between actor and playgoer in purely material terms. The *success* or pragmatics of the play's theory of performance is not what is at issue here, but rather its character, in its full-blown idealism or "promise."[9]

Pursuing a sense of the play's transaction with its audience in material rather than spiritual terms, I mimic the play's own modus operandi, which is consistently to render the divine (and other complex discourses such as that of the law) into terms that are "plaine," "honest," "wholesome," and "sweet" for consumption and comprehension by "the general." To put this another way, the play consistently presents the high-flown, the philosophical, the abstract in what Hamlet calls "examples gross as earth" (4.4.46). In fact, the play engages in a relentless materializing of everything it discusses. Turn to almost any line of this text and you will find the immaterial or the abstract given material form. The text bestows upon the abstraction time either anatomical or architectural form (it is "out of joint" [1.5.191]), and those other abstractions, the false and the true, find themselves figured as fish: "Your bait of falsehood takes this carp of truth" (2.1.62). There is a decided tendency in this text not only to render things material, or give them forms and figures, but to turn one form after another into what we might call, echoing the text, "baser matter" (1.5.104); and in an environment in which everything is being rendered material in one way or another, reason becomes the ability to distinguish thing from thing, or one form, from another: "when the wind is southerly," Hamlet informs Rosencrantz and Guildenstern, "I know a hawk from a handsaw" (2.2.321–322). The line also suggests that certain winds, or forms of air, make possible a rationality or perspective that Hamlet would otherwise lack, a matter to which I shall return. In fact, in this play so insistently about the material, even thinking exerts a material force: it is a "cudgel[ing] of [the] brains" which produces effects elsewhere in the body: thinking, Hamlet tells us as he considers what can happen to a lawyer's skull after his death, makes the bones ache (5.1.87).

One important result of the text's tendency to construe everything as the product of material exchanges or friction between material bodies is that the Hamlet who unfolds before us insistently pursues questions of identity in what we might regard as the simplest, or the earthiest, of terms. Not only does Hamlet regularly consider how everything ultimately returns to dust, he himself continually performs a linguistic equivalent of this material turn, posing high-flown questions about being and action in language that a ten-year-old could understand. With a mere ten words, for example—"And yet to me what is this quintessence of dust?" (2.2.277–278)—Hamlet presents one of the most pressing questions about identity in terms that foreground his own materiality along with his alienation from it, an alienation that makes possible the crucial disjuncture between self-as-object and self-as-reflexive-thinker from which Hamlet wrings so much linguistic payoff. The insistent materialization of everything taking place under the "majestical roof fretted with golden fire" (2.2.270–271), that is, both the earthly and the theatrical space, means that even those aspects of identity that we would deem the most abstract and intangible (soul, conscience, memory) are "limed" for us (3.3.68), made material through metaphor, that trick of language through which word is made flesh in familiar terms. This concern with ways in which to give complex thought material form extends beyond the language of the page to the semiotics of the stage, so that what the spectator experiences in the Globe is the by-product of a material aesthetic—that is, an aesthetic that everywhere turns one form into a "baser" or simpler one not only to ensure the widest possible communicability of the text, but also to draw its audience into an experience—one sensual and physiological—through which it participates in material processes of transformation.

The play's language catches its spectators or auditors up in this materializing tendency in its talk of various forms of feeding or consumption. This talk insistently reminds playgoers of their own embodiment, and perhaps the fact that they are making their bodies available for some kind of transaction simply by taking their place in the theater. In its plainest terms, playgoers are induced to imagine that they will ultimately be, like Alexander the Great, nothing more than "dust" in a "bunghole" (5.1.193–194). Elsewhere, this rhetoric reminds playgoers not only of their own physicality and mortality but also of the ways in which their embodiment is caught up in political forms of consumption: "We fat all creatures else to fat us, and we fat ourselves for maggots. Your fat king and your lean beggar is but variable service—two dishes, but to one table" (4.3.21–23). The play's critique of sociopolitical dynamics in terms of the ingestion of one form of matter by another casts Hamlet's claim that he eats air as political: eating air, he removes himself from the material circuit that makes some men fat while leaving others lean, and places only men like Osric, who are "spacious in the possession of dirt," at the king's table (5.2.75).[10] Hamlet fashions a political discourse in which the king is made an object and stripped of the mystery whereby he exerts his power over others and claims certain feeding privileges denied to others: "The king is a thing," he informs Rosencrantz and Guildenstern—"of nothing," he adds, when Guildenstern presses him for elaboration (4.2.25–27). This thing he desires to turn into the "offal" with which he may fat "kites" (2.2.518–519). The "fine revolution" threatened in all of this—Hamlet attributes substance and meaning to beggars along with their bodies, while depriving the king of the same—is one of the things that makes Hamlet the "hectic" in Claudius's blood (4.3.65); figuratively crammed with Hamlet, Claudius is in desperate need of a cure. But I am interested in the obverse of all this: not how Hamlet conceives of Claudius's unjust "fatting" of himself at others' expense, but the play's compensation for the operations of the polis in terms of the fare it serves up to its audience. The action of the play will culminate in Hamlet finally taking revenge upon Claudius but in the course of these representations of action, what does the audience consume? Joining Hamlet in his eating of air, the audience will take in a substance that nourishes them more than any fare they could have if they too had a "crib . . . at the king's mess" (5.2.73–74). Eating the air they will take in a substance, moreover, that renders them active rather than passive, allowing them to imagine a more positive transaction with other bodies or materials than that which Hamlet imagines in his talk of the king's progress "through the guts of a beggar" (4.3.30).

I am certainly not the first scholar to suggest that playgoers in the Globe were ingesting various forms of matter as they took in a play. Scholarly discussion has so far, however, focused on what Sir Francis Bacon called "visibles" and "audibles." On the impact of these two "species" of matter, Bacon wrote:

> The *Species* of *Visibles* seeme to be *Emissions* of *Beames* from the *Obiect seene;* Almost like Odours; saue that they are more Incorporeall: But the *Species* of *Audibles* seeme to Participate more with *Locall Motion,* like *Percussions* or *Impressions* made vpon the *Aire.* So that whereas all Bodies doe seeme to worke in two manners; Either by the *Communication* of their *Natures;* Or by the *Impressions* and *Signatures* of their *Motions;* The *Diffusion* of *Species Visible* seemeth to participate more of the former *Operation;* and the *Species Audible* of the latter.[11]

Bacon's statement is vague, especially in regard to "visibles," which somehow communicate their natures by a form of "emission" he can describe at best by way of simile: they pass into the spectator "like Odours," or as if they were scents or smells. The species of "audibles" has proved more tractable material for both sixteenth-century and contemporary theorists, precisely because of the "percussions" that Bacon attributes to them here. The idea of direct material transfer from actor to playgoer of sound is captured most famously, perhaps, in John Webster's description of the "excellent actor" as a figure whose riveting of playgoers' attention lets Webster imagine he sees lines of transmission between the actor's body and playgoers' ears: "he charms our attention: sit in a full theatre, and you will think you see so many lines drawn from the circumference of so many ears, while the actor is at the center."[12] The "percussions" that move along those lines between actor's body and playgoers' ears have been pursued by both Joseph Roach and Bruce Smith. Joseph Roach has famously read the transaction between actor's body and playgoers' ears in terms of kinetic energy—the actor's voice and gestures both create waves of sound and motion that infiltrate playgoers through their ears to exert a physical force inside them, stirring up their passions.[13] More recently, Bruce Smith has argued that the Globe serves as a physical instrument for the transmission of sound, in which every playgoer's body becomes a smaller instrument through which sounds play and resonate.[14]

Smith's argument is important for moving us away from an idea of the theater as predominantly discursive arena. He suggests that with sound the playgoers communicate materials that are prediscursive: playing with a phrase from Wright's *Passions,* he argues that by "hearing green" the playgoer in the Globe may enjoy the viscerality of the theatrical experience simply by thrumming with "audibles" and without processing them into phonemes.[15] I wish to go beyond the idea of the theater as a place where a material transfer of theatrical representations takes place through the conduits of eyes and ears, and beyond the idea of the Globe as an organ for the transmission of sound, in pursuit of a material and a theatrical experience that is more ephemeral and more elusive. I start by not resting content with Bacon's simile, "like Odours." Let us use *Hamlet*'s relentless materializing to cut through that simile. *Hamlet* makes literal what is figurative in Bacon and Roach to provide a theory of performance that reads the exchange between actor and playgoer in terms of the actual infusion of one body with the materials of another, through breath.

The terms in which *Hamlet* discusses the species of "visibles" and "audibles" are, as we might expect from my earlier discussion of the materializing tendencies of the play, elemental. It presents "visibles" in gritty terms, or should I say, terms of grit: the spectacle that the Ghost presents, for example, is a "mote . . . to trouble the mind's eye" (1.1.112). Horatio's metaphor imagines "visibles" as things that can get inside one, causing in their transit into another form of matter some friction or rub. The body of the "visible" may be microscopic, a "mote," but it produces physical effects: seeing makes the eyes ache. Given that this is a play in which a character digs a grave, we may imagine many actual motes going into circulation, depending on whether the playing company makes a property out of that substance of which Hamlet keeps speaking and the vigor with which the actor digs. But the play is also concerned with that other species of matter that Bacon designates, "audibles." In the course of objecting to Rosencrantz and Guildenstern's attempts to make him a tool for their own advancement, Hamlet focuses on that other species by imagining his own body as a "little organ" or "pipe" upon which they attempt to play (3.2.362–364). The act of blowing that would be required for them to play upon him as a pipe would result in sound, but the sound would be a by-product of their breath passing through him: "Give it breath with your mouth," Hamlet says (3.2.352–353). Neither words nor sounds are the primary material here. The material of which both sounds and words are composed is, as Ophelia tells us, "sweet breath" (3.1.98).

When we focus on the transaction between actor and playgoer in the Globe as the transmission of breath, we find another answer to the question that Thomas Wright raises in *Passions of the Minde in Generall* as he considers the immense power of the passion that can be communicated in performance: "what qualities carie simple single sounds and voices, to enable them to worke such wonders?"[16] Working toward an answer, Wright claims that passion in an orator, actor, or any other "perswader" seems to him to "resemble the wind a trumpeter bloweth in at one end of the trumpet."[17] As his description continues, the simile shifts into metaphor ("the passion proceedeth from the heart, & is blowne about the bodie, face, eies, hands, voice . . .")[18] but it is only elsewhere that he approaches the issue in material rather than figurative terms, writing that "sound it selfe . . . is nothing else but a certaine artificiall shaking, crispling or tickling of the ayre (like as we see in the water crispled, when it is calme, & a sweet gale of wind ruffleth it a little . . .)."[19] This last statement provides support for theories (both sixteenth century and of our own moment) that posit that sound through its "crisplings" stirs the passions of the hearer. But I would like us to think of the air not, as Wright does, as the thing that is stirred or blown about by something else, but rather as the thing that stirs. Air, wind, or breath is not simply the medium, carrier, or agent of sound and words; in its issuance, in the theatrical arena, from actors' mouths, it is a propulsive force. The matter that emanates from actors is not "like odours" and does not simply "resemble the wind"; it *is* the "sweet breath" of which all of their enunciations, whether they are verbal or prelinguistic, are composed.

In a text where characters regularly make use of ejaculations such as "hum," "pooh," and "ha," the play suggests that nonverbal forms of communication have matter in them, or rather carry matter that is neither sound nor words. Not only can the "windy suspiration of forced breath" (1.2.79) express passion (grief, in the context of Hamlet's assertion that he does not simply *seem* woeful), it may emit, exude, or simply comprise matter: "There's matter in these sighs" (4.1.1) Claudius informs Gertrude when he finds her heaving after her confrontation with Hamlet. The sighs carry some sense that he wishes her to unfold in words, but the sighs are also the vehicle for matter of another kind, the passion with which Hamlet's words have filled her, a passion so great that it is crowding out her own breath. Hamlet, himself suffering from the effects of another's passionate communication (the effects, that is, of "incorporeal air" as mysteriously embodied in his father's ghost), also experiences the impact of sighs, at least according to Ophelia's report: he breathes a sigh of such force in a visit to her that it seemed to "shatter all his bulk / And end his being" (2.1.94–95).

Gail Kern Paster's extensive work on the humoral body and the "ecology of the passions" helps us understand the physiological force that the actor playing Gertrude is feigning when confronted by Hamlet. As "passion's slave," Hamlet is the victim of his own physiology, stirred into a state of great excitation, disturbance, and distraction by his encounter with that thing of air, his father's ghost. "The narrative of physiology is," Paster writes, "one of assimilation of nature's raw matter—its food and water and air—into the stuff in which consciousness must lodge, the bodily stuff of self."[20] This assimilation requires an intermixing of "nature's raw matter" with the body's humors (black bile, yellow bile, blood, and phlegm) in the "containing vessels" of the body's arteries, and "the compression of incorporated air and fire moving along the liquid streams of [these] containing vessels" makes possible action.[21] It also causes "explosions of air and fire within the body's dense liquidity" that may manifest itself in overly forceful outward action, as Paster's quotation of Bacon suggests: "wee knowe that simple *Aire,* being preternaturally attenuated by *Heate,* will make it self Roome, and breake and blowe vp that which resisteth it."[22] Dealing with the effects of the "winds of passion" inside him that have been stirred up the Ghost, Hamlet speaks of himself as having been plunged into "Vulcan's stithy" (3.2.83). In more recent work Paster provides a detailed reading of the First Player's speech about Pyrrhus which shows how Pyrrhus, as a thing "roasted in wrath and fire," becomes a figure for Hamlet's physiological state after his encounter with his father's spirit.[23] The air is the agent here, stirring or "exagitating" one person's spirits so that he in turn stirs or "exagitates" another's.[24] But the communication of passion in the form of breath between actor and playgoer need not work such deleterious effects. In fact, we could argue that when Hamlet advises the players not to "saw the air" (3.2.4) around them with their hands, he is seeking to ensure a gentle, non-coercive transfer of breath from actor to playgoer. When the actor "saws" the air, he risks subjecting the playgoer to an onslaught of kinetic energy, perhaps even risks altering the nature of the thing being transferred: with the sawing, the "sweet breath" may become something else entirely, a barrage of motion waves that disperse it before it ever reaches the playgoer. It may also do a kind of violence upon the person who receives it: "Ayre so carued," Wright writes, "punisheth and fretteth the heart."[25] In the language of Shakespeare's text, it serves up to the playgoer a "whirlwind of . . . passion" (3.2.6) that he or she may not have the power to ingest. The play represents the effects of such airs or such a "whirlwind" in a decidedly negative inflection en route to ensuring that its own "chameleon's dish" (3.2.92) will be "wholesome" and "sweet" (2.2.385), the product of its own players "us[ing] all gently" (3.2.5).

The play cultivates the sense that the matter in sighs and the matter of breath may be communicated to playgoers or infused through them gently, as something already "well digested," by appealing to another of their senses, the sense of smell. "Affection (or passion) poureth forth it self by all meanes possible," Wright notes;[26] and while Wright believes that the most powerful of the senses for the transmission of passion is sight ("no sense hath such varietie of objects to feed and delight it . . . no sense sooner moueth"),[27] and though he devotes a great deal of attention, as Smith has noted in his reading of *Passions,* to sound, he also suggests the importance of smell to what he calls the "discoverie" of passions. "Passion smelleth," he writes.[28] The remark suggests that as passion percolates through the body (a "machine," according to Hamlet [2.2.124]), it gives off an, odiferous by-product or a chemical stink. Shakespeare knows this: he has Claudius attribute a rankness to his "offence" of killing his brother, which "smells to heaven" (3.3.36). Writing of the difficulties that insincere men or those who dissimulate pose to those who would discern their true natures or motives, Wright claims that his readers can smell their way to the truth: "in all suiters presents," he suggests, by way of example, "a man of a bad sent may easily feele a smell of profit, which perfumeth those gifts."[29] Attributing to objects a scent or perfume, Wright gives passions a body, matter or substance in the form of odors that makes them discernible even to a man of "bad sent." This matter will allow him to apprehend or *feel* the smell of profit in the gifts. The wonderful catachresis of "feele a smell" not only underscores the physicality of smelling one's way toward apprehension or understanding, it also marks for us the invisible transit of material in the act of breathing, material that we can *feel* even if our sense of smell fails us.

In addition to indicating that smells can offend (Hamlet recoils from the stink of Yorick's skull, for example, at 5.1.190 ["And smelt so? Pah!"]), all three of *Hamlet*'s texts present scent, as Wright's text does, in relation to gifts or presents. In 3.1, Ophelia informs Hamlet that he is to take back his letters and the tokens of love that he has given her for their "perfume" is "lost" (3.1.99). In other words, for the benefit of her father and Claudius, Ophelia pretends that she can no longer feel the smell of Hamlet's gifts; this act, in which she dissociates herself from her own passions, will lead eventually to her madness and drowning; but the reference invites playgoers to think of objects as exuding some invisible matter that may be apprehended by smell, and perhaps *only* by smell. The most important reference to scents comes from the Ghost, about a third of the way through the long speech to Hamlet in which he explains how he was murdered. Brought up short in his tale-telling by his recognition that morning is approaching, the Ghosts says, "But soft, methinks I scent the morning air" (1.5.58). Scenting the morning air, the Ghost may not only be breathing it in, but in a now obsolete meaning also exhaling it.[30] A thing of air himself, he is therefore a medium or organ for air's transmission, and the actor who stalks onstage to personate him gives body to that which he himself exudes in motes (on first encounter, Hamlet suggests that the Ghost either trails "airs from heaven or blasts from hell" [1.4.41]). Scenting the air, the Ghost also feels smells, as the typographical appearance of "scent" as "sent" in both Q2 and the Folio underscores, for "sent" draws our attention to the word's etymological roots in French (in the verb "sentir") and Latin (in the verb "sentire"): to scent is to feel or perceive.[31] Performing for playgoers the act of scenting or feeling smells, the actor playing the Ghost on the Globe's stage (Shakespeare, as legend would have it) draws the audience's attention to the importance of the act of breathing, especially in the space of the wooden O, which becomes, with the single word of "scent," a vehicle for feeling and apprehension through smell, but also the medium for the transmission of scent and breath to others. Drawing breath, the actor takes in not only a scent or perfume but also the air that carries it; exhaling it, he perfumes it in turn, as he returns to the environment around him what he took from it. The performance of the act of "scenting" stimulates the audience's sense of smell and its ability to scent, priming its members to understand the air of the theater as perfumed—filled, that is, with the breath of the actors, which they may "scent," ingest or, as Hamlet's suggests, "eat." The "miraculous organ" in which they find themselves and of which they are a part functions, then, not only as a globe or head filled with words that may stir them to intellection, as Hamlet suggests the Ghost does, but also as another body part: a pair of lungs that scatters throughout its environment a "baser matter" in the form of perfume.

What work does this air or breath do? Let me first consider the ways in which it does *not* work. In its suggestion that playgoers may, like Hamlet, "eat the air" or feed on what is transmitted by it, the play goes well beyond any idea of the theater tied to mimesis. It also goes beyond the transmission of breath for or as language. The play, I suggest, although it exploits what mimetic representation can offer, is also suspicious of the kinds of effect to which mimesis lends itself, and Hamlet is of course famously dismissive of words. The fact that Hamlet is himself the instrument of mimetic principles at their most coercive should not deter us from accepting some of his other ideas about the function of the theater. As Robert Weimann has noted, this is a strange play in which both Hamlet and Shakespeare articulate an "equivocal position": "the demand for 'reform' and the refusal to comply with it in one and the same play is," for example, "largely unparalleled."[32] In Hamlet's hands, the mimetic character of the theater becomes a weapon that he uses both to provoke some show of Claudius's guilt and to threaten him (the *Mousetrap* shows a nephew poisoning his uncle). He uses mimetic principles even more aggressively with Gertrude as he holds up a glass wherein she may see the inmost part of her. Hamlet is in fact so forceful with Gertrude that he renders her breathless: when he asks her to swear not to tell Claudius about his confrontation of her, she assures him that she could not if she wanted to: "Be thou assured, if words be made of breath, / And breath of life, I have no life to breathe / What thou hast said to me" (3.4.197–199). Hamlet has gone too far. To borrow a word that Wright uses when writing of passion's forcible effects upon an auditor, Hamlet's confrontation of Gertrude, an exhibition of mimetic principles wrested to coercive ends, threatens to "exanimate" her (175). Using mimetic principles to such ends, Hamlet veers from the project that the Ghost has assigned him, a project that involves a purgation of the state through a bringing-to-account of Claudius. What the audience experiences here, palpably, even if they are too far away to see what might easily appear here, the actor's breath upon the mirror, is the forcefulness of one practice of mimesis. Given that Hamlet also fails to achieve the effects that Thomas Heywood will later claim for mimesis in his *Apology for Actors* (1612) as he aims to demonstrate the moral utility of the theater (Gertrude is not prompted to any show of guilt in relation to the murder), the scene thus seems, as Jane Tylus has suggested, to "militate *against* the very 'work' theater is ideally supposed to perform as a discoverer of hidden passions."[33] But that is not the work that this play, I am arguing, sets out to do. Hamlet's roughness with Gertrude constitutes a practice of mimesis that the play's theory of performance as an exchange of breath counters. Articulating a theory of its exchange with the audience in terms of the eating of air, the feeling of smells, the drawing of breath, the play offers an idea of the theater as an organ for an exchange that works to fill playgoers with breath in its most positive character rather than expose them to any kind of force that would compel it from them. The breath that the actors transmit works to the very opposite effect that Hamlet pursues with Gertrude: it does not exanimate, but inspires. It motivates and mobilizes. The organ of the theater operates as a pair of lungs that takes through that "canopy" that is no proper roof at all a material that, harnessed by the actors in their acts of breathing and speaking, passes outward to the audience, who may receive the breath as "mutes," but who do not remain mute; they receive the breath as "patients," as materials that are acted upon, but what they receive renders them active, or rather creates in them the capacity or the potential to become that which they observe: the breath makes them "capable" by turning them all into potential actors.

Wright helps us further this line of thinking. Advocating that his readers turn to the theater, and to players in particular, for models for their own passions, he suggests that they go to the theater to learn how to act—not on the stage, but in the world. His language posits a circuit of exchange in which the players, basing their personation of action on their observation of the passions around them, make themselves into superlative models of passionate action for others:

> The first is, that we looke vpon other men appassionate, how they demeane themselues in passions, and obserue what and how they speake in mirth, sadnesse, ire, feare, hope, &c, what motions are stirring in the eyes, hands, bodie, &c. And then leaue the excesse and exorbitant leuitie or other defects, and keepe the manner corrected with prudent mediocritie: and this the best may be marked in stage plaiers, who act excellently; for as the perfection of their exercise consisteth in imitation of others, so they that imitate best, act best. And in the substance of externall action for most part oratours and stage plaiers agree: and only they differ in this, that these act fainedly, those really; these onely to delight, those to stirre vp all sorts of passions according to the exigencie of the matter.[34]

What begins with the actions of men and women in the world (those who act "really," in Wright's wording) finds itself perfected by players on the stage (those who "act fainedly") and the "fained" becomes the model for the "externall action" of those who act "really." What the playgoer receives, then, in Wright's view, when they go to the theater, are lessons in acting for which they were the source material. The refinement of the "externall action" in which they are always engaged comes back to them from the players. The exchange is thus two-way, and in its double character offers a challenge to subjectivity, for what the actor personates, whether he is confined within the bounds of the O or walking London's streets, performing his actions "really," is always already someone else, or the many bits of sundry other persons which he cobbles together in an inheritance from others that has no proper point of origin, no proper author, no one person. What passes between actors and playgoers, then, in the exchange of breath, that material that allows for the expression of passion, is no particular idea of subjectivity, and no discursive end. "We move," Wright writes, comprehending himself as a player too, if only in terms of his grammar: " . . . we moue, because by the passion thus wee are moued, and as it hath wrought in vs so it ought to worke in you."[35] In its intransitivity (the players move others, but to no particular object or end), Wright's formulation suggests that what the players transmit as they perform passion is the principle of action: they are moved, in turn move, and make possible further moving in those moved. *Hamlet*'s famous formulation for action spoken by the first Clown—action is "to act, to do, to perform" (5.1.12–13)—goes a step beyond Wright's formulation, both in terms of its grammar and what it is actors do, liberating action from both subject and object, stripping it naked, leaving it all verb. It untethers action from any particular source and any particular end, rendering it a pure, enlivening force that can be accessed, through the act of breathing, by all. The material through which all of this is accomplished is unconfined and unconfutable. It may move through bodies with a certain power or energy, as the actor's breath does when the. Ghost's voice booms through the wooden O in the opening act, but, like the Ghost's voice, it is simultaneously everywhere and nowhere, all around them and yet in no one place. It may gather force as it moves through the enclosed spaces of the actors' bodies and the shell of the theater itself, and take on or carry other material as it does so (including sound, as Smith has argued so persuasively), but, in its ideal formulation, it is always free and unrestrictive: available to all, coercive with none.

Indeed, within the physiological terms that Gail Kern Paster has so extensively elaborated, within the theatrical space, each and every playgoer becomes a "containing vessel," in which this breath stirs up the animal and vital spirits to make possible action. The breath—or the air of the chameleon's dish of which they all eat—excites the physiological processes in which they are all "stithies." The work that they engage in is both individual and collective. Each playgoer must deal with the effects of the passionate transmission—that is, take in the passion received from the actors in the exchange of breath, and bear any potential negative consequences, en route to permitting the purgative effects of the stirring up or enlivening of their own passions. If we note, along with Stephen Orgel, that the Greek word that signifies the thing from which playgoers are released or relieved in the experience of catharsis is "pathemata," and that this word, usually translated as "sufferings," "implies, literally, passive action," or as Orgel paraphrases it, "what happens to you, as opposed to what you do," the theory of performance to which the play thus speaks might be understood as an elaboration of Aristotle's theory of catharsis: where they join the actor playing Hamlet in his eating of the air, and when they weep at the character's death, playgoers make themselves available for a physiological alteration that frees them from the inaction or passivity that "pathemata" connotes to "make them capable."[36]

If we take all of this literally, as Gail Kern Paster urges us to do, we might imagine playgoers engaged in a larger process of collective purification. The play repeatedly draws our attention to one distillate of the physiological processes that playgoers may experience as the play unfolds, the salt that gets left behind on playgoers' cheeks when they weep. This weeping is a result of the tragic action. Within the fiction, Hamlet's action of killing the king figuratively clears or purifies the "pestilent congregation of vapors" (2.2.272–273) in Denmark; and the represented purgation, by provoking real-world physiological effects that include but are by no means limited to crying, may refine or purify the air that playgoers "scent." Within the "ecology of the passions," Paster notes, breath "moves into and out of the body," and in its ambiguity makes our constitution ambiguous; we are the product of both internal and external forces, and the product of parts that are always our "own" (bones, flesh, organs) and something that we share with others (the air that we draw in with our breath).[37] This suggests that both our capacity to act and our physical being are always tied both to the ecological system within us (that tempestuous interaction of air, fire, and water that makes meteorological metaphors so apt for their description) and the ecology without, that environment that one finds without, as one crawls, as Hamlet puts, it between heaven and earth. In the Renaissance, the circulation of materials between these two environments—that of the individual's body and that of the larger physical environment in which he or she is situated—was understood, as Paster has argued, literally: "That which is bodily or emotional figuration for us, preserved metaphors of somatic consciousness, was the literal stuff of physiological theory for early modern scriptors of the body," she writes as she urges us to resist the tendency to let "semantic differences between past and present discourses of the body . . . occlude early modern habits of bodily sensation and self-experience . . . and lead us to substitute figurative where literal meanings ought to remain."[38] As I noted at the outset, the play's own relentless materializing also encourages us to resist a metaphorical turn. If we are as obstinately literal in our conception of the exchange as the First Clown is, within the fiction, about other things ("How absolute the knave is!" [5.1.129]), we might argue that within the space of the theater, both actors and playgoers are joint contributors to a process of ingestion, digestion, and refinement of the air that circulates between them that results ultimately in its purification. The notion that what Hamlet calls "more rawer breath" (5.2.108) might be refined, in the collective "stithy" of the theater, into something more delectable is clearly idealistic, and certainly no virulent antitheatrical writer or preacher would have acknowledged it as a genuine possibility. But the invitation that the play extends to playgoers is that each of them might become a pipe through which a sweeter air might flow.

The connection between the exchange of breath in the theater to which the play speaks and Hamlet as the instrument of purgation was beautifully suggested in Trevor Nunn's 2004 production of the play for the Old Vic. Nunn used the material of breath in a pointed way in relation to Hamlet's act of killing the king. This act has important legal aspects that I pursue at greater length elsewhere.[39] Let me here offer simply the upshot, which is that Hamlet, as he strikes at Claudius, is in the terms of the case that the Clown nonsensically redacts in his presentation of the "three branches" of action, *Hales v. Petit,* a dead man walking: he is already killed, but still capable of taking action against Claudius. At the moment that Hamlet discovers that he is killed, and just before he seizes the opportunity to act, Hamlet inhabits a strange liminal space and moment between life and death. He is about to die, but is in some sense at this moment at his most alive, for he is free to take action against Claudius not only in "perfect conscience" but also without anyone, including any representative of the law and his own accusatory self, being able to "charge" him with anything at all. In that moment, the young actor playing Hamlet in Nunn's production, Ben Whishaw, took a sturdy, deep, deliberate breath, the performance of which was inescapable. The audience watched the actor/character breathe, and then the breath result in an action: Whishaw rose, stepped forward, and touched Tom Mannion, the actor playing Claudius, with his foil so gently, so lightly, that the foil barely connected with Mannion's body. By preceding these actions with such a deliberate performance of the act of breathing, Whishaw and Nunn turned the moment and the play into an exhibition of contemporary Shakespearean performance as a vehicle not for Shakespeare's "voice" (as Bill Worthen has shown us so many contemporary acting manuals advocate)[40] but for the replaying of the circulation of the material in which Shakespeare and his fellow actors dealt, the material of breath.

The text of *Hamlet* offers its most explicit and its final expression of the idea of the theater as a place for the exchange of breath in Hamlet's final speech. As the play draws to a close, Hamlet requires that Horatio continue to "draw breath" in this harsh world awhile so that he may tell Hamlet's story (5.2.331). Horatio conceives his role as storyteller, as executor of the legacy Hamlet has left him, as a passing on of Hamlet's voice and breath: he will speak "from his mouth whose voice will draw on more" (5.2.375). Speaking from Hamlet's "mouth," Horatio becomes a vessel for, or pipe whereon, that voice may play, but more important the figure for the transfer of Hamlet's breath to others. He functions as the audience's proxy, eating once of the air that exudes from Hamlet with his final utterance, in that string of O's that Bruce Smith has called Hamlet's "omega."[41] This omega is not, however, only an expression of Hamlet in sound or as sound, as Smith suggests. The string of O's signifies the moment in which the actor looses Hamlet's breath, setting it free for uptake and safe-keeping by Horatio. With that string of O's, the actor playing Hamlet performs the loss of the character's life, but as he does so, or to do so, must let loose his own breath. Hold up your hand before your mouth while breathing Hamlet's string of O's and you will feel a gentle variant of the exhalation of breath that the actor is called upon to perform. The character's breath and the actor's exhalation are in fact enfolded, and that which is "fained" and that which is "real" here collapse into one another; in the fiction, the character dies and in the space of the Globe the actor playing him passes on something material to the constituency around him—not something "like Odours," not something that "resembles the Wind"—but breath itself. As a result, two things occur: the character who imagined that he would be happy "bounded in a nutshell" becomes, within the larger shell of the theater, a kind of food, a figurative nut meat, for playgoers; at the same time, along with that "fained" food, or the imaginary consumption, the playgoers in the Globe who scent the air for the perfume or exhalation of the actor take in something that is not "fained" at all, the breath that is set loose to disperse among them in motes.[42]

With this loosing of the actor's breath in the play's closing moments, the play simply makes explicit what has been occurring during the entire passage of the actors' two hours' traffic upon the stage (or four hours, as the case may be). The play in performance has been offering up to its constituency from its start a fare that not only takes the character of its interaction with the audience well beyond the bounds of mimesis, but also takes it beyond Wright's goal for all those who deal in passionate presentations, which is to find the most effective way of communicating passion to "the common people."[43] By appealing to their sense of smell and encouraging them to believe that they are partaking of a particular delicacy, the play not only reminded playgoers that they were processing machines, but invited them to feel what would otherwise be so usual with them, so common, that it would go unnoted, unmarked, the progress of air through the matter of the body. The act of breathing would thus become one means of experiencing the subtle way in which we are continuously infiltrated by materials from outside us and would thus unsettle or make more tenuous the apparent or provisional integrity of human identity as it is defined in or around the vessel or machine of the body. The invitation of the play, then, to eat the air or scent it is an invitation to experience a heightened sense of one's own embodiment along with a paradoxical liberation from it: the process of "feeling smells" or of experiencing the felt progress of air through the machine of one's own body induces a sense of participation in a larger body, a body united and constituted by the breath that passes in a continual state of flux through one and through others in an endless scattering and dispersal, and reconstitution and remembering, that challenges the integrity of individuals even as it animates and revitalizes them.[44]

If, then, the play is, in performance, the occasion for a form of "breathing time" (5.2.156), a form of recreation in which playgoers may experience the propulsive, animating and generative force of breath, and find themselves, through the act of breathing, or their eating of the "chameleon's dish," made part of a larger "miraculous organ," the sensual experience afforded by smell or the physicality of using the diaphragm to take the breath of actors into the machine of the body is unique to the moment of performance: words in printed form may conjure up images in the mind's eye and sounds in the mind's ear, but there is no substitute for the materiality of the breath exchanged within the Wooden O. On the page, Hamlet's final string of O's may hint at the passage of breath onstage, but it cannot act, do, or perform it. The participation in the theater's "breathing time," is in short utterly and completely ephemeral: it is the "perfume and suppliance of a minute" (1.3.9). But by capturing some idea of this ephemeral aspect of the Shakespearean theater for us, the play as printed suggests why it pleased all in performance: all playgoers needed to do to have the core of its theatrical experience, and partake of its finest fare, was "scent the air" for the actor's loosed breath. Then they too might become, in Shakespeare's "stithy," things of "quick sail" (5.2.101).

When we recall that the voice and breath that the actor playing Hamlet passes on or disperses to the audience has its origin within the fiction in the Ghost, and its origins as theatrical representation in the person of Shakespeare, the loosing of the breath that playgoers capture when they "scent the air" has implications for our understanding of the character of Shakespearean authorship. This play makes play-going about the giving away of words and breath—for a price, it is true, the price of the penny given at the gate, but for a price not commensurate with what is yielded in return. In the sense that the price paid cannot equal what is bestowed in return, the play in performance is a gift, and the gift is in large part a sharing out of the writer and his conceptions.[45] The aesthetic of the play thus counters materialist arguments that would construe the Shakespearean theater as thoroughly embroiled in, and unable to extricate itself from, market forces. I suggest that Hamlet's disavowal of a proprietary relationship with words—to Claudius's claim "These words are not mine," Hamlet retorts "No, nor mine now" (3.2.94–96)—stands, at least in relation to this play, as a gesture of disavowal on Shakespeare's part: the organ of the O takes his words and disperses them to all gathered there, and as they part from him, whether or not they issue from his own mouth, in the part that he takes on actor, or from other actors' mouths, the words are no longer his own. With this play, Shakespeare uses the "aire" to "set passions aloft,"[46] and that air or wind, in the form of each of the actors' breaths, disperses both words and breath for eating by all of the playgoers gathered there. With that dispersal, the perfume of the gift infuses through the Globe and scatters.[47] We cannot "scent the air" as playgoers in the Globe did to "recover the wind" that was set free there (3.2.340): the perfume is lost. It was always lost, for at the end of each performance the "wind" moved out the Globe's large mouth, back to the air beyond its shell again; and the playgoers moved out the other points of egress in that body, that shell, in which they had been all temporarily bound together in a sharing of space and breath, to scatter too.[48] We can, however, use the artifact of the text to articulate the remains of the theatrical experience, and reconstruct our sense of the gift, the thing shared, by recapturing an idea of what *Hamlet* offered up to playgoers, for their "breathing time."

Notes

I would like to thank Will West and Stephen Deng for their comments on an earlier version of this paper at the 2004 meeting of the Shakespeare Association of America. Their comments were instrumental in turning me in the direction that I pursue here.

    1. This and all other references to the play are, unless otherwise noted, to *The Tragical History of Hamlet Prince of Denmark*, ed. A. R. Braunmuller (Penguin, 2001).

    2. Annabel Patterson, *Shakespeare and the Popular Voice* (Oxford: Basil Blackwell, 1989), 13–14. Patterson seeks to mediate between opposing views of the Shakespearean theater as represented by the work of Ann Jennalie Cook and Walter Cohen, Cook arguing that Shakespeare wrote for a "privileged" educated audience and Cohen that the Shakespearean theater catered to a "social heterocosm" that included "artisans and shopkeepers" and was in turn shaped by their desire for a populist and nationalist theater (15–17). She also resists Stephen Greenblatt's theory of containment ("We need to return to a less impersonal, less totalitarian account of how Shakespeare's theater probably functioned" [25]). To do this, she argues that Hamlet, a transgressive and radical character, speaks in a "mocking, dynamic, subversive, popular, and 'general' voice" (98), and that the play opposes "academicism," then and now (29–31), and that with this voice, and its critique of certain ways of thinking, the play speaks simultaneously to "the judicious few" and

the "underprivileged many" (100). She posits that the play displaces philosophical speculation to restore to playgoers "the ground, the trust in material reality, that philosophical speculation had excavated way" (118). Here I pursue *the means* by which it does so.

3. See Steven Mullaney, "Mourning and Misogyny: *Hamlet, The Revenger's Tragedy* and the Final Progress of Elizabeth I, 1600–1607," *Shakespeare Quarterly* 45:2 (1994): 139–162, esp. p. 144.

4. Stephen Gosson, *The Schoole of Abuse* (London, 1587), STC 12098, 50.

5. Ibid., 52.

6. For one discussion of culinary metaphors in antitheatrical rhetoric, see Jeremy Lopez *Theatrical Convention and Audience Response in Early Modern Drama* (Cambridge: Cambridge University Press, 2003), 27–31.

7. For Anthony Dawson's discussion of the ways in which Shakespeare's theater offered Shakespeare's first audiences an experience related to and perhaps a substitution for their experience of Christ's real presence in the Mass, see chapter 1, "Performance and Participation" 11–37, in Anthony Dawson and Paul Yachnin, *The Culture of Playgoing in Shakespeare's England: A Collaborative Debate* (Cambridge University Press, 2001). P. A. Skantze recapitulates Dawson's arguments in terms of a "secular transubstantiation" in *Stillness in Motion in the Seventeenth-Century Theatre* (New York: Routledge, 2003), 15.

8. Those who wish to argue that Hamlet offers its audience an experience of breath or air that is spiritually or religiously inflected could argue that it extends a Catholic theatrical tradition of creating an experience of the devine in the form of the Holy Ghost through appeals to the senses that is best epitomized in the medieval drama in the *Digby Play of Mary Magdalene*.

9. In "'A History of the Air': Shakespeare and the Evaporating Self," a paper delivered to the Shakespeare Association of America in March 2002, Carla Mazzio discussed the toxicity or noxiousness of the air that playgoers had to breathe in Elizabethan and Jacobean London in relation to texts by Shakespeare, Bacon, and Donne. In that paper, she raises the possibility that the Shakespearean drama may have offered a "restorative poetics"; through weeping, she suggests, audience members may have brought about an "elemental alteration, self-evaporation, a 'clearing of the air' of the self, soul and environment."

10. Robert Weimann's suggestion that "air" puns on "heir" puts another political aspect of the statement into play. Hamlet is left eating air as the heir, that is, as someone whose own claim to the throne has been preempted, at least temporarily, by Claudius's. Weimann discusses the kinetic energies that are embodied and released in Hamlet, but not the implications of this statement for the play's theory of performance. See *Author's Pen and Actor's Voices: Playing and Writing in Shakespeare's Theatre,* ed. Helen Higbee and William West (Cambridge: Cambridge University Press, 2000), 176–177.

11. Francis Bacon, *Sylva Silvarum,* qtd. in Bruce R. Smith, "Hearing Green: Logomarginality in *Hamlet,*" Conclusion, *Early Modern Literary Studies* 7.1 (May, 2001): 5.1–7 <URL: http://purl.oclc.org/emls/07-1/logomarg/conclus.htm>, 4.

12. John Webster, qtd. in Joseph Roach, *The Player's Passion: Studies in the Science of Acting* (Newark: University of Delaware Press, 1985), 32.

13. See chapter 1 of *The Player's Passion,* especially 44–45.

14. See Bruce Smith, "Hearing Green: Logomarginality in *Hamlet,*" Physical Frame. *Early Modern Literary Studies* 7.1 (May 2001): 2.1–4 <URL: http//purl.

oclc.org/emls/07-1/logomarg/physic.htm>, 2. See also Smith's more recent essay, "Hearing Green," in *Reading the Early Modern Passions: Essays in the Cultural History of Emotion*, ed. Gail Kern Paster, Katherine Rowe, and Mary Floyd-Wilson (Philadelphia: University of Pennsylvania Press, 2004).

15. See Smith, "Hearing Green: Logomarginality in *Hamlet*," Physiological Frame. *Early Modern Literary Studies* 7.1 (May 2001): 3.1–3 <URL: http://purl.oclc.org/emls/07-1/logomarg/physiol.htm>, 2.

16. Thomas Wright, *The Passions of the Minde in Generall*, ed. Thomas O. Sloan (Urbana: University of Illinois Press, 1971), 168.

17. Ibid., 174.

18. Ibid.

19. Ibid., 170.

20. See Gail Kern Paster, "Nervous Tension: Networks of Blood and Spirit in the Early Modern Body," 106–125, in *The Body in Parts: Fantasies of Corporeality in Early Modern Europe*, ed. Carla Mazzio and David Hillman (New York and London: Routledge, 1997), 116.

21. Ibid., 110.

22. Ibid., 108–109.

23. Gail Kern Paster, "Roasted in Wrath and Fire: The Ecology of the Passions in *Hamlet* and *Othello*," 25–76, in *Humoring the Body: Emotions and the Shakespearean Stage* (Chicago and London: University of Chicago Press, 2004), esp. 34–40.

24. The word is Robert Burton's translation of a passage on air in the work of Levinus Lemnius, as quoted in Paster, "Roasted," 41.

25. Wright, *Passions*, 170.

26. Ibid., 176.

27. Ibid., 151.

28. Ibid., 177.

29. Ibid., 255.

30. *OED*, entry for "scent" v. <http://80-dictonary.oed.com.webvoy.uwindsor.ca:2048/cgi/entry/00215171>. The obsolete meaning is the third definition that the *OED* offers: "3. To exhale an odour, to smell. [So F. *sentir.*] Now *rare* or *Obs.*" (October 27, 2004).

31. *OED*, entry for "scent" v., <http://80-dictonary.oed.com.webvoy.uwindsor.ca:2048/cgi/entry/00215171> (October 27, 2004).

32. See Weimann, *Author's Pen*, 123.

33. Jane Tylus, "'Par Accident': The Public Work of Early Modern Theater," 253–271, in *Reading the Early Modern Passions*, 269.

34. Wright, *Passions*, 179.

35. Ibid., 176.

36. Stephen Orgel, "The Play of Conscience," 129–142, in *The Authentic Shakespeare and Other problems of the Early Modern Stage* (New York and London: Routledge, 2002), especially 133–134.

37. Paster, "Roasted," 41.

38. Paster, "Nervous Tension," 110.

39. "Hamlet's Cause," in *Shakespeare and the Law*, ed. Karen Cunningham and Constance Jordan (New York: Palgrave, forthcoming).

40. See chapter 3 of W. B. Worthen, *Shakespeare and the Authority of Performance* (Cambridge: Cambridge University Press, 1997). Worthen quotes the

actor Simon Callow on the experience of acting as the "incomparable feeling" of having "another person . . . breath[e] through your lungs" (144).

41. See Smith, "Hearing Green: Logomarginality in *Hamlet*," Dramaturgical Frame. *Early Modern Literary Studies* 7.1 (May 2001): 4.1–4 <URL: http//purl.oclc.org/emls/07-1/logomarg/dramat.htm>, 3.

42. The line "O God, I could be bounded in a nutshell, and count myself a king of infinite space—were it not that I have bad dreams" occurs only in the Folio. See the *Riverside Shakespeare*, 2.2.254.

43. Wright, *Passions*, 175.

44. The process of "feeling smells" therefore works to a very different end from civilizing processes that work to establish various kinds of propriety, inculcate certain forms of behavior, and uphold the integrity of the individual. In "Acting with Tact," Mazzio discusses how civilizing processes give rise to the mode of behavior we call "tact," which encourages sensitivity to "a kind of vulnerable air in the space between persons." Tact, we could argue, treats the "vulnerable air" between bodies as a body in its own right to discourage contact or make any move toward contact through touch tentative; the process of "feeling smells" breaks "tact" down, as it involves intimate contact between bodies at a remove. See Mazzio, "Acting with Tact: Touch and Theater in the Renaissance," 159–186, in *Sensible Flesh: On Touch in Early Modern Culture*, ed. Elizabeth D. Harvey (Philadelphia: University of Pennsylvania Press, 2003), esp. 186.

45. Robert Weimann also writes of the economic exchange that takes place in terms of some kind of return to the audience: "that audience, which had not come empty-handed, did not leave empty-minded. Their contribution, a profitable commodity, was rewarded with a volatile sense of 'imaginary puissance.'" His emphasis falls, however, on what Shakespeare's company gets rather than what it gives: "What remained in the theatre was the sum total of all the pennies paid, together with the desire and the need to have more of them from returning audiences." See *Author's Pen*, 216–217.

46. Wright, *Passions*, 168.

47. Here I extend Bruce Smith's notion of the dispersals that take place in the Globe. In "Hearing Green," Smith offers a descriptive formula by which sound leads to "spiritus," which is in turn dispersed through the entire space. He may write of sound, and I, of breath, but clearly the phenomena of which we write, though they differ crucially, are very intimately related. See Smith, "Hearing Green," Physical Frame, 1. Weimann's discussion of digestion in relation to the prologue to *Henry V* and the Globe's space is also a useful point of reference here. I extend his discussion of the ways in which the Globe's space digests things by applying it specifically to the dispersal of breath. See Weimann, *Author's Pen*, 75.

48. Both Smith and Weimann write of the Globe's "canopy," Smith focusing on the actual canopy above the stage and Weimann the canopy of the air to which Hamlet refers. Smith focuses on the actual canopy to explain how the shell of the Wooden O contributes to the acoustical properties and experience of plays in performance: "the presence of a canopy, however, meant that sounds originating under that canopy were reflected from top to bottom as well as from side to side, producing a more diffuse, harder to locate sound," he writes. See "Hearing Green," Physical Frame, 2. Weimann suggests that Hamlet's reference to the canopy of the air "conjoins the global circumference of this 'goodly frame the earth' with the protruding place of the stage as a 'promontory' jutting out into the pit. . . . "

(*Author's Pen*, 215). Imagining the canopy as a mouth through which the air outside the theater is ingested and then released again gives us another way of talking about Hamlet's claim that "excellent plays" offer up matter that is "well digested."

AMY COOK

Staging Nothing:
Hamlet *and Cognitive Science*

> Ham. Do you think I meant country matters?
> Oph. I think nothing, my lord.
> Ham. That's a fair thought to lie between maids' legs.
> Oph. What is, my lord?
> Ham. Nothing. (3.2.115–119)[1]

In *Hamlet*, few things are as powerful as nothing. Nothing is seen by the watchman Barnardo at the start of the play. Nothing lies between Ophelia's legs. Nothing makes the player king weep for Hecuba. Nothing is the thing that makes up the king. Nothing comes up thirty times in *Hamlet*.[2] The presence of nothing in the text calls attention to the absence that nothing is supposed to stand for. Cognitive linguistics challenges a stable definition of nothing, illuminating the things from which no things spring. In performance, *Hamlet*'s destabilization of nothing goes even further, pointing to the something that each particular nothing is. Staging nothing both sheds light on a major debate within cognitive linguistics and calls attention to the traditional assumption of a suspension of disbelief.

The Way We Think
In a 2001 issue of *SubStance*, a "Dialogue" took place between Ellen Spolsky on one side and John Tooby and Leda Cosmides on the other, regarding the

SubStance: A Review of Theory and Literary Criticism, Volume 35, Number 2 [110] (2006): 83–99. Copyright © 2006 Amy Cook.

ways literature may be evolutionarily adaptable. While both sides agreed on the value of literature, and used science to make an argument for it, the gulf between the two theories turned out to be fairly wide. Tooby and Cosmides follow a computational model of the brain derived from the work of Noam Chomsky and Steven Pinker; Spolsky argues with cognitive scientists such as Eleanore Rosch and George Lakoff for an embodied brain. The paradigm shift between seeing the brain as a computer, with input undergoing algorithmic processing, and viewing it more as an organism, shaping and being shaped by its environment, is beginning to have profound impact on various fields. Until the debate is settled, any application of cognitive science to the humanities should foreground the paradigm in which it operates. Rather than rehearse the debate here, I will use the scientific work that best helps me explain the persistent presence of nothing in *Hamlet*. Perhaps the process of applying the various theories can operate as a kind of natural selection, with "survival" being awarded to the one more fit to explain the aesthetic, emotional, and cognitive experiences that matter the most to us. Research in cognitive linguistics and emotion has provided a kind of barium milkshake to my thinking on theater, coloring and illuminating an experience that had seemed invisible.

In *Philosophy in the Flesh: The Embodied Mind and its Challenge to Western Thought*, George Lakoff and Mark Johnson argue that the "very structure of reason itself comes from the details of our embodiment" (5). One of the consequences of understanding language and cognition as coming from an embodied experience of the world is that there is no transcendental truth that thinking and language attempt to capture and represent. Our basic-level metaphor "More is up," for example, comes from experience pouring liquid into a container; our basic-level metaphor of the container structures our understanding of space, and comes from an experience of our body as having an inside and an outside.[3] While some argue for a weaker version of this embodied paradigm—that abstract concepts are based on representations of experience-based domains, rather than direct experience, as Lakoff would argue—it addresses our inability to talk about abstract concepts such as time and life without using metaphors. In *The Metaphors We Live By*, Lakoff and Johnson argue that certain thoughts are contained and defined by the metaphor we use to talk about them. For example, a metaphor like "Time is money" will systematically lead to entailment metaphors ("Time is a valuable commodity") and our relationship to time becomes defined by this coherent system of thinking of time. This is how, in our society, time can be "spent" or "wasted" and time is seen as something one has for one activity but not another. Metaphors illuminate some elements of the abstract concept and hide others, since a metaphor will only map some information from the source domain (money) to the target domain (time).

However, metaphor theory has its limits. For example, in *Women, Fire, and Dangerous Things*, Lakoff uses the example of the term "social lie" to explore the category of "lies" (74). While the idea of a social lie illuminates the graded way we categorize lies (some are intentional deceits while others are untruths spoken unknowingly or untruths spoken to protect a social contract), he admits that he does not know how the meaning of a social lie comes from the term, since the modifier "social" fails to explain completely the sense of the phrase. What Lakoff's conceptual metaphor theory (CMT) fails to account for, conceptual blending theory (CBT) explicates clearly. CMT views meaning metaphorically, such that information from one domain (source) gets mapped onto a second domain (target) to understand the target domain in terms of the source. In *The Way We Think*, Gilles Fauconnier and Mark Turner argue that there are many things that cannot be explained by an analysis of mapping between two domains. They use Fauconnier's mental space theory to envision informational blends.[4] Blends are constructions of meaning based on projection of information from two or more input spaces to a blended space, such that the blended meaning contains information and structure from more than one space. The meaning of "social lie" depends upon projecting information regarding lying and information regarding the rules of social etiquette into a blended space. In this way, a "lie" is not understood through mapping information from "social" onto our understanding of "lie;" rather, both spaces contribute information to the final understanding. What is so rich about this theory is how it explains so much creative elaboration of metaphoric thought. Pulling apart these blends in language reveals hidden spaces and assumptions.

The blended space is like a stage set with props and characters or a *commedia* script awaiting enaction and improvisation. Double-scope blends create emergent meaning by combining structural information from both input spaces. For example, In *The Literary Mind*, Turner explores stories, from Jesus's dying for our sins to the children's story *The Runaway Bunny*. In each case, there is information in the blended space that is not present in either of the input spaces but is a result of the blend. In the example of Jesus dying for our sins, the input space of Jesus as being without sin is blended with the input space of human beings who are sinful. In the blend, his death expiates the sins of mankind. His death becomes dramatic, meaningful, and iconic because we understand it neither literally nor metaphorically[5] but as a blend; the blend then shapes how Christians think of the cross, suffering, death, and sin. Blending theory exposes unconscious assumptions that pervade our language. Seeing "nothing" as a blend, for example, allows us to question its provenance and think about the matter from which its absence springs.

Nothing as a Mental Construct

Birthed by thought, nothing is something made "so" by thinking: nothing does not exist; we have no material proof of it; we must therefore construct it. Conceptual blending theory unpacks the seemingly stable idea of nothing and exposes it as a blend of multiple mental spaces, with an emergent structure capable of begetting a lineage of thoughts specific to the particular somethings blended into nothing. Fauconnier and Turner argue that this articulation of a gap is more than just a function of language; it is evidence of how we construct blends by projecting information from two or more mental spaces into a blended space and then are able to use what was a non-thing as a thing:

> Inside the blend, this new element can be manipulated as an ordinary thing, and the usual routines of language for referring to things can be deployed. In the case of "the missing chair," the missing chair is a thing in the blend that, viewed from the outside, is a non-thing. It can be pointed to and takes up physical space. It inherits its physical characteristics of being a gap from the "actual" input, in which there is not a chair in the corresponding position. We suggest it is no accident that expressions like "nobody," "nothing," and "no luck" are ordinary noun phrases for picking out things in a space. That is why it is easy to get them in all the normal places in grammatical constructions: "He was seen by no one," "I had no money," "No brains is your problem," "I expect no one to understand me," "He has a no-nonsense attitude." (241)

Once we have created the blended space that is nothing, it can take on many of the characteristics of something, just as "missing chair" has many of the characteristics of "chair." This is its emergent structure; nothing takes on a powerful meaning by the selective projection of absence from the place of a particular substance. In discussing the case of "zero," Fauconnier and Turner refer to the invention of zero; though initially a place holder for the absence of number, it became a number in its own right and was used in the same mathematical functions of other numbers.[6] This is the same powerful nothing that the Chorus references at the start of Shakespeare's *Henry V*, capable of standing in for a million in the right space: "since a crooked figure may / Attest in little place a million, / And let us, ciphers to this great account, on your imaginary forces work" (Prologue, 15–17). A zero in one place may be a cipher, but it only takes six of them placed after a one to make a million.

Hamlet's Nothing

During the badinage before the play within a play, different shapes of nothing surface between Hamlet and Claudius and Hamlet and Ophelia. With

Hamlet's typical word-play, Claudius's question about how Hamlet is doing becomes a question about how he is eating, and Hamlet responds that he is eating the nothing that he is being fed: "I eat the air, promise-crammed. You cannot feed capons so" (3.2.93). Claudius responds that he has "nothing with this answer, Hamlet. These words are not mine" (3.2.95), as if Hamlet's words, hurled at him, missed their target, and Claudius failed to catch them. Claudius declares the answer "nothing" since it is not something to him. Hamlet, out-blending Claudius, insists that the words, once spoken, defy proprietary control: "No, nor mine now" (3.2.97). Hamlet gives shape and meaning back to the nothing of his words by locating them apart from the speaker or hearer, like the "missing chair" evoked in reference to absence.

Similarly, Ophelia dodges Hamlet's question about "country matters" by echoing Claudius's retort to the petulant prince: "I think nothing, my lord" (3.2.116). Again, Hamlet manipulates "nothing" into something, calling Ophelia's nothing "a fair thought to lie between maids' legs." In Hamlet's dexterous use of words, nothing is suddenly the genital space, and Ophelia's nothing must be viewed through the mental space of the penis's thingness. Compared to Hamlet's thing, Ophelia's is absent; but both are made mentally visible through Hamlet's language.

What becomes of Ophelia's nothing when it is embodied onstage? Hamlet's language disrobes Ophelia by drawing the audience's attention toward what is or is not between her legs. But disrobed, out of costume, Ophelia must be the actor portraying her, since Ophelia requires the loan of an actor's body to become corporeal. In Elizabethan England, the theatrical convention of the boy player adds another layer of the blending that occurs: the actor playing Ophelia did not have "nothing" between his legs. The theatrics of the language on the page call to a reader's mind the genitals of the characters; embodied onstage, the theatrics of the language call to mind the genitals of the actors. The eroticization of boys dressed as women, things masquerading as nothings, was one of the main concerns of antitheatricalists of the time.[7] Shakespeare breaks the illusion of Ophelia's sex because in performance it is more powerful that he/she is both. Shakespeare's "nothing" exposes a presence in a space designated as empty. This presence in absence is the emergent structure of *Hamlet*'s nothing. The performance of language onstage changes the dynamics of meaning through the networks of spaces evoked and blended in the process of understanding.

Theater's Blend of Fiction and Reality

Despite the growing wave of exciting work in literary studies to incorporate research from the sciences into examinations of literature, so far there has been very little work done within theater or performance studies to use the cognitive sciences to put pressure on our understanding of plays in performance.[8] From understanding that the man onstage reciting "to be or not to be" is simultaneously an actor, a character, and a historical figure, to feeling moved by Hamlet's death but not moved to jump onstage, theatrical blends illuminate some of the same cognitive illusions used in our daily life. Onstage everything is a hybrid: part representation, part the thing itself. When Shakespeare writes "Who's there?" it is fiction; when the actor says it onstage, it is partially fiction and partially a real question asked by a real man in a real situation. He is neither completely one nor the other, and this both/and status gives him a particular power. Coleridge introduced the idea of a "willing suspension of disbelief" to explain the power that unreal events and people can have to evoke real emotions; theater theory, performance analysis, and reviews rely on this metaphor to discuss the phenomenology of theater. Suspension of disbelief has become the predominate narrative of theater theory, yet it is untenable, given current cognitive linguistic theory and research in emotion.

Suspension of Disbelief

In *Great Reckonings in Little Rooms*, Bert States argues that "The presentational basis of theater rests upon a double pretense: the play pretends that we don't exist (the fourth wall convention) and we pretend that the play does (the willing suspension of disbelief)" (206). This formulation sees theater as rising out of denial; it is the emergent structure of nothing. To suspend disbelief creates disbelief as a presence that haunts our reception of theater; the logic goes that in order to enjoy fiction we must hold in abeyance the knowledge that it is not true. This allows us to feel in reaction to what is happening onstage, but not to act based on what is happening on stage. Suspension of disbelief remains a defining feature of how we speak of being "carried away" or "transported" by a successful narrative.

Considering how central this idea of suspension of disbelief is to our understanding of fiction, particularly theater, it is astonishing how little interrogation it has received. Most scholarly pressure placed on "suspension of disbelief" relies on an assumption that thinking and feeling are separate mechanisms and that engagement with fiction is a special state, requiring a special interruption of normally functioning mental assays capable of determining truth value. The argument of Tooby and Cosmides depends on just such a separation between fiction and non-fiction: "Most especially, fiction when communicated is not intended to be understood as true—as literally describing real events in the world accurately" (12). As Spolsky points out, however, plenty of people misapply fiction to reality:

> One can think not only of King Lear and his daughters, but of the conflict faced by a young man who needs (according to one

of his cultural stories) to drink beer of an evening, even though, according to another story, he needs to drive his date safely home. If only there were an evolved mechanism that would inform the fellow that the first story is a local, cultural fiction, and the second a matter of fact. [. . .] the evidence is that humans *do* confuse the two [fictional worlds and real worlds] frequently, subject, as they are, to powerful stories and their powerful interpreters. (187)

According to Tooby and Cosmides, suspension of disbelief suggests that we have a way of bracketing our reception of fiction such that cognitive input during a fictional event is not confused with the truth. Spolsky argues that bits of information within stories are projected differently into different situations—with fictional information often being projected to nonfictional situations—which is how we can know that there is truth in *King Lear* without *King Lear* being true. Spolsky does not pursue within her article the implications of this statement, but they bear on our understanding of suspension of disbelief. The conceptual blending theory of cognitive linguistics challenges our belief in suspension of disbelief and makes way for a new understanding of the nothing that makes *Hamlet*'s player king weep for Hecuba, and makes the play the thing to catch the conscience of the king.

Two theoretical interrogations of suspension of disbelief are Eva Schaper's complication of our definition, and Norman Holland's application of neuroscience to the phenomenon, though neither sufficiently challenges the assumptions on which the concept is based. Schaper investigates the relationship between suspension of disbelief and emotions, suggesting that without the first, "we could not avoid the puzzle resulting from being moved by what we do not believe ever really happened or ever existed" (31). She cannot discount the experience of emotions in response to a fictional world, but is troubled by the assumption that either what we are reacting to is illusory or how we react is illusory: "Suspension of disbelief, whatever it may amount to in detail, gains plausibility only if we assume that there is a requirement that being genuinely moved presupposes holding beliefs about the object of such emotions, and the notion of suspension of disbelief meets that requirement" (34). She begins to dismantle suspension of disbelief, arguing that belief may be more nuanced than "suspension" suggests. She nonetheless does not question the assumption that in order to feel something we have to believe the stimulus that causes the emotion actually exists.

It is not necessary to believe that Horatio literally held Hamlet in the chambers of his heart—miniaturized, presumably—in order to be moved by Horatio's reaction to Hamlet's dying plea, just as it is not necessary to believe that either Hamlet or Horatio actually exists. When our best friend reports that she has "reached a dead-end" in her career or that her end is near, we do not need to believe that her life is literally a path or that time is literally located in space to understand—and react emotionally to—her concern that she is not progressing or that she does not have much time left to live. If it is not necessary to understand the sentence literally in order to understand it emotionally, then why insist that disbelief is suspended when something is spoken onstage? Why are we so committed to the belief that we believe?

Norman Holland follows up his earlier use of psychoanalysis to explain suspension of disbelief with an application of neuroscience research.[9] He argues that when we stop paying attention to our bodies, our plans, etc., as we do in a theater or when reading a book, we cut off the connection between our emotions and our prefrontal cortex. We still feel the emotions, but they no longer go to the prefrontal cortex for reality testing and planning. The planning that is done in the prefrontal cortex requires that we "imagine a future and a past for an object, neither of which is true now . . . And as long as we do not plan to move while reading a book or watching a play or movie, we do not test the reality of what we are perceiving. Thus, we willingly suspend disbelief. The minute we do plan to move, we, as we say, break the spell" (4). His formulation explicitly expands suspension of disbelief, arguing that it is the same thing that occurs when we imagine hypotheticals or counterfactuals. To suggest that one state is a "spell" wherein we have willingly suspended disbelief is to underestimate the power and ubiquity of this particular state.

Holland's summation that "we can feel real emotions toward unreal fictions, because two different brain systems are at work" (6) continues what I see as a false dichotomy between real and unreal in emotions and situations. To argue that normal situations that evoke emotions are reality-tested is to presume that "reality" is important to emotions. When someone cries because she did not receive an expected call from her boyfriend, she, like the player king, is crying over nothing, since the lack of a call suggests nothing in and of itself. The fictional world wherein such a lapse hints at betrayal or lack of interest is not reality-tested either. The fact that we use fictional pieces of information to construct a non-fictional account of a situation that generates our emotions does not decrease or alter the emotions we experience.

This dichotomy is unnecessary in theories of embodied cognition, since the brain is seen as constantly composing narratives to function and make sense of its environment. Outside of the debate between embodied cognition and computational cognition, neuroscientist V. S. Ramachandran isolates an anomalous brain condition which, he argues, points to how the brain tells itself "the truth" in an undamaged state. Ramachandran reports on cases of anosognosia, wherein patients do not believe that they have suffered the injuries that they have—usually paralysis due to stroke or other cerebral damage impacting the right hemisphere of the brain. These patients concoct extraordinary stories to explain away the evidence of their paralysis, or to avoid providing the evidence. They will say that they lifted a tray with a paralyzed arm even though the doctor witnessed that the arm did not move, or they will deny a request to move the arm claiming that, rather than paralysis, their denial comes from preference. Ramachandran suggests that the key to understanding this syndrome is its relationship to hemispheric differences between the right and left brain. The left hemisphere, he suggests, is responsible for creating a "'belief system,' a story that makes sense of the available evidence" (134), and the right hemisphere collects potentially contradictory information and then periodically forces a revision of the script to fit the latest collected data. If the right hemisphere sustains damage, he argues, the left hemisphere need not revise its story because the right hemisphere is no longer recognizing contradictory data. Ramachandran's story of a hemispheric "devil's advocate" may seem speculative, but his research on patients with anosognosia suggests that the notion that we feel real emotions only about what we believe to be real fails to explain the everyday impact of "fictional" stories ("I'm fat" or "Cordelia must not love me") or the extraordinary impact of hemispheric damage.

While Ramachandran's theory explains a severe case of brain damage, Fauconnier and Turner's theory of "living in the blend" explains cognitive and linguistic leaps in articulation and comprehension that happen every day. Like Holland's elaboration of suspension of disbelief, "living in the blend" explains being "carried away" at the theater, but unlike Holland, Fauconnier and Turner speak of *living* in the blend, with the assumption that both thinking and feeling are requisite for living. Similar to Erving Goffman's conception of the "operating fiction" (26) used to process and understand a given situation, Fauconnier and Turner's reformulation does not tie the process to fiction or belief. The use of fiction as the controlling agent, though, presupposes a factual set of terms with which the fiction deals. This is an assumption that "living in the blend" avoids, because it relies on the conceptual process that constructs temporary matrices for understanding anything. The degree of truth is irrelevant to what makes a blend useful or emotionally evocative.

Fauconnier and Turner discuss a severe case of depression studied in Berlin in the 1980s. Sufferers had purchased lottery tickets—for "fun," rather than with any real hope of winning—and then felt crippling depression when they lost. Their symptoms were like those of someone who had lost a home or a loved one, suggesting that since purchasing their tickets, the lottery hopefuls had been living in a fantasy of having won. When the reality of not winning destroyed this, it also took away what the fantasy had brought them: "The amazing thing is that the fantasy world seems to have had profound effects on the psychological reality of the real world, given that the patients had no delusions about the odds of winning, and said so clearly" (231). The woman who sent a note to Burbage after his performance in *Richard III*, asking that he "come to her" by the name of Richard, was hoping to continue to live in the blend of Richard Burbage and Richard the hunchbacked king (see Sorlien, 10). Women who vie to catch the bride's bouquet have blended the bouquet with a husband, living in the blend that to catch one is to procure the other. The limits of these blends differ; while it would not be uncommon for the bridesmaid to feel happy at catching the bouquet, it would be cause for concern if she began sending out invitations with only the ritual flowers as fiancé. Fauconnier and Turner's formulation of "living in the blend" does not restrict itself to fiction, but allows room for the extensive and powerful experience—both linguistically, conceptually, and emotionally—of what has fallen under the misleading and restrictive category of "suspension of disbelief."

What's Hecuba to him?

Ham. Is it not monstrous that this player here,
       But in a fiction, in a dream of passion,
       Could force his soul so to his own conceit
       That from her working all his visage wann'd,
       Tears in his eyes, distraction in's aspect,
       A broken voice, and his whole function suiting
       With forms to his conceit? and all for nothing!
       For Hecuba!
       What's Hecuba to him, or he to her,
       That he should weep for her? (2.2.545–554)

Hamlet's concern that the player weeps for Hecuba while he, with "the motive and the cue for passion," does nothing, suggests an interesting relationship between emotions and fiction. Hamlet sees his own reality as more likely to prompt real feelings (and, he assumes, actions) and is outraged that he is not drowning the stage with tears. Hamlet rages about being dull and "unpregnant of my cause" and Shakespeare crams the speech with extra syllables and interrupted lines, contradicting Hamlet's claim that he is "muddy-mettled" and says "nothing":

Who calls me villain, breaks my pate across,
Plucks off my beard and blows it in my face,
Tweaks me by the nose, gives me the lie i' th' throat
As deep as to the lungs—who does me this?
Ha! (2.2.567–571)

The first three lines above begin with a spondaic and then trochaic feet, shifting the usual rhythm of the iambic foot that stresses the second syllable to a rhythm that stresses the first syllable. The third line interrupts the iambic rhythm further, shoving extra unstressed syllables into the line with a troche in the first, third, and fourth foot. While "Ha!" can also be printed on the following line, either option forces the actor into the emotion of the moment, either giving him (or her) a gap or pause of nine syllables before continuing with "'swounds" or creating a spondaic first foot with "Ha! 'swounds" and then ending on a feminine ending with "be." Hamlet's soliloquy expresses and exposes his own emotions; finding himself moved by the player's performance of emotions, he transforms the "nothing" of his response into a plan. The fiction of the theater, he decides, is the way to capture the truth of the king's guilt. Emotion, like the "direction" best discovered through "indirection," is best assayed through the performance of emotion.

The performance of emotion is not necessarily the same thing as emotion. The player king performs emotions in reaction to a story of a woman's emotions in reaction to her dead husband. While he clearly shows the biological effluvia of emotions—he cries, turns pale, etc.—we do not know whether he *feels* the emotions he shows. Similarly, while Shakespeare expresses Hamlet's emotions in verse and the actor performs Hamlet's emotions in performance, the audience of *Hamlet* does not know whether or not the actor playing Hamlet actually feels the emotions he conveys.

Elly Konijn studied empirically whether actors experience the emotions that they convey their characters to be feeling. She finds that the emotions experienced onstage are aroused by the "situational meaning-structure of the performance situation, rather than by the emotions of the character" (65); i.e., onstage, actors feel the emotions associated with acting in front of an audience (challenge, nervousness, concentration, tension, etc.), regardless of what emotions the character is supposed to be feeling or the emotions the actor is performing. This is true, she finds, regardless of whether or not the actor considers him/herself to be "method" and mimetic in style, or presentational and detached. The emotions experienced by the actors are related to the task at hand for them, not to the experience being had by their characters: "During a *performance*, however, the demands of the actual context of acting—in front of an audience—will prevent the actor from losing himself in character-emotions" (78). The actor and character have different feelings, merged perhaps by an expression of feeling; the emotional goal of theater—the experience that suspension of disbelief is called upon to explain—is the ability of an audience member to have the same feelings as the character, midwifed through the performance of the actor. In order, then, to understand how this could possibly be the case, it is necessary to complicate our understanding of emotions.

Emotions, Aristotle argued, are the key ingredients in tragedy, since any dramatic narrative must contain events arousing pity and fear in order for the audience to experience catharsis. The scholarly debate on catharsis has been cacophonous, but few theater theorists have asked what "pity and fear" are. They can be forgiven, since until recently, even neuroscientists privileged reason over the study of emotions. When emotion was studied as part of the brain, it was seen as part of "the lower neural strata associated with ancestors whom no one worshiped" (Damasio 1999, 39). The limbic system, the general term for the emotional centers of the brain, was thought to act alone, deep in the brain. One was taught that it was the forebrain that understood math, and the "reptilian brain" that was afraid.

In *Descartes' Error,* Damasio defines emotions as a "collection of changes in body state that are induced in myriad organs by nerve cell terminals, under the control of a dedicated brain system, which is responding to the content of thoughts relative to a particular entity or event" (139). Sensory input is sent directly to the thalamus, responsible for shunting any potentially alarming information to the amygdala, the body's alarm mechanism. Emotional stimulus is sent directly from the thalamus to the amygdala, which prepares a physical response, as well as being sent to the sensory cortex where the information is assessed. Once the sensory cortex has assessed the stimulus, it will send inhibitory or excitatory information to the hypothalamus, which sends and receives messages to and from the rest of the body. The messages involve neurotransmitters and hormones to alter the body state, resulting in symptoms such as sweaty palms, dry mouth, increased heart rate, flushing or pallor, constriction of the stomach, and relaxation or tension of muscles. These responses occur in order to protect us, as, for example, an increased heart rate will be necessary if one needs to flee.

A racing heart, however, could mean panic, rage, or love. Although there may be subtle differences between panic and love in the overall chemical changes in the body, Damasio argues that the primary difference lies in the assessment of the body state by the cerebral cortex. He calls this assessment *feeling,* and defines it as the experience of the emotion in the body juxtaposed with images, memories, and knowledge of the stimuli. The body's physical reaction is not specific to a feeling; in order for the feeling to register with the person, the specific mix of bodily changes must be assessed in light of other information. The racing heart and constricted stomach is assessed as love because of the candlelight and the dilated eyes of the person across the table. In another situation, the same experience feels like food poisoning. Whereas emotions generally can be perceived by a bystander, feelings are internal and private—mental states evoked by the physical reaction of emotions.

Humans do not need to experience something in order to have an emotional reaction to it. A spectator might experience fear when seeing Oedipus walk onstage with bleeding eyes, or upon hearing the cry of pain from offstage; the stimulus resembles those patterns that require immediate physical response, and therefore the amygdala is alerted. The emotions could also be aroused by the mere expressions of the actors. The amygdala is highly attuned to expressions of fear in others, with one part devoted to assessing facial expressions and one to tonal shifts in voice.[10] Perceiving emotion in others can be enough to generate them in the spectator. One study exposed subjects to another person making an expression of disgust; when the expression registered intense disgust, the subjects' own brains registered disgust, exciting the same neurons in the brain that become active when disgusted.[11] There is a growing body of evidence that humans are not a closed system, we react emotionally to expressions of emotions in others.

Damasio calls this the "as-if body loop" and argues that witnessing suffering in a loved one can evoke a biological response similar to actually experiencing such suffering. The body loop is the system for circulating information—hormonal, electrical—through the body, to alter the body's state under certain circumstances—fear, arousal, etc. The cognitive representation of the body's state recognizes changes as if they are going on in the body, even when they are not. This is necessary, Damasio argues, because it facilitates simulation; it allows us to experience emotions separate from the stimulus that initiates them, as in memory. Memory does not recall an exact replica of the person or event remembered, but an interpretation or version of the original (Damasio 1994, 100). This imitation of the memory is enough, however, to arouse the emotions associated with the original.

Theater depends upon the brain's ability to reconstruct the emotions associated with certain events. In its imitation of an action on stage, theater creates an imitation of an action in the brain that in turn creates emotion. A picture of one's mother evokes the emotions associated with her. Just as Aristotle's tragedy is an imitation of an action, the memory it recalls is an imitation of the original event or stimulus, which then evokes real emotions in response to the representation. The fear and pity that Aristotle associated with a reaction to tragedy onstage are mimetic, just as pity and fear in the spectator rely on mimesis in reaction to "real" events. If every feeling is a mental story created to explain a biological reaction, or emotion, then the feeling evoked by Hecuba need not be any different from the feeling evoked by remembering one's mother. Both are reactions to representations.

Research into the human mirror-neuron system sheds light on the power of theater to initiate an emotional reaction in the audience, mirroring emotions performed onstage. While Damasio's work is based on functional magnetic resonance imaging (fMRI) scans of patients with various brain abnormalities, electro-encephalographic (EEG) and magnetoencephalographic (MEG) readings of normal human brains suggest a system of mirror neurons that react to specific actions in others. Rizzolatti and Craighero document activation of the premotor cortex in persons watching someone perform an action or even a meaningless gesture.[12] Other studies have shown that activation of the mirror-neuron system occurs when subjects witness actions forming the intended action, like reaching for the telephone. Both studies indicate that not only do humans have a mirror-neuron system similar to that in monkeys,[13] but that ours is more advanced and probably plays a large role in our ability to imitate others. Research on mirror neurons suggests that there is a system in the brain to facilitate learning, compassion, and connection to others. Our traditional ideas about why we are moved by theater or the fictional (or true) stories of others must begin to consider the work being done in the sciences.

Not Nothing

Ger.   To whom do you speak this?
Ham.   Do you see nothing there?
Ger.   Nothing at all; yet all that is I see. (3.4.131–133)

Hamlet asks if Gertrude sees nothing and she confirms that she sees nothing; they are in agreement: Hamlet points to nothing and she sees it. Gertrude's insistence that "all that is I see" makes nothing part of all that is, something *Hamlet* insists on throughout. On stage, of course, Hamlet is not pointing to nothing, but to the ghost, embodied by an actor—perhaps Shakespeare in the original—whom he calls nothing, yet whom the audience definitely sees. Nothing is there, onstage, and has the power in its ghostly absence to provide the cue for passion and bloody thoughts. Blending theory illuminates the network of mental spaces primed and operating within Shakespeare's play. It allows us to find content previously obscured by the blends that construct seemingly "literal" meanings. Any application of cognitive science should recognize the power of the embodied actor to alter and play with the meaning of language. As a character, Ophelia might have nothing between her legs, but onstage she has something very particular between her legs.

Further, cognitive linguistic theory complicates and challenges traditional theories of suspension of disbelief and clear distinctions between truth and fiction. When nothing takes the stage, the lines get blurred. To base our theory of fiction on a division between fact and fiction, something and nothing, is to reify binaries between literal and metaphoric, thinking and feeling, which current scientific research does not bear out. Many of the witnesses of the September 11th attacks on the World Trade Center began their description by saying "It was like a movie." The real thing had to be compared to a fictional world in order to be understood. We could argue that this means that suspension of disbelief is required for belief, but this explodes the term out of usefulness while acknowledging that belief is not necessary for belief. If our brains are wired to react to intended gestures in others, and our emotions can be triggered by events not happening to us directly, than watching Hamlet react to the player's story of Hecuba mirrors our reaction to Hamlet's determined seeing of nothing. It feels like it is there, so it must be there. The truth of the ghost or the thing—non-thing—between Ophelia's legs is all in the mind of the beholder. Theater teaches us to see and feel for nothing, and that is something.

NOTES

1. All quotations from *Hamlet* are from *The Arden Shakespeare*, 1982.

2. As opposed to the 32 times it is referenced in *King Lear*, which has received more critical attention for its "nothing." For an examination of *King Lear* in light of debates circulating at the time of atomism and divisibility, see Crane, 2004. She points out that around 1600, the Aristotelian notion that what is visible behaves similarly to what is not visible began to give way, through questions about condensation and evaporation, to theories of atomism that posited invisible forces. She compares this "intuitive physics" with the "basic image schemas" of George Lakoff and Mark Johnson, wherein our language system reflects concept of physics, such as a cause is a physical force.

3. See Lakoff 1987, 271 and Lakoff and Turner 1989, 19.

4. Mental spaces are packets of information constructed on the fly, in which information is organized. For more on mental space theory, see Fauconnier, *Mental Spaces*.

5. To understand it metaphorically would mean projecting information from a source space onto a target space to understand the target in terms of the source. Jesus's physical death is not understood in terms of our sins or his sinlessness; to understand his death as relieving our sins requires a blend of information from the ideas of death as being an end to earthly suffering, our having sins, and Jesus being without sin.

6. See Fauconnier and Turner, 244. For a brilliant book-length study on how cognitive linguistics illuminates the development of something as "literal" as mathematics, see *Where Mathematics Come From* by Rafael Núñez and George Lakoff. They argue that mathematical concepts are all products of the human mind and the language necessary to express them; zero does not exist separately but rather is "seen" as a number through a shift in perception.

7. For more on the antitheatricalist attention to cross-dressing, see Barish, 132–154, and Reynolds.

8. Some excellent applications of cognitive science in literary studies include the work of Mary Thomas Crane, Donald Freeman, and F. Elizabeth Hart. Some notable exceptions to the silence within the theater field include Bruce McConachie's article on image schemas and theater history and his forthcoming book with Hart, *Performance and Cognition* (Routledge), and forthcoming work by Rhonda Blair examining Stanislavsky from a cognitive perspective.

9. Psychoanalysis, he originally argued, sees suspension of disbelief as a "regression to the stage in infancy when, according to psychoanalytic theory, the child feels the boundaries between itself and mother as blurred, uncertain, and

permeable" (2–3). In conclusion, however, he appears to move to use neuroscience to complement his earlier psychoanalytic reading, hoping, it seems, that the two may not be contradictory but that perhaps neuroscience may provide some empirical proof of psychoanalytic theories: "The willing suspension of disbelief takes us back to a time when our limbic systems had begun to function, infancy" (6).

    10. See Carter, 85.

    11. See Phillips.

    12. Although I know of no specific study or evidence, this information seems to call into question another assumption of suspension of disbelief, cited by Tooby and Cosmides that "fictional worlds engage emotion systems while disengaging action systems" (8).

    13. See Rizzolatti et al, 2001 and Kohler et al, 2002.

WORKS CITED

Barish, Jonas. *The Antitheatrical Prejudice.* Berkeley: University of California Press, 1981.

Carter, Rita. *Mapping the Mind.* Berkeley: University of California Press, 1998.

Crane, Mary Thomas. *Shakespeare's Brain: Reading with Cognitive Theory.* Princeton: Princeton University Press, 2001.

———. "The Physics of *King Lear:* Cognition in a Void." *The Shakespearean International Yearbook 4: Shakespeare Studies Today.* Ed. Graham Brodshaw, Tom Bishop, & Mark Turner. Aldershot: Ashgate, 2004; 3–23.

Damasio, Antonio R. *Descartes' Error: Emotion, Reason, and the Human Brain.* New York: Avon, 1994.

———. *The Feeling of What Happens: Body and Emotion in the Making of Consciousness.* New York: Harcourt, 1999.

Fauconnier, Gilles. *Mental Spaces: Aspects of Meaning Construction in Natural Language.* Cambridge University Press, 1994.

———. "Compression and Emergent Structure." Manuscript.

Fauconnier, Gilles and Mark Turner. *The Way We Think: Conceptual Blending and the Mind's Hidden Complexities.* New York: Basic Books, 2002.

Freeman, Donald C. "'Catch[ing] the nearest way': *Macbeth* and Cognitive Metaphor." *Journal of Pragmatics* 24 (1995); 689–708.

Goffman, Erving. *Frame Analysis: An Essay on the Organization of Experience.* New York: Harper, 1974.

Hart, F. Elizabeth. "Cognitive Linguistics: The Experiential Dynamics of Metaphor." *Mosaic* 28, 1995; 1–23.

Holland, Norman. "The Willing Suspension of Disbelief: A Neuro-Psychoanalytic View" PsyArt: A Hyperlink Journal for the Psychological Study of the Arts, article 020919. Available http: http://www.clas.ufl.edu/ipsa/journal/2003_holland06.shtml, February 4, 2005.

Kohler E, Keysers C, Umiltà MA, Fogassi L, Gallese V, Rizzolatti G. "Hearing sounds, understanding actions: action representation in mirror neurons." *Science* 297 (2002); 846–847.

Konijn, Elly. "The Actor's Emotions Reconsidered: A Psychological Task-Based Perspective." *Acting (Re)Considered: A theoretical and practical guide.* Second Edition. Ed. Phillip B. Zarrilli. London: Routledge, 2002; 62–81.

Lakoff, George. *Women, Fire, and Dangerous Things: What Categories Reveal about the Mind.* Chicago: University of Chicago Press, 1987.

Lakoff, George and Mark Johnson. *Metaphors We Live By.* Chicago and London: University of Chicago Press, 1980.

———. *Philosophy in the Flesh: The Embodied Mind and its Challenge to Western Thought.* New York: Basic, 1999.

Lakoff, George and Mark Turner. *More Than Cool Reason: A Field Guide to Poetic Metaphor.* Chicago: University of Chicago Press, 1989.

McConachie, Bruce A. "Doing Things with Image Schemas: The Cognitive Turn in Theatre Studies and the Problem of Experience for Historians." *Theatre Journal* 53.4, 2001; 569–594.

Phillips, M. L. et al. "A specific neural substrate for perceiving facial expressions of disgust," letter to Nature, 389:6550 (1997); 495–497.

Núñez, Rafael and George Lakoff. *Where Mathematics Comes From.* New York: Basic, 2000.

Ramachandran, V. S. and Sandra Blakeslee. *Phantoms in the Brain: Probing the Mysteries of the Human Mind.* New York: Quill, 1998.

Reynolds, Bryan. "The Devil's House, 'or worse': Transversal Power and Antitheatrical Discourse in Early Modern England." *Theatre Journal* 49. Johns Hopkins University Press, 1997: 143–167.

Rizzolatti, G., Fogassi, L., & Gallese, V. "Neurophysiological mechanisms underlying the understanding and imitation of action." *Nature Reviews Neuroscience* 2: (2001); 661–670.

Rizzolatti, Giacomo and Craighero, Laila. "The Mirror-Neuron System." *Annual Review of Neuroscience,* 27 (2004); 169–192.

Schaper, Eva. "Fiction and the Suspension of Disbelief." *British Journal of Aesthetics,* 18:1 (1978: Winter); 31–44.

Shakespeare, William. *Hamlet.* Ed. Harold Jenkins. London: Arden Shakespeare, 1982.

Sorlien, Robert Parker, ed. *The Diary of John Manningham of the Middle Temple, 1602–1603.* Hanover: University Press of New England, 1976.

Spolsky, Ellen. "Why and How to Take the Fruit and Leave the Chaff." *SubStance* 94/95 (2001); 177–197.

———. "Dialogue: Ellen Spolsky Responds to John Tooby and Leda Cosmides." *SubStance* 30.1&2 (2001); 201–202.

States, Bert O. *Great Reckonings in Little Rooms: On the Phenomenology of Theater.* Berkeley: University of California Press, 1985.

Turner, Mark. *The Literary Mind: The Origins of Thought and Language.* Oxford: Oxford University Press, 1996.

Tooby, John and Leda Cosmides. "Does Beauty Build Adapted Minds? Toward an Evolutionary Theory of Aesthetics, Fiction, and the Arts." *SubStance* 94/95 (2001); 6–27.

———. "Dialogue: John Tooby and Leda Cosmides Respond to Ellen Spolsky." *SubStance* 30.1&2 (2001); 199–200.

LINGUI YANG

Cognition and Recognition:
Hamlet's Power of Knowledge

Knowledge is power.

—Francis Bacon

Almost as an intellectual manifesto of modernity, Bacon's conception of knowledge as power is integral to the Renaissance discourse of the mind-body relationship in the formation of subjectivity. The early modern knowledge of self marks the beginning of modern epistemologies. Modern philosophers can trace the development of all epistemological modes to their early modern intellectual ancestors, who looked back still further at the Greek thinkers to challenge the orthodox mythological ways of knowing humanity. There were inevitably debates over the cognitive process among early modern intellectuals simply because they referred to different knowledge systems. Experimental philosophers such as Bacon relied more on practical experience for the abstraction of knowledge than theologists and skepticists such as Montaigne, who doubted contemporary teachings about the humanities *(studia humanitatis)*.[1]

Shakespeare must have been aware of his era's debate about knowledge and power and dramatizes some arguments in his plays. Various models of early modern epistemology permeate *Hamlet,* in particular, a play that dramatizes the epistemological dilemma of the Prince. The Hamletean predicament

Foreign Literature Studies/Wai Guo Wen Xue Yan Jiu, Volume 28, Number 117 (February 2006): pp. 16–23. Copyright © 2006 *Foreign Literature Studies.*

is so omnipresent in the Western history of epistemology—especially concerning the relationship between mind and body—that cultural philosophers must point back to the play for evidence of human knowledge. Thus, seen in the context of early modern discourses of knowledge and power, the play comments on the process of knowing and the embodiment of social consciousness. At the same time, some modes of the early modern conception of knowledge have been reinstated or elaborated by later thinkers such as Descartes. The play, then, has become a reflecting screen on which numerous cultural imprints are projected. As a result, we can map out a cultural psychology through examining modern interpretations of the play. *Hamlet* is a cultural trope or a mirror through which Cartesian intellectuals introspectively examine the human soul and psychoanalysts explore the consciousness. First of all, it is a play of human self-knowledge and the predicament that knowledge has caused:

> What a piece of work is a man, how noble in reason, how infinite in
> faculties . . . how like an angel in apprehension, how like a god!
> . . . And yet to me what is this quintessence of dust?
> (2.2.280–283)

For Hamlet, knowing is suffering because there is a substantial gap between knowing and action, and between the mind and the body. The intellectual world is impotent in the reality of flesh ("quintessence of dust"). Hamlet is perplexed by the gap between the material world and the ideal world and by the impotence of moral rationality.

Renaissance intellectuals had a clear vision of the power of knowledge in the construction of social and moral ideals. For Machiavelli and Bacon, knowledge is an empowering force and means of control. Machiavelli's knowledge must open the way to immediate and practical conquest, and the desires for control and conquest "give man his reason for being, his soul, his *virtu*" (D'Amico 163). Prospero's use of magic—a special form of knowledge—for his control of the island might be a response to the Machiavellian conception of knowledge. Prospero has made a successful experiment by transferring the learning from his books into control over Caliban and the islanders. However, Prospero's wish to retire belies Machiavellian desires for lasting power. Like Lear, another aging Shakespearean ruler, Prospero seeks comfort in retirement. Unlike Lear, Prospero knows human limitations, and his abandonment of power suggests a happy resolution in a romance denouement. On the other hand, Lear's self-knowledge has come too late to save him from the turmoil of his last days. His ignorance of both the world and of himself seems to be rooted in his conviction in the absoluteness of power. In *Hamlet*, the separation of knowledge from political power informs the portrayal of Claudius and

Hamlet. The former sounds more Machiavellian than the latter, who indulges himself in intellectual meditation. Knowledge of both reality and of himself does not give Hamlet power, but rather weakens his action.

Shakespeare's explorations into the process of cognition in *Hamlet* reflect on the early modern modes of knowledge—the eye of the mind and mirror of the intellect—which emerged in the Renaissance (Rorty 38–69). According to Rorty, the Renaissance derived the distinction between the eye of the body and the eye of the mind from Greek philosophy, which paved the ground for the Cartesian separation between mind and body. However, I would argue that the Renaissance humanists were influenced more by the Aristotelian notion of knowledge than the Platonic one, on which Descartes relies. In Aristotle's conception of knowledge, as Rorty also notes, "intellect is not a mirror inspected by an inner eye. It is both mirror and eye in one" (45). Renaissance theorists seem to follow the Aristotelian conception of "mirror and eye in one" better. For instance, Sir Philip Sidney sees an interaction of mind and body in the "accurate" representations of an object rather than the dualism Descartes developed. It is this Renaissance conception—rather than Cartesian dualism—that emphasizes the "close affinity in the Western philosophical tradition, between the process of conceptual thought and the function of vision; even more specifically, between the perception of the self and the function of the mirror" (Armstrong 244). What the mind's eyes see, however, is the mirror—representations of the object.

Sidney draws his aesthetic knowledge or "theory of the mind" from Aristotle and gives it moral power. In Sidney's debate against contemporary refutation of the "active" function of poetry, he feels the urge to present a moral value for art. He endows the poet with the intellectual power to move people—to make better people—by promoting moral judgment. For the poet's "heavenly poesy . . . showeth himself a passionate lover of that unspeakable and everlasting beauty to be seen by the eyes of the mind" (Sidney 607). The moral part of Sidney's theory may have shown some Platonic influence. Nonetheless, writing in a context of the Elizabethan transformation to Protestantism, Sidney must summon the ghosts of both Aristotle and Plato to fight against a conservative, theological devaluation of art. Much of Sidney's discussion of Plato purports to refute the abusers of poetry, who allude to Plato's banishing the poets out of his commonwealth. Addressing Plato's dialogues, Sidney compares beauty to skin and knowledge (philosophy) to what is inside to explain the relationship between aesthetic attractions and art's intellectual function (606). The metaphors have actually indicated a cognitive process from bodily experience to mental assimilation. And the aesthetic principle Sidney uses to explain such a relation between the "skin" and the "inside" is Aristotelian. He defines poesy in Aristotle's term of imitation—imagery which represents life ("a speaking picture") so as to "teach and delight" (Sidney 608) spectators. Delight may be both the means and part of the end of literature. Tragedy teaches people by "stirring the affects of admiration and commiseration" (Sidney 614). The term "commiseration" seems to have been derived from Aristotle's "pity and fear" in the cathartic process. At the end of the process, the audience "recognizes" the lesson about life that the tragic protagonist's suffering has enacted. This recognition (knowledge) provides release and satisfaction, which is a process that may be explained in modern physiological terms. The final release of the adrenaline surge that the stage spectacle has excited and intensified through plot development may produce some pleasure. Consequently, the best tragedian quenches the watchers' desire to know what happens to the protagonist and transforms the suffering knowledge into a fear about the bitter world. Thus the power of drama is realized through the audience's watching; drama/stage provides the mirror through which the audience sees human weaknesses and elevates their visual experience to moral rationality.

Shakespeare's perception of the power of drama informs contemporary discourses of theatrical power in *Hamlet*. As his protagonist articulates, drama works on the audience's organic perception. Successful performances "[c]onfound the ignorant, and amaze indeed / The very faculties of eyes and ears" (2.2.505–506). The Elizabethan debate over the power of the theater became more severe in the Jacobean era when Thomas Heywood argued against Puritan anti-theatrical pamphleteers such as Philip Stubbes in his *Apology for Actors* (1612)[2]. Heywood recounted a woman's confession—upon watching a play—that she has poisoned her husband. The immediate effect of the theatrical spectacle may have resonated in Hamlet's "mousetrap", through which he explores dramatic power. The Prince directs a play called "Murder of Gonzago", the play-within-the-play, and catches Claudius's conscience (2.2.584–592). For Hamlet, drama is a mirror "held up to nature" (3.2.17). Claudius's irritated response has confirmed Hamlet's doubt about his father's death and the Ghost's narrative about the cause. In this example, the mirror's gaze back at the audience's gaze, as Armstrong elaborates, has ended up with the observer's identification with what is in the mirror (218). I would suggest that Shakespeare's use of identification through the mirror participates in the contemporary discussion of drama "dramatically"—by using the play as a form of argument. The dramatist explores a different knowing process through Hamlet's handling of the frustration that his self-mirroring has revealed.

Hamlet's mirror identification is at the center of his problem in knowing himself. Before he became "mad", the Prince was a mirror—a "glass of fashion" (3.1.145) because he was identified as a copy of the royal father and would be the heir to state power. But the loss of the father has caused a gap in this identification even before the play begins. Although he still bears his father's name—and he is still considered the person "most near" to the throne—Hamlet feels alienated from both the father and power. Therefore he can only "see" his father's image in his "mind's eye" (1.2.185). Seeing the ghost of Old Hamlet—the original copy of his identity—he must "remember" (1.5.95, 97)—re-member or re-impress—the father's forgotten image onto the mind. Later on, when Hamlet allegedly forgets the ghost's command when chastising Gertrude, he sees the ghost again in her chamber while she cannot (3.4.131–134).

The Prince's reliance on the mirror-drama for self-identification seems to have confirmed Jacques Lacan's psychoanalytic modes of identity construction. For Lacan, as for Sigmund Freud and Ernest Jones[3], the play is a primary instance of psychoanalytic theories, albeit Lacan's mode moves beyond the Oedipus complex. In his "Desire and the Interpretation of Desire in *Hamlet*," Lacan establishes a symbolic identification between the ego and its ideal image in the mirror stage of psyche formation, in which the ego at once has the desire to destroy the ideal other in the mirror and depends on it for fixing his own identity. The paradox in the imaginary identification is further shifted to the identification with the phallus in a process of objection through the mirror. The image of the father represents the phallus, the signifier of power in a psychoanalytic, rather than political or biological, sense. Hamlet confronts a more complicated situation since the person who has taken the place of the phallus is a fake king—the real phallus is absent. The frustrating fact is that "[t]he body is with the king, but the king is not with the body" (4.2.24). As a result, the desire for fighting the phallus becomes a permanent frustration. Lacan explains Hamlet's inaction thus:

> The very source of what makes Hamlet's arm waver at every moment, is the narcissistic connection that Freud tells us about in his text on the decline of the Oedipus complex: one cannot strike the phallus, because the phallus, even the real phallus, is a *ghost*. (50)

Revising Freud's Oedipus complex, Lacan emphasizes the "narcissistic connection" in the subject's castration complex. And when the center of desire transfers from the subject in the mirror to the object as mirror, the phallus as the signifier of power acquires its psychic value. As with Freud's panlibidinal mode of psychoanalysis, Lacan's phallus-centered interpretation of *Hamlet* approaches epistemological problems by starting with bodily experience, a process that moves from sexuality to cognition.

Therefore, Freud's psychoanalysis and Lacan's post-psychoanalysis provide a mode of knowing that contrasts to the classic epistemology of Aristotle. Levy points out the distinction between Freud's and Aristotle's modes of knowledge by noting that "to Aristotle, in contrast to Freud, the defining

urge is *cognitive*, not sexual" and that "in the classical schema, man is a rational animal, not an Oedipal one" (118). Reading the play in the opposition of
the two epistemological modes, Hamlet's "[b]estial oblivion" as against "godlike reason" (4.4.35–40) cannot partake the operation of the brain's "normal"
faculty. Only the "noble and most sovereign" (3. 1.159) or the faculty of "apprehension" (2.2.306) is qualified for the "noble" mind. However, Hamlet's
skepticism is toward both bestial and noble qualities as he problematizes his
own "capacity" to think rationally—"my wit's diseased" (3.2.313).

Regardless of the contrast between the two modes, Levy delineates
—arguably—a similar process of knowing in Aristotle's and Freud's
epistemologies—both subsuming the particular in the universal. In both modes
of epistemology, the two dimensions—body and mind—are prominent and in-
teractive, I would argue. They represent contrastive procedures—one emphasizes
transferring knowledge from mind to body, and the other vice versa—which are
equally significant to Hamlet's mental process. Moreover, as active as these two
elements is a third dimension of epistemology—culture, relatively independent
of the other two yet interacting with them—which is neglected by applicants of
the previous modes. All the three together form a cycle.

We must consider all of them to understand fully such epistemological
complexity as *Hamlet*. Biological determination and rational abstraction (as
in Renaissance humanism and in the idealism of Descartes and Kant) cannot
exhaust its complexity even by working together. Recent philosophical and
cognitive studies have shown that the functions of mind, body, and culture are
indivisible. Through experiments Andy Clark found that "brain, body, world,
and artifact" are "locked together in the most complex of conspiracies" and
that "mind and action are revealed in intimate embrace" (33). Epistemological
behavior, like other human behavior, is "largely determined by culture, a largely autonomous system of symbols and values, growing from a biological base,
but growing indefinitely away from it" (Dennett 491).[4] These new findings
in cognitive science and philosophy have not only proved a dialectic relationship or interaction between mind and body but also singled out the function
of culture or ideology in human cognition. In cultural materialist terms, when
ideology acquires its relative autonomy in the form of consciousness, it comes
back to form bodily experience. Ideology functions in our consciousness not
only as a set of abstract concepts but also as "structures of feeling" (Williams
132). Culture enters the structuring process of mind and oversees the action
of body.

A more complete knowing process has three stages, in which concrete
and abstract, particular and universal, material and immaterial elements in-
teract. The whole lively process may not appear in this order although it can
be mechanically described as follows for convenience. First, the learning subject approaches the object and is *impressed* with an initial physical perception

of the object. Or, the object leaves an imprint on the subject's nervous system with perceivable features—its visual and acoustic characteristics, for instance. The subject may be active or inactive in this stage of information processing. Secondly, almost at the same time as it is received, the information is classified and encoded in the brain. Thirdly, the new information is instantly greeted by old information, which is already there ("memories"), and then is let in or expelled. The process may start from and end at any phase, and sometimes one of the stages may not be discernible. The operation of the code depository (the established information system of the brain) plays a crucial role in the processing of new codes and in determining possible actions or reactions to the outcome that the newcomer and its alien input system have brought. In psychoanalytic terms, the depository may be the unconscious, or in Marxism the ideological field, or more generally the cultural background.

Hamlet's perception of his father's death begins with a doubt about the cause, which is yet to become clear. Then he sees the Ghost and is informed of the murder. He needs confirmation for the ghost's story. Yet after he has already "seen" the evidence, he cannot decide to engage in revenge. The problem is that he cannot exert a concentrated action. He simply ponders it and vows to remove what is in his "memories". There, complex, convoluted, and conflicting cultural factors crowd into his rationalization of such an action. Thus, a cyclical process of epistemology—body-mind-culture—will be conducive to the understanding of Hamlet's dilemma. Actually, the cultural element in the knowing process has been submerged by rationality, or the unconscious, or the phallus in the classical, psychoanalytic, and post-psychoanalytic modes since it is not always ostensible. Hamlet's moral rationality and its frustration are only meaningful in the context of the cultural transformation of early seventeenth-century England. The symbolic phallus is a cultural image locked in the individual psyche. The phallus as signifier makes its sense in the condition of social gendering; the privilege of the phallus's center position reflects the stratification of sexuality in patriarchal society. Culture, along with mind and body, plays a significant role at the third stage, where Hamlet's self-knowing process breaks down and is lost in impasse. Although his brain has received the experience of his father's death and registered it in the bank of ideological data, it fails to direct his bodily action. In a self-reflective mood, he articulates his epistemological paradox: "I do not know / Why yet I live to say this thing's to do" (4.4.43–44).

The play provides plenty of evidence of cognitive fracture at this stage. Much of the fracture is evident in his reflections on time. For Hamlet, the "time is out of joint" (1.5.189). His knowing capacity (cor)responds to this rupture in time. The political chronicle is out of joint because of his father's unnatural death, since for Hamlet time is linked by the continuation of his father's body—part of his memories. As Charnes observes, in the "patrilinear

successive monarchy, the passage of political time is inseparable from biological time: the father's body is the political calendar of king-father's body as
chronicle in patriarchal society" (193). The gap in the royal chronicle results
in disorder in his "distracted globe" (1.5.96). The old "records" are supposed to
be the basic data to be used to process incoming information. However, the
apparition's narrative of the unnaturalness—his father's body being killed in
light and his spirit suffering in purgatory—is so appalling and so devastating
that the new message tends to delete the old. On the table of his memory,
"[a]ll saws of books, all forms, all pressures past" were "copied" (impressed) on
his brain (1.5.100–101) when his father was King. Now in the face of the unnatural cause, the "naturally" formed memories must be "wiped away" (1.5.97)
together with King Hamlet's chronology. And now his father's ghost wants
him to remember the new "word" (revenge); his father continues to govern his
memory, yet from the supernatural sphere.

    However, it is as impossible for him to replace his memory as it is for
him to set the time right in the conflicting conceptions of naturalness. Even
before he "sees" the Ghost, he senses the unnaturalness in the continuation
of the courtly timetable: "funeral bak'd meats . . . furnished forth the marriage
tables" (1.2.180–181). The images of abnormal succession provide poisonous
food for the brain's right order. Jumbled informational vehicles coming in
from all directions overwhelm the narrow path. The old and new memories have imposed ideological convolution upon his brain and jammed the
crossroad of his neural traffic with numerous impossibilities in temporal and
historical time. His mother's haste and incestuous union with his uncle has
battered the ideal memory of the "perfect" model of happy royal parents for
the young Prince. But now the royal body has been contaminated; the flesh
is "sullied".

    The only hope to purify it so as to restore its integrity has been maimed
by his mother's lust since she is already in Claudius's "incestuous sheets"
(1.2.57). Morality, along with time, is out of order as the result of the death
of the legal royal head. Even if he killed Claudius, he is unable to fix the
time's moral joint and renew the mother for the ghost father. In Gertrude's
chamber, Hamlet pushes her to the mirror and lets her compare images of
her two husbands. He warns Gertrude to stay away from Claudius's "enseamed bed" and gradually develop the habit of chastity—not to be "stewed
in corruption" (3.4.92–93). Hamlet's concern over impure sexuality is further shown in his attitude toward Ophelia; he alienates her and orders "Get
thee to nunnery" to purify the body and avoid the possibility of breeding
sinners (3.1.121–122).

    But he knows that it is not possible to cleanse the polluted moral time
since the morality that governs the kingdom's political body is still in a diseased state. The new king—his new "father"—is carrying on the political

time by holding the royal order. He calls Claudius "mother" and explains that father and mother are one flesh (4.3.47–50). The father and kingly body is not there—only a fake in his place to carry on political time. In another sense, mother and father together make history continue by producing male heirs who will succeed to the throne. Hamlet is the legal heir—the best product of the father-mother union—and yet is deprived (pos oned) of the right to the throne. In this way, political time is misplaced: the false father takes the place of the son. The new father-mother reunion leaves more impossibility to Hamlet. The whimpering lamb must starve since "the grass still growing" (3.3.322).

Hamlet's disappointment and the ghost's order seem to accelerate his urge to revenge. However, his perception of cultural fractures has led to cognitive stagnation. He suffers from a failure to reach the last level in the cycle of experience-reason-practice. Rationality loses the guiding role to experience and even becomes an obstacle to practice; he blames himself for his inertia upon seeing the Norwegian army's march to battle. Hamlet's cognitive fracture is demonstrated in his skepticism, which anticipated Descartes. Hamlet's realization of the impossibilities fails to offer him the "name" for action. He gives up the chance to kill Claudius while the latter is at prayer because moral rationality defuses action. His reasoning deletes the meaning of his action—killing does not fulfill revenge but rather sends the enemy to heaven. In Lacan's terms, the object of avenging action—the power center—is empty. The lack of signifier blocks a transition between objection and subjection. In Marxist terms, his knowledge fails to become the guide to revolutionary practice. To be sure, there is always a gap between knowledge and practice. The gap can never be fixed since it dwells in the gray area of cognition. Consequently, Hamlet practically takes a providentialist stance toward the absoluteness of life's failure—"[t]he readiness is all" (5.2.160).

Hamlet's recognition of his impotence in the face of woeful reality leaves a perpetual dilemma that, as a typical Hamletean legacy, continues to perplex generations of intellectuals who attempt to rip the cognitive Sphinx whose body is incongruent with its head. The prince's knowledge, determined by the cultural forces surrounding him, seems to have limited his power of action; the intuitive force that drives Laertes's rebellion has been tempered with Hamlet's ethical ratiocinations. This is why he has been identified by intellectuals of several generations after him as their spiritual ancestor. They share with him the conundrum of mind-body separation and the frustration of knowing themselves. As a result, Hamlet has accompanied the epistemological discourses from the early modern to the modern, and perhaps the postmodern, times. Hugh Grady aptly summarizes Hamlet's position in the history of modern intellectuality as such:

Hamlet, who came into being as a carrier of the new form of malleable, protean subjectivity identified by Hegel and Burckhardt as the hallmark of modernity, and who served centrally as the emblem and signifier of art and subjectivity throughout the classical bourgeois era, now emerges into a new century re-newed, uncannily ourselves, yet once more challenging our own understandings of our world, its past, and its uncertain future. (18)

Surely, Hamlet is at once an affirming emblem of modern subjectivity and challenging signifier of "things standing . . . unknown" (5.2.287). The vexing postmodern recognition, like that which renders Hamlet's learned "thoughts . . . nothing worth" (4.4.67), acknowledges the complexity of Hamletean cognitivity and the inadequacy of some available *sciences* of knowledge about ourselves and our world. Hamletean discourses must carry on.

NOTES

1. See Burke, especially 7–18.
2. For a discussion of the debate and of how the opposing parties configure the good/evil effects of theatrical transactions, see Armstrong 216–218.
3. See Freud and Jones.
4. Recent Shakespearean studies have incorporated findings of cognitive research and cultural philosophy. Mary Crane studies how culture and body work together to form Shakespeare's early modern subjects in *Shakespeare's Brain: Reading with Cognitive Theory*. Especially, Ellen Spolsky's book *Satisfying Skepticism: Embodied Knowledge in the Early Modern World*, to which I am greatly indebted for this study, provides penchant showcases of early modern skepticism and their implications in Shakespeare's plays, particularly *Coriolanus* and *Othello*. Spolsky suggests that in the early modern period, versions of skepticism—"the entanglements of brain, body, and culture—were felt by some to be a sickening disappointment" (4).

WORKS CITED

Armstrong, Philip. "Watching Hamlet Watching: Lacan, Shakespeare, and the Mirror/ Stage." *Alternative Shakespeares* 2. Ed. Terence Hawkes. London: Routledge, 1996. 216–237.

Burke, Peter. *Montaigne*. New York: Oxford University Press, 1981.

Charnes, Linda. "The Hamlet Formerly Known as Prince." Grady 189–210.

Clark, Andy. *Being There: Putting Brain, Body, and World Together Again*. Cambridge: MIT Press, 1997.

Crane, Mary. *Shakespeare's Brain: Reading with Cognitive Theory*. Princeton: Princeton University Press, 2001.

D'Amico, Jack. *Knowledge and Power in the Renaissance*. Washington, DC: University Press of America, 1977.

Dennett, Daniel C. *Darwin's Dangerous Idea: Evolution and the Meanings of Life*. New York: Simon, 1995.

Freud, Sigmund. *The Interpretation of Dreams.* Trans. James Strachey. New York: Penguin, 1976.

Grady, Hugh, ed. *Shakespeare and Modernity: Early Modern to Millennium.* London: Routledge, 2000.

Jones, Ernest. *Hamlet and Oedipus.* London: Gollancz, 1949.

Lacan, Jacques. "Desire and the Interpretation of Desire in *Hamlet.*" *Yale French Studies* 55–56 (1977): 11–52.

Levy, Eric P. "The Universal versus Particular: Hamlet and the Madness in Reason." *Exemplaria* 14 (2002): 99–125.

Rorty, Richard. *Philosophy and the Mirror of Nature.* Princeton: Princeton University Press, 1979.

Sidney, Philip. "The Defense of Poesy." *The Renaissance in England.* Ed. Hyder E. Rollins and Herschel Baker. Prospect Heights, IL: Waveland Press, 1992.

Spolsky, Ellen. *Satisfying Skepticism: Embodied Knowledge in the Early Modern World.* Burlington, VT: Ashgate, 2001.

Williams, Raymond. *Marxism and Literature.* Oxford: Oxford University Press, 1977.

PAUL MENZER

The Tragedians of the City?
Q1 Hamlet *and the Settlements of the 1590s*

The title page to the 1603 Quarto of William Shakespeare's *Hamlet* (Q1) advertises that the play has been "acted . . . in the Cittie of London."[1] Andrew Gurr has recently suggested that City playing was forbidden in 1594; since Shakespeare's *Hamlet* debuted in 1600/1601, Q1's "Cittie of London" must therefore be read as a figural locution.[2] As W. W. Greg has noted, "That Shakespeare's play had been acted in 'the Cittie of London' cannot be literally true: the only performances were presumably at the Globe, which was in Southwark."[3] This conclusion relies upon a paradox: "Cittie of London" had a literal meaning; therefore, the reference to the "Cittie of London" here cannot have a literal meaning. Presumably, Q1's "Cittie" claim is merely a title-page topos. Rather than conclude that the phrase cannot mean what it says, however, we might recognize that *Hamlet*—either Shakespeare's play or the Chamberlain's Men's earlier play of the same name—might well have appeared within the City walls, at Cross Keys Inn in Gracechurch Street or elsewhere. Recognition of a City performance of *Hamlet,* for which I am arguing, would also exemplify a larger phenomenon: City playing evidently continued, despite repeated attempts to suppress it in the mid-1590s.

Three explanations can account for the phrase "the Cittie of London" on Q1 *Hamlet*'s title page. First, the title page uses standard boilerplate copy. Second, the words recall Chamberlain's Men performances of the earlier *Hamlet*

Shakespeare Quarterly, Volume 57, Number 2 (Summer 2006): pp. 162–182. Copyright © 2006 The Johns Hopkins University Press.

at Cross Keys. Third, Shakespeare's *Hamlet* did indeed play in the City, despite attempts to suppress such events. This last possibility, which I propose here, would revise our understanding not only of *Hamlet*'s performance history but also of theatrical practice and its regulation in the last decade of the sixteenth century. To weigh these alternatives, this essay first examines other title pages of plays that advertise City performances, pursues the precise coordinates of the "Cittie of London" in early modern English usage, and finally challenges the position that City playing must have ceased in the mid-1590s.

I. Title Pages and the Stages of London

Title pages are advertisements. As Peter Blayney points out, title pages often include the location of the bookseller.[4] Hung upon signposts in the City with other advertisements, title pages pointed readers to a specific place where they might transact a commercial exchange. Playbills functioned in much the same way. As Tiffany Stern has recently argued, title pages and playbills were proximate forms in both design and display.[5] Both advertised publications—one textual, one theatrical. Posted within the City, Q1 *Hamlet*'s title page advertises the text of a play performed within the walls and presumably available for purchase nearby. The marketing function of the title page—like its textual cousin the playbill—demanded geographical specificity.

Title-page claims for City performances are rare in the period. Of the 836 title pages of plays in English compiled in W. W. Greg's *Bibliography of the English Printed Drama to the Restoration* (covering the years 1512 to 1689), only 8 refer to the City of London. Other than a 1606 reprint of *Mucedorus* (originally published in 1598) and a 1631 reprint of *Fair Em* (originally published around 1591),[6] the designation disappears completely from new plays printed after 1603. Furthermore, no printed play before the 1590 octavo of Marlowe's *Tamburlaine* includes the claim. The 1603 *Hamlet* then caps just over a decade's worth of printed plays that claim performances in or about the City of London. In the thirteen years between the 1590 printing of Marlowe's *Tamburlaine* and the quarto of Shakespeare's *Hamlet*, only six other plays refer to the City on their title pages: *The Troublesome Reign of King John* (1591), *Fair Em*, *Edward the Second* (1594), *A Knack to Know an Honest Man* (1596), *Edward the Third* (1596), and *Mucedorus*.[7]

In nearly every case, the designation can be read literally, for the texts can be linked to companies known to have played in the City. The earliest extant title page to make such a claim is Christopher Marlowe's *Tamburlaine*, which boasts of several urban locations: "Tamburlaine the Great . . . | . . . | *Deuided into two Tragicall Dis-* | courses, as they were sundrie times | shewed vpon Stages in the Citie | of London."[8] *Tamburlaine*'s title page locates the play on the "Stages" of the City, which at this point could have been any of the four inns known to host plays: the Bell, the Bull, the Bel Savage, and the Cross Keys. The play's debut is usually assigned to late 1587, when the Rose was under construction, but there is no evidence that either the first or second part of *Tamburlaine* appeared at the Rose until 1594.[9] The Admiral's Men may have been at James Burbage's Theatre in November 1587, and they did play there in 1591.[10] Evidence for their presence at the Bel Savage comes considerably later, in 1633, when William Prynne refers to *"the visible apparition of the Devill on the Stage at the Belsavage Play-house in Quene* Elizabeths *dayes"* during a performance, apparently by the Admiral's Men, of *Dr. Faustus*.[11] The play's 1604 quarto assigns it to the Admiral's Men, although Prynne does not specify which company the devil disturbed. It is also generally evident that the Admiral's Men played in these inns, for on 6 November 1589, the Lord Mayor wrote Burghley to describe an encounter with both the Admiral's and Strange's players. As will be developed more fully below, the early winter date is significant:

> It appered vnto me, that it was your honours pleasure I sholde geue order for the staie of all playes within the Cittie, in that mr. Tilney did vtterly mislike the same. According to which your Lps. good pleasure, I presentlye sent for suche players as I coulde here of, so as there appered yesterday before me the L. Admeralles and the L. Straunge's players, to whome I speciallie gaue in Charge and required them in her Maiesties name to forbere playinge, vntil further order mighte be geuen for theire allowance in that respect: Whereupon the L. Admeralles players very dutifullie obeyed, but the others in very Contemptuous manner departing from me, went to the Cross keys and played that afternoon[.][12]

The Admiral's Men may have complied on this occasion, but it is clear that they had been playing "within the City," for the Lord Mayor tried to suppress their doing so. *Tamburlaine*'s title page certainly tells true when it boasts of its City stages.

In the case of *Fair Em*, there is no reason to read the claim that the Lord Strange's Men performed it in the City as anything other than factual. The play's performance dates from around 1591, when the company was known to be at Cross Keys, as indicated by the Lord Mayor's letter above. The quarto, tentatively dated 1591, asserts that the play is printed "As it was sundrietimes publiquely acted in the | *honourable citie of London, by the right honourable* | the Lord Strange his seruaunts."13 The company can be traced to two suburban playhouses as well, the Theatre in 1590–1591 and the Rose in 1592–1593,[14] but the comedy of *Fair Em* clearly graced the stage of a City inn.

Of the several companies that played in and about London in the 1580s and 1590s, the Queen's Men can be most decisively placed in the inns. On 28 November 1583, they received permission to play "at the sygnes of the Bull in Bushoppesgate streete, and the sygne of the Bell in Gratioustreete and no-wheare els."[15] Eight years later, *The Troublesome Reign of King John* appeared in a quarto that records the play's City credentials:

> <THE> | Troublesome Raigne | of *Iohn* King of *England,* with the dis- | *couerie of King* Richard Cordelions | Base sonne (vulgarly named, The Ba- | stard Fawconbridge): *also the* | death of King *Iohn* at | *Swinstead* | *Abbey.* | *As it was (sundry times) publikely acted by the* | *Queenes Maiesties Players, in the ho-* | *nourable Citie of* | London.[16]

The latest reference to a Queen's Men performance at a London inn is 1588, when, following Tarlton's death that year, a spectator memorialized the great clown and recalled his appearance at Bel Savage in "a sorowfull newe sonnette, intituled Tarltons Recantacion uppon this theame given him by a gentleman at the Belsavage without Ludgate."[17] If *The Troublesome Reign of King John* was part of the Queen's Men's repertory in the early 1590s, however, there is no reason to think it was exempt from the Queen's Men's "consistent performance pattern" of touring in the provinces in summer and early autumn before moving to "the city inns sometime in November."[18] If Sampson Clarke were to affix the play's title page to his stall behind the Royal Exchange in 1591, his City customers would be reminded that the play had once been acted in their midst.

In 1594, the title page of Christopher Marlowe's *Edward the Second* claimed that Pembroke's Men had often played it in the City:

> The troublesome | raigne and lamentable death of | Edward *the second, King of* | England : with the tragicall | *fall of proud* Mortimer: | As it was sundrie times publiquely acted | *in the honourable citie of London, by the* | right honourable the Earle of Pem- | *brooke his seruants.* | *Written by* Chri. Marlow *Gent.*[19]

Of the companies discussed here, Pembroke's has perhaps the most obscure history. The company can only be located with any real precision at the Swan in 1597.[20] Most pertinent to this discussion, Pembroke's Men cannot be found in any of the City's inns during these years. However, we have no reason to suppose that a then-typical performance circuit of City, suburb, touring, and possibly court excluded Pembroke's players. Indeed, it would be surprising if this short-lived but popular company did not enjoy the City privileges of their fellows. The title page enticement to prospective buyers suggests that they did.

Of course, there is no statutory reason to challenge the title-page claims for City performances of plays acted and published before the end of 1594. Such performances were perfectly legal—if not uncontested—during those years. The plays discussed above would certainly have been acted in the suburbs (at the Rose, the Theatre, Newington Butts, and elsewhere), but they would just as certainly have been performed in City inns and innyards. In sum, no reason exists to take pre-1595 title-page claims for City playing as anything other than the truth. What, then, of the four post-1594 play texts—*A Knack to Know an Honest Man, Edward the Third, Mucedorus,* and *Hamlet*—that advertise City performances?

Of this group, Q1 *Hamlet* is the only one with a known post-1594 textual and theatrical history to claim a City of London performance. The publication of the other three may fall after 1596, but their title pages either refer to performances that predate 1594, as does *Mucedorus,* or employ the preposition "about" to signify performances "without" the City in the suburbs. Title pages were evidently careful when making City claims, and both *A Knack to Know an Honest Man* and *Edward the Third* claim performance not in but "about" the City.

As we will see below, just as the phrase "in the City" was used with precision, so was the phrase "about the City." In terms of theatrical regulation, "about" could mean not "throughout" but "outside," as in John Stow's reflexively precise use of this word when he describes the "Wall about the Cittie of London" in his *Survey of London.*[21] In the documents of control that passed between the Privy Council, the Lord Mayor, and the justices of the peace for Surrey and Middlesex, the inclusive phrase "in and about the City of London" recurs when the theaters of greater London are the topic. *A Knack to Know an Honest Man,* then, does not claim a City performance when its title page describes it as "A | PLEASANT | CONCEITED COME- | die, called, A knacke to know | an honest Man. | As it hath beene sundrie times plaied about the | Citie of London."[22] The play's editor, H. De Vocht, expressed his reservations about the phrase: "Whether it was ever publicly performed actually within the precincts may perhaps be doubted."[23] But to be precise, the title page does not claim performances within the precincts. When *A Knack to Know an Honest Man* appeared in 1596, its title page could recall performances quite literally "about"—i.e., outside—the City, specifically, on the Bankside.

In fact, the performance history of *A Knack to Know an Honest Man* does nothing to contradict its title page's precise use of "about the citie of London." Henslowe's *Diary* indicates that the Admiral's Men performed *A Knack to Know an Honest Man* exclusively at the Rose, a theater indeed not "in" but "about" the City of London. The play premiered on 22 October 1594 and played twenty-one times before its last recorded performance on 3 November 1596.[24] The play opened just five months after Lords Howard and Hunsdon apparently agreed that the Chamberlain's Men should play at the Theatre and the Admiral's Men should play at the Rose.[25] Again, the title page appears to advertise the play's provenance quite carefully and specifically.

Similarly, the anonymous 1596 quarto of *Edward the Third* includes "about"—*"As it hath bin sundrie times plaied about | the Citie of London."*[26] The play was almost certainly written and performed between 1589 and 1592 and belonged to either the Admiral's or Pembroke's Men.[27] *Edward the Third* dates from a period when companies moved seasonally in and out of the City, but its title page is quite specific in placing it outside.

On the other hand, *Mucedorus* clearly claims pride of place in the City. Despite a publication date of 1598, *Mucedorus's* claim to have been "plaide in the honorable Cittie of London" may nevertheless be taken as true:

A | Most pleasant Co- | medie of *Mucedorus* the kings | sonne of *Valentia* and *Amadine* | the Kings daughter of *Arragon*, | with the merie conceites | of *Mouse*. | Newly set foorth, as it hath bin | *sundrie times plaide in the ho-* | *norable Cittie of London*. | Very delectable and full | of mirth.[28]

One of its editors has allowed that "[i]t is almost impossible to date precisely the original composition of the play," but most critics have settled on 1590 or thereabouts.[29] Reasonable conjecture can push the date earlier or later by a few years, but the initial performances of *Mucedorus* could have been in the City. The 1598 title page may well recall performances during years when City playing was tolerated, however grudgingly.

Unlike *Edward the Third* or *Mucedorus*, Shakespeare's *Hamlet* could not have been played in the City when such playing was legal—if City playing was indeed outlawed in 1594. Q1's title page may then advertise a performance that could not legally have taken place:

THE | Tragicall Historie of | HAMLET | Prince of Denmarke[.] | By William Shake-speare.
  As it hath beene diuerse times acted by his Highnesse seruants in the Cittie of London : as also in the two Vniuersities of Cambridge and Oxford, and else-where
[device 301] | At London printed for N. L. and Iohn Trundell. | 1603.[30]

Because a City performance of Shakespeare's *Hamlet* does not fit comfortably within the parameters of traditional theater history, no one has taken Q1's claim seriously. In fact, although we may expect exaggeration from advertisements, Q1 *Hamlet*'s title page, like the majority of early English dramatic title pages, follows a fairly standard and factually rigorous formula: title (invariably), author (maybe), company that performed and owned the play (usually), place of playing (often), publisher (nearly always), year (usually), and place of sale (often). The immediate question is the factual specificity of title pages when the "place of playing" was "the City of London." By examining what the term denoted in 1603, we can read the topographic claims of title pages more carefully. If the term "City" specifically implied the territory within London's walls (or the "bars," which were the gates that formed a barrier into the city and marked its official boundaries), we can reassess the performance history of Shakespeare's *Hamlet* and the regulatory effectiveness of the Corporation of London.

II. The "Cittie of London" and the "Grammar of Place"

The "Cittie of London" was not a vague phrase in London, circa 1603. Then, as now, the term referred to the 677 acres (just over one square mile) ruled by the Lord Mayor and Corporation of London, who owed their privileges to a royal charter dating from the thirteenth century.[31] Contemporary use indicates that the "City" referred precisely to those quarters within its legal limits, outside of which Southwark fell (although the suburb was annexed as a ward, or borough, in 1550). Some of the best evidence for this definition is John Stow's *Survey of London*, which chronicles the City and its suburbs in boggling detail. In "A Table of the Chapters conteyned *in this Booke*," Stow lists the various wards that he will describe, along with chapters on the "wall about the Citie of London," the rivers and other bodies of water "seruing the Citie," the bridges "of this Citie," the gates that punctuate the wall of "this Cittie," and so forth.[32] Throughout the text, he draws sharp distinctions between within and without and between what does and does not constitute part of the City.

When Stow trains his survey outside London's walls, his terminology makes clearer still the distinction between City and suburb, a distinction particularly important to my argument: "Hauing spoken of this citie, the originall, & increase.... I am next to speake briefly of the Suburbs, as wel without the gates, & wals, as without the liberties."[33] The suburbs are not part of the "citie"; instead, Stow writes that "Bridge warde without" consists of the "*Borough* of Southwarke" in the "*county* of Surrey"; he moves on to the "*Liberties* of the Dutchie of Lancaster*" and the hospitals of the "Citie and suburbs."[34] Not only does Stow clearly consider Southwark apart from the City of London, he consistently calls it a borough. Stow's use demonstrates that when he refers to the City of London, he means precisely that, notwithstanding Southwark's post-1550 status as a ward. In fact, the language of the 1550 charter that brought Southwark under City control repeatedly stresses the geographical difference. As David J. Johnson writes, "Whether or not they had an alderman, Bridge Ward Without had an existence in the minds of its inhabitants as a community with its own identity."[35] Taxonomically, Stow's language is exact.

Stow's contemporaries support the precision of "City" as a geographical coordinate. The account of Elizabeth's coronation deploys the term with revelatory precision. On the day before her coronation, Elizabeth passed through the City from the Tower on her way to Westminster, viewing a lavish civic spectacle along the way. As she moved to leave the City of London, a tract entitled "The passage of our most drad Soveraigne Lady Quene ELYZABETH through the Citie of LONDON to WESTMINSTER, the daye before her Coronation, Anno 1558–9" tells us that

> On the South side [of the last pageant at Temple Bar] was appoynted by the Citie a noyse of singing children ; and one childe richely attired as a poet, which gave the Quenes Majestie her farewell, in the name of the hole Citie. . . . At which saying, her Grace departed forth through Temple Barre towarde Westminster, with no lesse shoutyng and crying of the People, then she entred the Citie. . . . Thus the Quenes Hyghnesse passed through the Citie.[36]

The precise phrasing denotes a threshold between one jurisdiction and another, from the City of London to the City of Westminster. On 15 March 1603—the year Q1 *Hamlet* appeared—James I also passed through the City. Thomas Dekker, in "THE MAGNIFICENT | ENTERTAINMENT GIVEN TO | KING JAMES, AND | QUEENE ANNE HIS WIFE, AND HENRY FREDERICK THE PRINCE, | Upon the Day of His Majesties Triumphant Passage (from the Tower) through his Honorable | Citie (and Chamber) of London," again distinguishes the corporate entity of London from its neighbors: "The *Citie of Westminster* and *Dutchy of Lancaster* perceiving what preparation their neighbor Citie made to entertaine her Soveraigne, though in greatnes they could not match her, yet in greatnes of love and duetie they gave testimonie that both were equall."[37] Dekker emphasizes competition among the City of London, the City of Westminster, and the Duchy of Lancaster, and competition relies on separation and difference.

Every town, as Fernand Braudel famously observed, wants to be "a world apart," and the growth of London's suburbs threatened the City's autonomy.[38]

What Lawrence Manley calls the "neofeudal tenor of the civic ethos" required not just an actual but also a perceptual topography that insisted upon a City exclusive of the suburbs.[39] Containment motifs such as walls and gates recur in the works of such sixteenth- and seventeenth-century topographers as William Camden, John Norden, John Speed, and John Stow. What Cynthia Wall calls the "grammar of space" in these topographies presents a London "fixed and stable, *contained* by place."[40] Manley observes that King Lud appears in "countless descriptions" to renew London's walls and gates, sacralizing the City of London's foundational shape against change, a triumph of space over time.[41] In addition to the pocked crescent of walls and gates that enclosed the City to the east, west, and north, Speed refers to the "south-bounding Thames" that demarcated the extent of the City.[42] As James Howell writes, it divided the City's "Members and homogeneal parts" from her "heterogeneal, or Suburban parts."[43] Perceptually, literally, legally, and administratively, the City of London was a different place from the borough of Southwark, and contemporary uses of "City" reflect this fact.

Even, or especially, in the regulation of plays and players the distinction held between City and suburb. As is well known, the regulation of players was a long-standing point of contention between the Privy Council and the Corporation of London. Particularly between the opening of the Theatre in 1576 and the closing of the theaters in 1642, control over when, where, and how often the players might perform indexed a larger power struggle between the Privy Council and Guildhall. Within this contest, topographic distinctions between areas that the City of London did and did not control were critical. As early as 1549, the crown itself recognized that, in theatrical matters, the City of London required special handling. In the wake of the Kett rebellion, Edward VI issued a proclamation that banned playing for nearly three months. In it, he censured "a greate number of those that be common Plaiers of Enterludes and Plaies, as well within the citie of London, as els where within the realme" who "do for the most part plaie suche Interludes as contain matter tending to sedicion and contempnyng of sundery good orders and lawes."[44] While "within the realme" sounds all inclusive, the proclamation closed any loopholes by singling out the precinct of London.

This habitual phraseology persisted throughout the century in letters, minutes, edicts, and orders that attempted to regulate the stage. On 24 July 1582, for instance, the Lord Mayor replied to the earl of Warwick's letter of 1 July 1582, which had asked that his servant, John David, be allowed to play his prize, or compete in a public demonstration to qualify as a fencing master, at the Bull:

> I did not expulse your servant from playing his prize . . . only I did *restrain him from playing in an inn.* . . . I was indeed enforced

to restrain him from gathering public assembly of people to his play *within the City,* and never the less did allow him in the open fields. . . . [Now,] I have herein yet further done for your servant what I may, that is that if he may obtain lawfully to play at the Theatre or other open place *out of the City,* he hath and shall have my permission with his company, drums, and show to *pass openly through the City.*[45]

The Lord Mayor distinguished between the inns "within the City" and open places "out of the City," such as James Burbage's Theatre. This is a distinction we should observe as we turn to the struggle over City playing in the last decade of the sixteenth century and how Q1 *Hamlet* clarifies or disturbs that story.

III. The Forbidden City?

It is generally agreed that by 1594 players settled in houses north and south of the City—the Lord Chamberlain's Men at the Theatre, the Admiral's at the Rose, and the other active companies variously dispersed.[46] Was it then that the players finally abandoned the City's inns and innyards? Or did the companies continue to play in the City despite repeated attempts to stop them? The editors of *English Professional Theatre, 1530–1660,* summarize the evidence for a hard, mid-1590s suppression of City playing thus: "It is usually said that the authorities of the City managed to suppress the four inns in 1596, though no document expressly says so."[47] The evidence they present consists of Richard Rawlidge's *A Monster Late Found Out and Discovered* (1628), which recalls that soon after 1580 "the playhouses in Gracious Street, Bishopsgate Street, nigh Paul's (that on Ludgate Hill) . . . were quite put down . . . by the care of those religious senators."[48] The "religious senators" certainly *tried* repeatedly to "put down" the inns from the mid-sixteenth century on; their success in doing so in the mid-1590s is the question. (Rawlidge also refers to a mid-1580s injunction, which obviously failed.) The editors also note that two foreign visitors, Prince Ludwig of Anhalt-Cöthen (writing on 26 June 1596) and Johannes de Witt (writing in the same year), both mention four public playhouses, but neither describes inns used as theaters.[49] This is not terribly surprising. The purpose-built amphitheaters attracted wide comment from visitors in these years, who stressed the novelty and grandeur of the suburban playhouses. Smaller in size, inns that hosted plays would not so obviously attract the attention of foreign tourists. Furthermore, we know that de Witt visited during the summer, when the companies would be enjoying London's long evenings in their suburban playhouses. The argument for suppression is not strong, and ample evidence suggests that City playing went on well after the mid-1590s.

At the end of the sixteenth century, playing companies migrated from the suburban houses to City inns or innyards for the winter season whenever possible. At least, such was their desire. In a petition of disputed date but probably filed in November 1584, the Queen's Men petitioned the Privy Council to "permitt vs to excercise within the Cittye," "the season of the yere beynge past to playe att anye of the houses without the Cittye of London."[50] The Queen's Men considered the winter an unseasonable time to play in the suburbs; they therefore wished to play in the City. Far from being exceptional, this move to secure winter quarters sounds habitual.

The Corporation of London's grievances against City playing are familiar—crowded streets, noisy players, licentious playgoers—but why were players so eager to abandon large suburban amphitheaters for smaller City inns and innyards? In these years, companies apparently sought winter haven in the City in search of light as much as warmth.[51] After all, innyards were no warmer than amphitheaters, although the inns' large covered rooms certainly were. London's early winter dusk made the suburban theaters inconvenient for patrons who had not only to traverse frozen lanes but also to do so through the gloaming. In their reply to this request for a winter home, the Corporation of London suggested that the Queen's Men desist from playing altogether. Their terse response acknowledges the inconvenience of winter playing but also reveals the Corporation's reluctance to grant the players access to the City:

> If in winter the dark do cary inconuenience, and the short time of day after euening prayer do leaue them no leysure, and fowlenesse of season do hinder the passage into the feldes to playes, the remedie is ill conceyued to bring them into London, but the true remedie is to leaue of that vnnecessarie expense of time, whereunto God himself geueth so many impediments.[52]

(The answer implies, interestingly, that "London" does *not* include the suburbs.) The Corporation of London added a nearly impossible codicil to this sarcastic "remedie":

> That no playeing be on holydaies but after euening prayer : nor any receiued into the auditorie till after euening prayer.
> That no playing be in the dark, nor continue any such time but as any of the auditorie may returne to their dwellings in London before sonne set, or at least before it be dark.[53]

Particularly on holy days, this restriction left scant time for winter playing if audiences had to "returne to their dwellings" from the suburbs. The City's inns, closer to the population centers, made it far easier for patrons to return home before dark in the winter and provided the players a suitable answer to suburban inconvenience. The City's hostility to inn-playing therefore threatened the players' established solution to London's short winter evenings.

The redistribution of their liveried players to the Rose and the Theatre by 1594 may have satisfied Lords Howard and Hunsdon, but it did nothing to alleviate the company's winter needs, and both the Admiral's and Chamberlain's Men continued to seek winter quarters. In a letter of 8 October 1594, Carey, Lord Hunsdon, asked the Lord Mayor that his new company be allowed to perform at Cross Keys, the players' "accustomed" practice:

> Where my nowe companie of Players haue byn accustomed for the better exercise of their qualitie, & for the seruice of her Maiestie if need soe requier, to plaie this winter time within the Citye at the Crosse kayes in Gracious street. These are to requier & praye your Lo. (the time beinge such as, thankes be to god, there is nowe no danger of the sicknes) to permitt & suffer them soe to doe.[54]

As Gurr notes, we cannot know if the Lord Mayor complied. If so, the response is lost. Carey seemed confident of success, however; in closing, he notes that he is "not dowting of your willingnes to yeeld herevnto, vppon theise resonable condicions."[55] If Carey's optimism was justified, it could have been in the winter of 1594–1595 that his company presented the earlier *Hamlet*, which they had played the previous June at Newington Butts.[56] Gurr argues that if the Chamberlain's players did perform at Cross Keys that winter, it would have been "the last occasion that the city inns were ever used for playing."[57] At any rate, the Lord Chamberlain's Men obviously desired to continue their accustomed winter residency at Cross Keys, even after securing the Theatre in 1594.

The Admiral's Men, at least, may have toughed it out at the Rose through the winters of the 1590s, with some notable exceptions, discussed below. However, their discontent with the Rose as a winter home is clear from the documents that accompanied their move to the Fortune in 1600. The Bankside theater apparently offered less-than-satisfactory winter shelter, since one rationale of the Admiral's Men for abandoning the Rose for the Fortune was that it was "scituate vppon the Bancke," which was "verie noisome for the resorte of people in the wynter time."[58] The desire for winter accommodations clearly persisted long after the establishment of the Rose and Theatre as the principal playhouses.

There is ample evidence to suggest that the players translated that desire into action. City playing, that is, evidently continued well after 1594, although it is not always clear which players were involved. Some of the clearest evidence comes from Thomas Platter, whose account of his visit to the Globe to see *Julius Caesar* on 21 September 1599 is well known.[59] Less familiar is Platter's description of London's "great many inns, taverns and beergardens scattered about the city, where much amusement may be had with eating, drinking, fiddling and the rest, as for instance in our hostelry, which was visited by players almost daily."[60] "Players" here translates Platter's *spilleut,* which in sixteenth-century German more commonly meant "play actors."[61] If so, Platter, lodged in Mark Lane in the middle of the City of London, describes the players' near-daily recourse to his inn during the autumn months of 1599. Perhaps we might distinguish here between the officially licensed activities of the Globe, Curtain, or Fortune and the fugitive inn-playing that City officials continued to harp on.[62]

The many surviving references to plays at night also argue for continued inn-playing after the mid-1590s, and it may be such performances that Platter enjoyed in Mark Lane. Since the outdoor theaters had no means of illumination, nighttime plays were presented in the large upper rooms of inns. Night playing has its own history of contention within the City. On 3 January 1569, the City issued an injunction to forbid plays "in anny house Inne or Brewhouse . . . after the howre of v of the Clocke in the after noenne at annye tyme betwene this and Shrovetyde nexte" (i.e., February 11).[63] On 11 January 1580, London's Lord Mayor singled out evening performances and issued an order for the arrest of players and the "owners of the houses" because of plays "plaied by night . . . begyninge about vij or viij of the clock in the eveninge and contynuinge untill xj or xij of the clock."[64] The Chamberlain's Men's 1594 promise to be done between four and five o' clock when they sued to use Cross Keys sounds like a reassurance against such objections. Nevertheless, later witnesses, such as Henry Crosse in *Vertues common-wealth* (1603), attest to "nocturnall and night Playes, at vnseasonable and vndue times."[65] City complaints, issued in the dead of winter, testify to an evidently popular phenomenon of playing after dark in London inns.

Even the Admiral's Men—although they apparently played at the Rose all winter in the 1590s—may have slipped into the City at night. Henslowe lent the company money "when they fyrst played dido at nyght the some of thirtishillynges wch wasse the 8 of Jeneway 1597 I saye. xxxs."[66] The performance did not take place at court and could not have been at the Rose: Henslowe records receipts of twelve shillings for the same day for a performance of "valteger."[67] The tantalizing suggestion is that the Admiral's Men double-dipped in the dead of winter, finding a warm, lit room in which to perform their second play of the day.[68] Similarly, Henslowe recounts a misadventure in March 1598 when the company obviously had performed in the City: "pd vnto the carman for caryinge & bryngyn of the stufe backe agayne when they played [as]in fleatstreat pryuat & then owr stufe was loste . . .

iiis."[69] This may indeed have been a private performance, but it demonstrates the Admiral's Men's willingness to venture into the allegedly forbidden City.

Evidently, playing in inns continued at least into the reign of James I, when the officially licensed companies became more firmly lodged in particular houses. As late as 1608 we learn of one William Claiton, an East Smithfield victualler, charged "for the sufferinge playes to bee played in his [house in] the night season."[70] And John Taylor, the water poet, recalled an after-supper performance of "the Life and Death of Guy of Warwick" by the earl of Derby's players at the Maidenhead Inn, Islington, on 14 October 1618.[71] That innkeepers must have welcomed the patrons drawn by the players suggests cooperation between the entertainment and hospitality trades of sixteenth- and seventeenth-century London. Although such performances may have been of dubious legality (as the court records attest), they point to a tradition of inn-playing that survived well after the mid-1590s.

Furthermore, the documents of control that passed between City and Court point not to a settlement but to a continued contest over City playing into the seventeenth century. After all, if City playing ceased in the mid-1590s, why did the Privy Council continually reassert the ban on City playing up to and after 1601? On 22 June 1600, citing the "abuses and disorders that haue growen and doe Continew by occasion of many howses erected & emploied in and aboute the Cittie," the Council reiterated that only two playhouses were sanctioned—the Globe and Fortune—and added that "especiallie yt is forbidden that anie stage plaies shalbe plaied (as sometimes they haue bin) in any Common Inn for publique assemblie in or neare about the Cittie."[72] As before, the precise phraseology is critical. While "sometimes" in early modern English could mean "formerly," as well as "occasionally,"[73] had City playing ceased in 1594, the winter of that year would have been the last occasion upon which City inns were *officially* allowed for playing, granted that the Chamberlain's Men gained access to Cross Keys. If the clampdown was effective, the Corporation's restatement of the ban six years later would indicate extreme diligence. More likely, the Corporation responded in 1601 to a felt need to suppress an ongoing phenomenon.

According to Roslyn Knutson, William Shakespeare's *Hamlet* premiered at the Globe in 1600/1601,[74] just when the Privy Council reasserted the ban against playing in the common inns. The Chamberlain's Men may have continued to flout the law through the winter of 1600/1601, because on 11 March 1601, Privy Council minutes record the following: "A letter to the Lord Mayour requiring him not to faile to take order the playes within the cyttie and the liberties, especyally at Powles and in the Blackfriers, may be suppressed during this time of Lent."[75] If the children's companies in the liberties—at Paul's, at Blackfriars—are singled out here, "playes within the cyttie" must refer to those performed at inns or innyards, such as the ones Platter recorded seeing almost daily two years before.

And City playing does not seem to have ceased after the winter of 1600/1601 (when Shakespeare's *Hamlet* was still relatively new), for the attempts to limit playing to two suburban houses also met with challenges. On 31 December 1601, the Privy Council wrote a stern letter to the justices of both Middlesex and Surrey that addressed recent complaints from the mayor "of the great abuse and disorder within and about the cittie of London by reason of the multitude of play howses." Irritation marks the Privy Council's letter:

> For whereas about a yeare and a half since . . . wee did carefullie sett downe and prescribe an order to be observed concerninge the number of playhowses and the use and exercise of stage plaies, with lymytacion of tymes and places for the same (namely that there should be but two howses allowed for that use, one in Middlesex called the Fortune and the other in Surrey called the Globe, and the same with observacion of certaine daies and times as in the said order is particularly expressed), in such sorte as a moderate practice of them for honest recreation might be contynued, and yet the inordinate concourse of dissolute and idle people be restrayned, wee do now understande that our said order hath bin so farr from taking dew effect, as in steede of restrainte and redresse of the former disorders the multitude of play howses is much encreased, and that no daie passeth over without many stage plaies in one place or other within and about the cittie publiquelie made.[76]

The final phrase is telling. No day passes, the Privy Council states, without many plays "within and about the cittie publiquelie made," despite the limits placed on playing.

This letter serves as a further reminder, as Richard Dutton has it, that "their notional authority at times exceeded their capacity to enforce their will."[77] The Privy Council also wrote the Lord Mayor at the end of 1601 and placed responsibility for the City's theatrical management with him, enjoining the aldermen to execute "our said order within the cittie."[78] The Privy Council acknowledges the Mayor's complaints about the "great abuse and disorder within and about the cittie of London by reason of the multitude of play-howses," but the council pointedly notes that

> it betokeneth your care and desire to reforme the disorders of the cittie, so wee must lett you know that wee did muche rather expect to understand that our order (sett downe and prescribed about a

yeare and a half since for the reformation of the saide disorders
upon the like complaint at that tyme) had bin duelie executed.[79]

City playing was a City problem, and the Privy Council deftly passes
the buck.

These and later letters attest to the continued popularity of plays both
"within and about" London into the early seventeenth century. In a letter
dated 31 December 1604, the Privy Council targets those players who have
revived or continued the seasonal migration to the City inns and singles
out City playing, "charging and streightlie comaunding all suche persons, as
are the owners of any the howses used for stage plaies within the cittie, not
to permitt any more publique plaies to be used, exercised or shewed from
hence-foorth in their said howses."[80] Most pertinently, such a letter, written in the dead of winter, reveals that the contentious issue of City playing
remained active.

It seems quite possible that the Chamberlain's Men continued to eke
out London's limited winter light in City inns throughout the 1590s and
beyond. The title page to Q1 *Hamlet* may then record winter performances
in the early 1600s, when the Globe served as a summer home and the Cross
Keys was an uncertain winter berth. When the King's Men finally gained
access to the Blackfriars in 1608, their Globe-in-summer/Blackfriars-in-
winter pattern was not a reinstatement but a continuation of an "accustomed"
practice of playing indoors in winter.[81] Glynne Wickham pondered this possibility thirty years ago, although he did not pursue it: "The only exception to
this [the suppression of City playing in 1597] which I would not be surprised
to find revealed by subsequent research is the Cross Keyes in Gracechurch
Street where the Lord Chamberlain's Company played in the winter of 1594–
1595, and where it may have been allowed to remain until it could recover the
Blackfriars to its own use."[82] Long disregarded as evidence, Q1 *Hamlet*'s title
page may bear out Wickham's hunch.

IV. Conclusion: Q1 *Hamlet*

Of the three possible explanations for the claims raised at this essay's outset,
only the third—that Shakespeare's *Hamlet* did play in the City—fully incor-
porates the evidence mustered here. The notion that Q1 included the phrase
"acted in the Cittie of London" for fashion's sake has been discounted on the
grounds that such claims were not fashionable: only eight of the hundreds of
extant plays published between 1512 and 1689 boast of performances in or
about the City. Of the eight, only six advertise performances *within* the City,
and in five cases there exists no reason to dispute those claims. Furthermore,
printed Chamberlain's or King's Men plays from this period seldom provide
the kind of geographical precision found in Q1.[83] James Roberts, who held

the copyright to Q1 *Hamlet* but did not print it, entered just five plays in the Stationers' Register, all within the period 1598 to 1603 and all belonging to the Lord Chamberlain's company. None bears the distinctive City of London designation. Valentine Simmes, not Roberts, printed Q1 *Hamlet*,[84] yet this designation never appears in the twenty-four new and reprinted plays that Simmes issued.

The title page may then lead us to ask whether its composer wittingly or unwittingly overreached in his claim for *Hamlet* "by William Shake-speare." In proprietary terms, the title page may not distinguish between original and later versions. After all, a play called *Hamlet* entered the Chamberlain's Men repertory after their formation in May 1594.[85] It was in the following fall that their patron wrote to the Lord Mayor and asked him to "permitt & suffer" the players to perform at the Cross Keys Inn "this winter time."[86] *Hamlet*—although not Shakespeare's—likely played at Cross Keys that season if the company gained access, for we know their repertory included a play of that name. The title page may fold those performances in with those of Shakespeare's play, maximizing its marketing reach.

If Q1's title page refers specifically to the post-1601 *Hamlet*, we are left to consider the intriguing possibility that the Chamberlain's Men continued their habit of performing at Cross Keys every winter up through at least 1601, when the company premiered a new version of an old play. If so, they played in the face of continued efforts to stop them. To assume that those efforts were successful, however, overemphasizes the Corporation of London's regulatory muscle.

When considering City playing, the period between 1594 and (at least) 1603 was probably far less settled than theater historians have allowed. The degree to which inn-playing was implicated in the City's economic life is currently under review, but recent work has shown that players and playing were deeply enmeshed in the City's business operations.[87] Attempts to expel the players threatened the City's entertainment and hospitality trades and evidently met with more resistance than has previously been recognized.

If the Q1 *Hamlet* title page means what it says, we have to reconsider our state of knowledge about theatrical practice at the close of the sixteenth century. The implications for repertory and economics are considerable. When companies migrated to the City's inns, did the repertory alter? Were plays shorter in the winter? How was money collected? What were the arrangements between the players and the innkeepers? How collusive were their dealings? Did unlicensed companies play in the evening? Was there an underground industry of unlicensed plays and players? These questions are beyond this essay's ken, but to ignore Q1 *Hamlet*'s title-page claim of City performances may be to ignore information about one of the earliest performances of Shakespeare's *Hamlet*, along with its broader implications.

NOTES

I am grateful to the participants in the 2005 Shakespeare Association of America Theater History seminar for their responses to this essay, particularly Roslyn Knutson, Lawrence Manley, and Tiffany Stern.

1. W. W. Greg, *A Bibliography of the English Printed Drama to the Restoration*, 4 vols. (Oxford: Oxford University Press, 1939–1959), 1:197(a). All title page quotations and dates of play publication are taken from Greg's bibliography and are cited by volume and entry number. Quotations of title pages follow Greg's conventions of typeface and lineation, including the use of vertical bars (|) to indicate line breaks.

2. Andrew Gurr, "Henry Carey's Peculiar Letter," *Shakespeare Quarterly* 56 (2005): 51–75, esp. 52. The proposed date for *Hamlet*'s first performance appears in Roslyn Knutson, *The Repertory of Shakespeare's Company, 1594–1613* (Fayetteville: University of Arkansas Press, 1991), 81. Throughout this essay, "City" with a capital "C" refers to the area under the control of the Lord Mayor. Importantly, it indicates London exclusive of the suburbs.

3. W. W. Greg, *The Shakespeare First Folio: Its Bibliographical and Textual History* (Oxford: Clarendon Press, 1955), 307.

4. Blayney writes, "The primary purpose of an imprint was . . . to inform retailers where a book could be purchased wholesale. . . . a potential customer who knew about the imprint might correctly deduce that the distributor's shop would be the one most likely to have copies in stock—but that was merely incidental" (390). See Peter W. M. Blayney, "The Publication of Playbooks," in *A New History of Early English Drama*, ed. John D. Cox and David Scott Kastan (New York: Columbia University Press, 1997), 383–422, esp. 390.

5. Tiffany Stern, "'On each Wall and Corner Poast': Playbills, Title-Pages, and Advertising in Early Modern London," *English Literary Renaissance* 36 (2006): 57–89.

6. Greg, *Bibliography*, 1:113, cites "?1591" as a publication date for *Fair Em*.

7. Two other plays in this period claim performances in London without referring specifically to "the City." However, since their title pages lack the precise phraseology considered here, I have not included them in this survey. They are *The Wounds of Ciuill War* (1594; STC 16678; Greg, *Bibliography*, 1:122) and *The Blind Beggar of Alexandria* (1598; STC 4965; Greg, *Bibliography*, 1:146).

8. Greg, *Bibliography*, 1:94–95(a).

9. David Bevington and Eric Rasmussen argue that *Tamburlaine* was written and performed in 1587–1588; see Christopher Marlowe, *Tamburlaine, Parts I and II; Doctor Faustus, A- and B-Texts; The Jew of Malta; Edward II*, ed. David Bevington and Eric Rasmussen (Oxford: Oxford University Press, 1995), ix. On the evidence that *Tamburlaine* was performed at the Rose, see Andrew Gurr, *The Shakespearian Playing Companies* (Oxford: Clarendon Press, 1996), 232.

10. Gurr (*Shakespearian Playing Companies*, 232) speculates that the Admiral's Men were "most likely" at the Theatre, "if not at one of the London inns," based partly upon his interpretation of the mysterious and possibly apocryphal stage accident—an onstage shooting—of 16 November 1587. The account of the shooting can be found in Glynne Wickham, Herbert Berry, and William Ingram, eds., *English Professional Theatre, 1530–1660* (Cambridge: Cambridge University Press,

2000), 277. For the presence of the Admiral's Men at the Theatre in 1591, see E. K. Chambers, *The Elizabethan Stage*, 4 vols. (Oxford: Clarendon Press, 1923), 2:136.

11. William Prynne, *Histrio-Mastix* (London, 1633), sig. Ggg4[r].

12. Quoted in Chambers, 4:305.

13. Greg, *Bibliography*, 1:113.

14. Gurr, *Shakespearian Playing Companies*, 274.

15. Quoted in Chambers, 4:296.

16. Greg, *Bibliography*, 1:101(a).

17. Quoted in Chambers, 2:382.

18. Scott McMillin and Sally-Beth MacLean, *The Queen's Men and Their Plays* (Cambridge: Cambridge University Press, 1998), 49. For a discussion of the Queen's Men and *The Troublesome Reign of King John*, see 88–89; for the activities of this company, see 224–226.

19. Greg, *Bibliography*, 1:129(a).

20. Gurr places them at Burbage's Theatre in 1592–1593, largely on the grounds that they could not have been at the Rose, according to Henslowe's diary; see *Shakespearian Playing Companies*, 270.

21. John Stow, *A Survey of London: Reprinted from the Text of 1603*, intro. Charles Lethbridge Kingford, 2 vols. (Oxford: Clarendon Press, 1971), 1:5.

22. Greg, *Bibliography*, 1:139.

23. H. De Vocht, ed., *A Knack to Know an Honest Man*, Malone Society Reprints (Oxford: Oxford University Press, 1910), v.

24. *Henslowe's Diary*, ed. R. A. Foakes and R. T. Rickert (Cambridge: Cambridge University Press, 1961), 25.

25. Gurr conjectures that this agreement, forming a duopoly, went into effect in May 1594; he argues that the putative document for this agreement has been lost. See *Shakespearian Playing Companies*, 65–66. See also n. 46 below.

26. Greg, *Bibliography*, 1:140(a).

27. Fred Lapides convincingly assigns the play to the Admiral's Men; see *"The Raigne of King Edward the Third": A Critical, Old-Spelling Edition*, ed. Fred Lapides (New York, London: Garland, 1980), 39–41; for a thorough review of the authorship question, dating, and stage history, see 1–63. S. Schoenbaum, in *Annals of English Drama, 975–1700: A Supplement to the Revised Edition* (Evanston: Northwestern University Press, 1966), 5, tentatively assigns the play to Pembroke's Men, citing MacD. P. Jackson's claim in "'Edward III,' Shakespeare, and Pembroke's Men," *Notes and Queries* 210 (1965): 329–331.

28. Greg, *Bibliography*, 1:151(a).

29. Arvin H. Jupin reviews theories about the possible date of *Mucedorus* in *A Contextual Study and Modern-Spelling Edition of "Mucedorus,"* ed. Arvin H. Jupin (New York: Garland, 1987), 1–5; esp. 1.

30. Greg, *Bibliography*, 1:197(a). Formatting of this title page reproduces that used by Greg.

31. Ben Weinreb and Christopher Hibbert, eds., *The London Encyclopaedia* (Bethesda, MD: Adler and Adler, 1986), 172–175, s.v. "City of London."

32. Stow, 1:xcix.

33. Stow, 2:69–70.

34. Stow, 2.52, 2.141; emphases added.

35. David J. Johnson, *Southwark and the City* (Oxford University Press, 1969), 153.

36. Quoted in *The Progresses and Public Processions of Queen Elizabeth*, ed. John Nichols, 3 vols. (London: John Nichols and Son, 1823), 1:38–60, esp. 56–58.

37. Quoted in *The Progresses, Processions, and Magnificent Festivities of King James the First*, ed. John Nichols, 4 vols. (London: J. B. Nichols, 1828), 1:337–376, esp. 337, 375.

38. Fernand Braudel, *Capitalism and Material Life, 1400–1800*, trans. Miriam Kochan (London: Weidenfeld and Nicholson, 1973), 382.

39. Lawrence Manley, *Literature and Culture in Early Modern London* (Cambridge: Cambridge University Press, 1995), 129.

40. Cynthia Wall, "Grammars of Space: The Language of London from Stow's *Survey* to Defoe's *Tour*," *Philological Quarterly* 76 (1997): 387–411, esp. 390.

41. Manley, *Literature and Culture*, 144.

42. John Speed, *The Theatre of the Empire of Greate Britaine* (London, 1676), quoted in Lawrence Manley, ed., *London in the Age of Shakespeare: An Anthology* (University Park, PA: Pennsylvania State University Press, 1986), 43.

43. James Howell, *Londinopolis* (London, 1657), quoted in Manley, *Literature and Culture*, 164. London's sprawl continually threatened facile notions of exclusivity and integrity. Therefore, a perceptual civic sense became increasingly strident, as the suburbs, with their casual laborers and unaffiliated artisans, outstripped the City of London in growth so that, as Howell complained, "the suburbs of London are much larger than the body of the City, which make some compare her to a Jesuit's hat, whose brims are far larger than the block" (*Londinopolis*, quoted in Manley, *London in the Age of Shakespeare*, 47).

44. Quoted in Glynne Wickham, *Early English Stages, 1300–1660*, 3 vols. (London: Routledge and Kegan Paul, 1972), vol. 2, part 1, 67 (2.1:67).

45. Quoted in Wickham et al., 299–300; emphasis added. The inns were in high demand for prize-playing in the 1570s and 1580s. The Bel Savage and the Bull appear frequently as fight sites in the records of the Masters of Defence of London, a guild of teachers of fencing; see Herbert Berry, *The Noble Science: A Study and Transcription of Sloane Ms. 2530, Papers of the Masters of Defence of London, Temp. Henry VIII to 1590* (Newark: University of Delaware Press, 1991); and O. L. Brownstein, "A Record of London Inn-Playhouses from c. 1565–1590," *SQ* 22 (1971): 17–24.

46. Gurr argues that Howard and Carey agreed to license two companies—the Admiral's and the Chamberlain's—and may have forbidden them to play in the City, although no record of such an agreement exists. The new arrangement would have settled a persistent struggle over City playing between Guildhall and the Privy Council. According to Gurr, this new deal deferred to the Lord Mayor by permitting no plays in the City whatsoever, and he concludes categorically that "the inns had been closed as places for staging plays seemingly by 1596 and certainly before 1598, when the duopoly was in full swing" ("Henry Carey's Peculiar Letter," 58). Gurr outlines the duopoly system in his *Shakespearian Playing Companies*, passim.

47. Wickham et al., 304.

48. Quoted in Wickham et al., 304.

49. Wickham et al., 304, 441.

50. Quoted in Chambers, 4:299. Chambers argues for the November 1584 date, stating that it must come after the collapse of the scaffolds at Paris Garden on 13 January 1583. It must also, he claims, follow the formation of the Queen's Men in March 1583. He concludes that "the petition was, on the face of it, written

at the beginning of a winter, and the most natural interpretation would place it in the winter of 1584" (4:299). That it follows their permit to play in the City only emphasizes how provisional and contested such claims were.

51. Wickham, however, argues that performances at inns were not in the yard but in interior halls; see *Early English Stages*, 2.1:186–196.

52. Quoted in Chambers, 4:301.

53. Quoted in Chambers, 4:302.

54. Quoted in Chambers, 4:316. See also Gurr, "Henry Carey's Peculiar Letter."

55. Quoted in Chambers, 4:316.

56. For a record of *Hamlet* at Newington Butts on 9 June 1594, see *Henslowe's Diary*, 21.

57. Gurr, *Shakespearian Playing Companies*, 66. In *The Best Actors in the World: Shakespeare and His Acting Company* (Westport, CT, and London: Greenwood Press, 2002), David Grote discusses this winter run at Cross Keys and concludes, "Thus, Shakespeare's company entered London rather like a modern fringe company, performing in a small, converted space rather than one of the regular theaters" (22). The analogy misconstrues the nature of Cross Keys and the other London inns. Far from being fringe theaters, the inns were not only geographically central but also figuratively so and were semipermanent fixtures of the London theatrical circuit.

58. Quoted in Chambers, 4:328.

59. *The Journals of Two Travellers in Elizabethan and Early Stuart England: Thomas Platter and Horatio Busino*, ed. Peter Razzell (London: Caliban Books, 1995), 26–27.

60. *Journals of Two Travellers*, 31–32.

61. The relevant phrase "as for instance in our hostelry, which was visited by players almost daily" reads "wie dann auch vast alletag in unser losament die spielleüt sindt" in Thomas Platter, *Beschreibung der Reisen durch Frankreich, Spanien, England und die Niederlande 1595–1600*, ed. Rut Keiser, 2 vols. (Basel, Stuttgart: Schwabe Verlag, 1968), 2:795.

62. In this light, we might revisit Platter's record of another trip to see a play: "On another occasion not far from our inn, in the suburb at Bishopsgate, if I remember, also after lunch, I beheld a play in which they presented diverse nations and an Englishman struggling together for a maiden" (*Journals of Two Travellers*, 27). Chambers (2:400) read this account as a reference to a performance at the Curtain, which was a few hundred yards north of Bishopsgate. Gabriel Egan suggests that Platter may have meant the Boar's Head, which was near Platter's inn but farther from Bishopsgate than the Curtain; see "Thomas Platter's Account of an Unknown Play at the Curtain or the Boar's Head," *Notes and Queries* 245 (2000): 53–56, esp. 54.

63. Quoted in Wickham, 2.1:194.

64. Quoted in Wickham, 2.1:191.

65. Quoted in Chambers, 4:247.

66. Henslowe, 86.

67. Henslowe, 55.

68. On the obscure performance history of *Dido, Queen of Carthage*, see H. J. Oliver, ed., *"Dido Queen of Carthage" and "The Massacre at Paris,"* by Christopher Marlowe (Cambridge: Harvard University Press, 1968), xxxi–xxxii.

69. Henslowe, 88.

70. John Cordy Jeaffreson, ed., *Middlesex County Records* (Old Series), 4 vols. (London: Greater London Council, 1972–1975), 2:47. Glynne Wickham writes that "it is worth remarking that most of the prosecutions of inn-keepers of which we have record are for permitting plays at night" (*Early English Stages*, 2.1:364n73).

71. Quoted in Chambers, 2:127.

72. Quoted in Chambers, 4:330–332.

73. The *Oxford English Dictionary*, 2d ed., s.v. "sometimes," 2b: "At one time; in former times, formerly"; see also 1a, "On some occasions; at times; now and then."

74. Knutson, 81.

75. Quoted in Chambers, 4:332.

76. Quoted in Chambers, 4:332–333.

77. Richard Dutton, *Mastering the Revels: The Regulation and Censorship of English Renaissance Drama* (Iowa City: University of Iowa Press, 1991), 112.

78. Quoted in Virginia Crocheron Gildersleeve, *Governmental Regulation of the Elizabethan Drama* (New York: Columbia University Press, 1908), 193.

79. Quoted in Gildersleeve, 193.

80. Quoted in Chambers, 4:334.

81. Gurr, "Henry Carey's Peculiar Letter," 64–65; the reference to "accustomed" practice is from Carey's letter (quoted in Chambers, 4:316). If we allow that Q1 *Hamlet* may indeed record a "Cittie of London" performance in the winter of 1600, we need to account for James Burbage's efforts to secure the Blackfriars in 1596. The residents of that liberty, at any rate, saw Burbage's actions as an effort to skirt City proscriptions against London playing. They petitioned the Privy Council in November 1596, claiming that "now all players being banished by the Lord Mayor from playing within the Cittie by reason of the great inconveniences and ill rule that follweth them, they now thincke to plant them selves in liberties" (Chambers, 4:320, 319). Indeed, it could be concluded that both Burbage's effort and this petition argue for the efficacy of the suppression of City playing; otherwise, why would Burbage invest enormous capital in a City playhouse? Burbage was not merely looking to find a permanent winter home—a replacement for the "accustomed" Cross Keys; he was looking for a playhouse for all seasons. An official effort to end City playing was not the only impetus for his innovative project. After all, the writing was on the wall: the Chamberlain's Men were losing the Theatre, and the Globe was not yet, so far as we know, even envisioned. Burbage's ingenious scheme was to move the Chamberlain's Men to the liberty of the Blackfriars, not merely to sidestep orders against City playing in the winter but to find them a permanent house. See also Gurr, "Henry Carey's Peculiar Letter," 51–52 and 75. The effort failed, and the Chamberlain's men moved to the Curtain and then in 1598–1599 to the Globe.

82. Wickham, 2.2:101n.

83. For instance, in 1601, Ben Jonson's *Every Man in His Humor* appeared, as follows: "EVERY MAN IN | his Humor. | As it hath beene sundry times | *publickly acted by the right* | Honorable the Lord Cham- | *berlaine his seruants*" [Greg, *Bibliography*, 1:176(a)]. In 1602, *The Merry Wives of Windsor* was printed with the following title page: "A | Most pleasaunt and | excellent conceited Co- | medie, of Syr *Iohn Falstaffe*, and the | merrie Wiues of *Windsor*. | . . . | As it hath bene diuers times Acted by the right Honorable | my Lord Chamberlaines seruants. Both before her | Maiestie, and else-where" [Greg, *Bibliography*, 1:187(a)].

84. See Stanley Wells and Gary Taylor with John Jowett and William Montgomery, *William Shakespeare: A Textual Companion* (Oxford: Clarendon Press, 1987), 396.

85. Henslowe, 21.

86. Quoted in Chambers, 4:316.

87. See David Kathman, "Grocers, Goldsmiths, and Drapers: Freemen and Apprentices in the Elizabethan Theater," *SQ* 55 (2004): 1–49; and "Citizens, Innholders, and Playhouse Builders, 1543–1622," *Research Opportunities in Medieval and Renaissance Drama* 44 (2005): 38–64.

BRADLEY GREENBURG

T. S. Eliot's Impudence:
Hamlet, *Objective Correlative, and Formulation*

You get more credit for thinking if you restate formulae or cite cases that fall in easily under formulae, but all the fun is outside saying things that suggest formulae that won't formulate—that almost but don't quite formulate. I should like to be so subtle at this game as to seem to the casual person altogether obvious. The casual person would assume that I meant nothing or else I came near enough meaning something he was familiar with to mean it for all practical purposes. Well well well.

—Robert Frost

When T. S. Eliot revised his English collection *Elizabethan Essays* for an American edition twenty-two years after its initial publication, he made a number of serious cuts.[1] In cutting "Shakespeare and the Stoicism of Seneca," "Hamlet and His Problems," and "Four Elizabethan Dramatists," he remarked that these essays "on re-examination embarrassed me by their callowness, and by a facility of unqualified assertion which verges, here and there, on impudence. The *Hamlet,* of course, had been kept afloat all these years by the phrase 'objective correlative'—a phrase which, I am now told, is not even my own but was first used by Washington Alston."[2] Eliot's greatest impudence, given the conclusions drawn in the other two essays, came, one assumes, in his insistence that *Hamlet* lacks an "objective correlative." This

Criticism: A Quarterly for Literature and the Arts, Volume 49, Number 2 (Spring 2007): pp. 215–239. Copyright © 2008 Wayne State University Press.

formula, attempting as it does to characterize the play's failure, the "prob-lems" of Hamlet tried and found wanting as a cause for his studied inaction, is a product that far exceeds Eliot's purported reviewing of two books on Shakespeare's tragedy and its protagonist. The essay is instead one of the steps in the poet/critic's efforts to clear the way for, while clarifying the genealogy of, his modernist project. Eliot's aggressive reading of this play has much to tell us about the role of the critic in configuring the identity of modernist poetic practice as well as demonstrating how the play lures read-ers, even one as astute as Eliot, into a fixation with its main character.

The formula-producing moments of Eliot's early theorizing on the rep-resentational practice of poetry are frequently articulated in the context of his work on Renaissance drama and early seventeenth-century poetry.[3] What is it about *Hamlet* the story and Hamlet the character that provokes him, in the midst of working out a genealogical schema for modernist poetics, to invent such "impudent" formulations?[4] To answer this question I will explore the essays and book reviews of the late 'teens and early 'twenties, where Eliot carefully constructs a relationship between modernist poetics and Renais-sance drama and poetry. Further, I want to argue that such a construction is exemplified in Eliot's reading of *Hamlet* where, in performing the very analy-sis he has just warned us about, he misses a crucial element in the represen-tational structure and strategy of the play. Eliot's "unqualified assertions," in other words, are impudent in their imprudence: his formulaic turn in "Ham-let and His Problems" marks a failure to attend to the dramatic functioning of Shakespeare's play.

The dramatic functioning I refer to is Hamlet's relentless construction of a Hamlet who is captivating and realistic, with a subjectivity so complex and fraught with psychopathology that this character has been called the first "modern subject."[5] What so consistently escapes critical scrutiny is how *the play* does this. What are the mechanisms the drama employs to construct such a character? Since Eliot's review essay opens with a response to just this question—"Few critics have even admitted that *Hamlet* the play is the pri-mary problem, and Hamlet the character only secondary"[6]—we might well expect him to take precisely this line of argument. In other words, how does the play succeed—or, in this case, fail—to dramatize a dizzying array of sub-jective responses to grief, maternal guilt, murder, oedipal desires, and so forth? Eliot's essay, and so much of the criticism that follows it, does not provide a response to this question, because after it offers to confront the "problem" of the play, it spends its greatest energy analyzing the problems of its main char-acter. Hamlet, it seems finally to suggest, is *Hamlet,* and so if one diagnoses the inadequacy of the protagonist's construction, one has fully understood how the play lacks what would otherwise complete it.[7]

Eliot uses *Hamlet* in the developing polemic of his modernist project to insist that the play can have a pernicious effect upon the writing of poetry itself. The subject trapped in repetitive rumination, unable to do anything other than think about thinking rather than act upon knowledge and experience, puts poetry in danger of following a mistaken practice that dissociates emotion and objects. The debate that this engenders between the so-called Classic and Romantic ways of thinking about and writing poetry is a debate about the status of the poet and representational practice. Eliot's version of modernist poetics insists that a particular artistic sensibility must hold sway. His reading of *Hamlet* is an important move in the effort to establish the modernist position in a debate over the role of a main character credited for founding a certain subjectivity: an either destructively ruminatory self-consciousness, or a liberating maker of a dramatic poetry that frees thought from its limiting material context.

What goes unexamined in both the Romantics' view of *Hamlet* and Eliot's is that Hamlet is not simply a character who can be taken at face value, as an avatar for the founding of an aesthetic practice. If the play has been treated as an Academy, where subsequent poets and dramatists come to hear the master speak, they have been listening to Socrates too closely and failing to read beyond him to the Plato who labors to produce such intellectual, rhetorical effects.[8] The danger of using Hamlet as a model—either positively or negatively—for aesthetic practice is that there is a tendency to elide the way *Hamlet* works to produce its main character. Though Eliot will begin his essay by pointing out that *Hamlet* is the problem rather than Hamlet himself, he nonetheless goes on to use the delaying, ruminating character as the focus of his criticism of the play as well as his real target: the poetry of the nineteenth century that dissociates sensibility. For Eliot, the mimetic work that *Hamlet*/Hamlet performs is a dangerous precedent for poetry in the potential misunderstanding by which its main character becomes a model for poetic practice rather than the play itself. Considered closely, the formula of "objective correlative" fails to name a true defect of the play, since Eliot, and everyone else, has no trouble feeling the effects for which the cause is supposedly missing (or inadequate). The mimetic work of the play does, of course, occur, but rather than analyze how this takes place, Eliot peers too intently at Hamlet as a "real" character, seizing on the psychological characteristics that he identifies as the model for the problems that come to beset poetry. Whether T. S. Eliot the poet is aware of this or not—and perhaps his self-critical charge of "callowness" falls just here—he is himself a tremendously effective producer of such effects.[9]

* * *

Critics of "Hamlet and His Problems" tend to treat it as a patient etherized upon a table, from which they feel able to surgically remove the idea of the "objective correlative," dissociating it from its context.[10] The essay itself is rarely discussed as having any bearing on *Hamlet* whatsoever, and has become little more than a vehicle for bringing into the critical vocabulary a conceptual formulation that has proved difficult and often unwieldy for criticism. It is surely one of Eliot's most epigrammatic, gnomically formulated pieces of literary criticism, and there have been a number of suggestions as to why this is.[11] One strong possibility is the influence of the philosophical thought of F. H. Bradley, on whom Eliot wrote his dissertation at Harvard (1916).[12] But no matter what we may think of the worth of Bradley's philosophy, attempting to explain the idea of the objective correlative as containing within itself its own logic, silently cutting its contextual ties to Shakespeare's play, misses what should be the most important point of all, which is the relation between the critical formulation and the array of elements and forces that Eliot's essay attempts to deal with.

"Hamlet and His Problems" appears in 1919, at the beginning of a series of critical essays that Eliot will publish ostensibly as reviews, though they quickly place themselves at the center of the polemic of literary modernism. It is remarkable that the essays for which he is best known, especially as they contain those critical phrases that will not fade back into the essays from which they are taken, are all published between the years 1919 and 1924.[13] In this period Eliot is most consciously trying to place both his poetry and the poetry of his generation in a proper genealogical relationship to the tradition that he prefers. To do so he makes a concerted effort to place modernism's poetic origin where it will have been before anyone has a chance to claim otherwise. Though legitimacy is not the only reason, it is an important one for a poet trying to avoid the clichés of what he felt to be the legacy of a certain strand of nineteenth-century poetry.[14] The goal is to build a bridge between his poetic method, his sensibility, and that of a classic tradition stretching from the ancients to John Donne and a few of his successors.[15] The break that occurs after the metaphysical poets is, for Eliot's needs, crucial for placing under erasure a period that can finally be brought to an end thanks to his critical labors and the poetry of his friends. The question of authority looms large here, and can, I think, be answered by looking at how the relationship between poetry and its representational structure is configured and understood to work in practice.

According to Eliot, if Shakespeare "had written according to a better philosophy, [he] would have written worse poetry."[16] Eliot is conspicuously unwilling to commit to such a singular devotion. The poet, in making his poem, cannot be doing something else, and this applies as well to the critic. This is, says Eliot, a matter for a philosophical discussion of belief, where we would have to see just how much of what a poet knows affects the poetry created.[17] But though we might talk about both, we cannot afford to talk about them in the same breath; to do so would be to make a judgment about a relationship between elements that cannot be fully understood to bear upon the poem itself. The larger point of this debate will be taken up in Eliot's discussion of "impersonality" in "Tradition and the Individual Talent," where the artist as unaffected, unreacting catalyst cannot be seen to be filling his work with inner personal traits.[18] But Eliot, as does almost every other critic of literature before and after, wanders into this gray area occasionally himself: we might compare his discussions of Shakespeare and Algernon Charles Swinburne and notice that there is rather less difference than one would think.[19] When it comes to the *Hamlet* essay, the difference becomes even less clear. It is worth noting at this point that Eliot's critical opinion of Swinburne is that he is "diffuse" and suffers from a love for the words rather than the objects and emotions that must be attended to for those words to comprise great poetry.[20] This rather Johnsonian critical posture is Eliot's way of saying that an improper relation to representational integrity—Shakespeare's punning at the expense of dramatic unity and balance, for instance, or Swinburne's logophilia—takes away from poetry as being coherent of sensibility.

Shakespeare is, on this model, seen as a writer who is able to hold together the demanding effort of synthesis that is required to avoid the poetry of dissociation or diffuseness. As an "instrument for transformation," Shakespeare is able to make poetry as the metaphysician makes metaphysics and the spider makes filament.[21] But something caused this direct relationship to break down shortly after Shakespeare's death. Something occurred that necessitates the shifting of attention and labor of the poet to criticism in order to remake poetry according to the proper tradition.[22] To be able to make poetry correctly, avoiding an improper relation between poet, object, emotion, and the world, it is a matter of making clear these relations as found in the poetry culminating in Shakespeare and Donne and, though with less balance, the metaphysical poets Eliot discusses in his Clark Lectures of 1926.[23] In short, poetry as Eliot sees it in a time of world war and rapid change, where the nineteenth century must be broken with decisively, is in desperate need of both a clearly defined origin in the tradition and a clear sense of its originating force in the world itself. For both of these points, poetry must become aware of its relation to an object in order to develop a representational practice that will give it a model for its place in the tradition as well as its place in the world. What Eliot tries to do is to effect a suturing break with the tradition as he finds it. And he finds it by redefining it for his own purpose.[24]

Though the Hamlet essay precedes it, Eliot's essay titled "The Metaphysical Poets" introduces the formula of the "dissociation of sensibility."[25] The formulaic thesis of this essay develops in a genealogical direction the similarly formulaic insights introduced in "Hamlet and His Problems." For what fails in *Hamlet* will be the measure for what goes awry with the poets

who follow the poets of the early seventeenth century. After Donne there is
a certain Hamleting of poetry that infects the ability of poets to maintain a
proper relationship between thought and feeling.[26] This is "something that
happened to the mind of England between the time of Donne or Lord Herbert of Cherbury and the time of Tennyson and Browning; it is the difference
between the intellectual poet and the reflective poet. Tennyson and Browning
are poets, and they think; but they do not feel their thought as immediately
as the odour of a rose. A thought to Donne was an experience; it modified
his sensibility."[27] From here he goes on to define the poet as one who "amal-
gamates" experience: "in the mind of the poet these experiences are always
forming new wholes." What is it that creeps in between association ("amalgamation," or the "mechanism of sensibility") and dissociation? The answer
seems to be that which sicklies o'er experience: reflection, or conscience, that
paling cast of thought. The delay or hesitation that follows bleeds action dry,
and on this model Laertes would be a much better candidate for possessing
the necessary equipage for *poesis* than Hamlet. But what is it about Hamlet,
as the insoluble problem of *Hamlet,* that threatens to unhinge poetry from
something to which it must stay fixed?

Eliot's formulation regarding dissociation has affinities with John Keats's
idea of "Negative Capability." Keats is praised by his contemporaries as having "direct sensuous apprehension of thought."[28] Eliot, though, lumps the Romantics together and applies dissociation to them in a judgment as violently
generalizing as it is unverifiable. But there is a distinction to be made between
the poetry and the writing about poetry, even if Eliot is not willing to acknowledge it. What Keats says about Shakespeare could be taken as affirming dissociation as a positive feature of his poetic practice—especially in the
case of *Hamlet.* So even if Keats's poetry does not suffer from dissociation
to the extent that Eliot says it does, there is still something in the Romantic
view of poetic practice that would affirm Eliot's judgment. I am not saying
that Eliot's polemical stance regarding the Romantics is correct, but that it
has enough justification to have made it possible to saddle them with having worsened a problem that the rest of the century followed and that only a
writer such as, and according to, Eliot—with both critical and poetic faculties
in synch—can find the means to overcome. "Negative Capability" is a formula
with strong associations to the very problem that lies at the heart of Eliot's
concerns in both of his formulations that I am discussing here.

In his well-known letter of December 22, 1818, Keats writes:

> [A]t once it struck me, what quality went to form a Man of
> Achievement especially in Literature & which Shakespeare
> possessed so enormously—I mean *Negative Capability,* that is
> when man is capable of being in uncertainties, Mysteries, doubts,

without any irritable reaching after fact & reason . . . This pursued through Volumes would perhaps take us no further than this, that with a great poet the sense of Beauty overcomes every other consideration, or rather obliterates all consideration.[29]

What Keats celebrates so effusively in his letters touching Shakespeare is the latter's ability to transform language through his chameleon-like ability to invent the apposite mood, character, or dramatic scene. The "negative" part of this formula involves an evacuation of personality that leads to an unfettered inventive facility for the creation of Beauty, and this Germanic capital should alert us to the primacy of the abstract notion over the subject who receives and delivers it. The transformation that occurs here is from writer to character or poetic conceit. This is, of course, a consummate formulation for Romanticism. Though Eliot never attacks this phrase of Keats directly, his theoretical criticism tends to utterly reject yet slyly affirm it. Eliot was neither shy nor laconic about his distaste for the ideals of the Romantic poets as a generation, but no doubt out of this "intellectual chaos" some order could be found.[30] I do not want to dwell any further on the reasons for this complex relationship of poetic minds other than to note that these formulae occur in relation to Shakespeare, produced as they are to try to come to terms—and invent terms is what they do—with his poetry and drama.

This is not a question so much of influence as it is an irrepressible problem of judging not only the poetic practice of Shakespeare but of how any poet works. Eliot, appropriately, seems to look favorably on negative capability when speaking of the poet's personality in "Tradition and the Individual Talent." His "continual extinction of personality" that poetry consists in is similar to what Keats has in mind when he thinks of the artist as having the ability to lose (or loosen) the self-consciousness that would otherwise be seen as placing its distinguishing mark on that which it creates.[31] In neither of these formulations are there any concrete details as to how the poet might go about this, or even which elements are involved. The only prescriptive direction in either of these formulations concerns the artist's facility for negating the personality traits or self-conscious emotions that interfere in the deft synthesis of language and the world. For Keats, this is an avoidance of "any irritable reaching after fact and reason," and for Eliot, the artist is an unaffected catalyst who brings together object and emotions that they might combine into new forms.

What Keats and Eliot have in common here is their insistence that poetry cannot function in the hands of a poet who would act like Hamlet when writing poetry. For both, to create a character like Hamlet, which is an admirable thing for poetry to aspire to, it is a necessary condition that the poet avoid acting as Hamlet does. To make this mistake, Keats and Eliot imply, would be to lose all connection with the poetic object, and with it the per-spective that opens up poetry to experience; the result of such a mistake is a poetry so thoroughly soaked in subjectivity that all it can do is call attention to itself. The "problem" with Hamlet and *Hamlet* turns out not to be neither the titular protagonist nor the play in itself but the example it sets loose in the world that poetry will imitate. The mimetic work taken up by the poets who come after the metaphysicals, Eliot will argue, is mistaken insofar as they act like Hamlet instead of Shakespeare.

In his essay "Shelley and Keats," Eliot comes very close to liberating Keats by comparing him to Shakespeare. The affinity again concerns whether the poet has a "philosophic mind" in the sense that the poet is "about his busi-ness" rather than sidetracked into distracting personal concerns.[32] Eliot opens his remarks on Keats with this:

> But I am not so much concerned with the degree of his greatness as with its kind; and its kind is manifested more clearly in his Letters than in his poems; and in contrast with the kinds we have been reviewing, it seems to me to be much more the kind of Shakespeare . . . His letters are what letters ought to be; the fine things come in unexpectedly, neither introduced nor shown out, but between trifle and trifle.[33]

The second sentence closely and purposefully echoes Keats's remarks on Shakespeare's *Sonnets*. But where Keats has Shakespeare saying fine things "unintentionally," Eliot has Keats doing so "unexpectedly." Eliot here cor-rects Keats gently by returning both writers to a sense of control over their material. Though he will argue for Shakespeare's loss of a particular kind of control in *Hamlet*—of an association of sensibility that fails to deliver an "objective correlative"—this argument is specifically confined to this play, since Shakespeare must remain a model for Eliot's revival of a poetry of properly integrated sensibility. Such a subtle shepherding of Keats's view of Shakespeare restores to Keats his Shakespeare-like ability to amalgam-ate elements that are perhaps impossible to bring into language. It is much the same with the glaring omission here of negative capability, coming as it does with its famous reference to Shakespeare as its source. If Eliot is avoid-ing it, it may be because it is both unpalatable and disruptive (it cannot be made to fit into Eliot's critical system), and because it resonates too closely with the imprecise argument marshaled against *Hamlet,* which culminates in the objective correlative. If Eliot is trying to save Keats the embarrass-ing judgment of "dissociation," then it is not only too much but also too close to home to bring together two formulations that scrutiny will perhaps find contradictory to the whole enterprise of the proper association of poet, emotion, and object that the poem must be in order to escape the tragic consequences of "rumination."

It appears, then, that negative capability and the dissociation of sensibility are two sides of the same coin. They both localize a fundamental question of poetry: how do poets deal effectively with the creation of new wholes out of the parts that are given them? How to balance the forces of emotion in and along with the resistance of language while attending to the proper relationship to the poetic object? However we choose to answer such questions, we will necessarily fall short of a formula, the equation, for the making of a proper poem. These formulae of Eliot and Keats are both in the negative, and this is perhaps because any positive hypothesis would be inconclusive. A formula stated positively would have to contain all possibilities by arresting the fluidity of poetic creation, its associational and combinatorial indefiniteness, into a fixed and thus fragmented thing. That negation is a necessity for defining poetic practice is a clue to the very structure of configuring such a formula in the first place. The necessity of the negative character of the formula here performs a function similar to that of the fetish: it is a denial by substitution.

In the conclusion to *The Use of Poetry and the Use of Criticism*, Eliot says:

> To me it seems that at these moments, which are characterized by the sudden lifting of the burden of anxiety and fear which presses upon our daily life so steadily that we are unaware of it, what happens is something *negative:* that is to say, not "inspiration" as we commonly think of it, but the breaking down of strong habitual barriers—which tend to reform very quickly. Some obstruction is momentarily whisked away. The accompanying feeling is less like what we know as positive pleasure, than a sudden relief from an intolerable burden.[34]

This theory of the conditions that enable poetry to come into being is also, of course, a restatement of Freud's pleasure principle. What is missing are the psychological mechanisms at work as well as the poetic practices that would allow the poet, given such moments, to capitalize on them. Eliot is not satisfied with periodizing the dissociation of sensibility by means of a physiological disturbance, though this is indeed open to him. The metaphysical poets have often been characterized as writing in the midst of a general cultural depression, as if England had floated into the doldrums and could only get out by way of civil war. Whether Robert Burton's *Anatomy of Melancholy* or Timothy Bright's *A Treatise of Melancholie* can be taken as the symptom of the time or not, it might have been more convenient to say that following the metaphysicals, emotional conceit had been exhausted and only a bloodless rhetoric was possible. But this is not how Eliot proceeds. His argument for what the poets from Donne to Lord Herbert of Cherbury and Andrew Marvell do takes a positive form, a method of concrete association, before diffusion and disjointure set in.

The claim for how metaphysical poetry manages to do something that is the culmination of Elizabethan drama and the end of a coherent sensibility hinges greatly on how "sensibility" itself is defined. The previous quotation I gave from this essay is the clearest definition we will get: "it is the difference between the intellectual poet and the reflective poet. Tennyson and Browning are poets, and they think; but they do not feel their thought as immediately as the odour of a rose. A thought to Donne was an experience; it modified his sensibility."[35] This is one of those moments in Eliot's literary criticism where, even if we can point out the fallacy, we are still able to see the point he is making and can perhaps even agree with it in part if not with the whole.[36] That Eliot states it with such authority and such sweeping inclusion does not make the exceptions disprove it but seems to sharpen our reading of the poets concerned to see how they make poetry in light of these criteria. The exceptions "prove" the rule by testing it; they show its applicability for thinking about poetry as fundamentally thinkable as a practice rather than as an undisciplined outpouring of feeling or an ornamental artistic practice. From here it is no stretch to suggest, as Eliot will, that *vers libre* can be justified by its intellectual scansion, its adherence to a deeper music.[37]

But let us consider closely what Eliot says here, for we can begin to feel the presence of *Hamlet* as a specter that attends this scene of differentiation. The intellectual is placed ahead of the reflective, and what Eliot means by this is that the intellectual contains within it a proper relation between thinking, feeling, and acting/experiencing. It is not that the reflective poet lacks any of these things, but that instead of going about the business of placing all of this in the service of poetry, the reflective poet allows a gap to appear that becomes a chasm into which he falls.[38] This gap or hesitancy allows the proper amalgamation of experience to escape, as thinking about something impedes setting it down with the energy that the poet's sensibility provides. For Eliot, Tennyson and Robert Browning do not *feel* their thought immediately, and by "feel" he means they do not translate such thought immediately into poetry. The implication is that these poets take the feeling as a thing in itself to be thought of, and that the poetry of this thought can somehow approximate such rumination. The danger seems to be that such a hesitation risks the separation of feeling from object that will not be able to put them back together in the form of the poem. The odor of a rose, once reflected upon, leads only down the path of association. Similes and metaphors might give a sense of the flower, but will not necessarily translate its singular immediacy. Such an object encountered in a poem that is properly correlated proffers an object—a rose, for example—*as* an emotion; the feeling is experienced as the content of the amalgamating words of the poem.[39] The consequence for failing to do this, as Eliot points out, is that "while the language became more refined, the feeling became more crude."[40] One is left then, potentially, with a reversion to the euphuistic poetry that Shakespeare's generation differentiated themselves from by first imitating and then mocking.

It should be clear by now that the model for the breakdown that begins early in the seventeenth century is that of the tragedy of the famous prince from Denmark. The metaphysicals, insulated perhaps from the theater by their time spent ferociously scribbling in their rooms, were the last to avoid "going Hamlet" in their poetry. For once hesitation comes to stand in for the immediate action dictated by experience, says Eliot, feeling is cast away to be replaced by refined language, by the poetic equivalent of delay. The problem this poses for Eliot's purpose of articulating an aesthetic methodology is in *Hamlet*'s unwillingness to cover over mimesis by delivering representation as a direct action of capturing objects and experience in poetic language. What Eliot fails to attend to in the play is its assault upon the simplistic idea that mimetic work consists in the direct apprehension of something in language that can be handed over to the audience or reader without some fundamental dramatization.

Mimesis is always a dramatic production. In Shakespeare's *Sonnets* as in *Hamlet*, the mimetic work that implicates the audience or reader in the production of the drama as an affective experience is the result of the poet or playwright's implicit knowledge of the very impossibility of capturing things or feelings directly, unmediated, in language. There is a far more complex structure to the crafting of drama and poetry in order to evoke an affective experience than simply "saying it like it is" or having some direct access to the objects of experience such that the poet can deliver them whole, with their "odour" intact. This has the smell of the prelapsarian about it, and instead of insisting that poets before a certain time were endowed with a power that was suddenly lost, it seems reasonable to suggest that their aesthetic praxis was different, and more to the liking of Eliot and the poetry and drama he would like to see written.

***

Let us return to Eliot's essay on *Hamlet*, in order to see how the formula that I have been speaking of, the "objective correlative," comes into being in relation to Shakespeare's dramatic practice. The essay begins with an important distinction: "Few critics have even admitted that *Hamlet* the play is the primary problem, and Hamlet the character only secondary."[41] Eliot begins by focusing on the dramatic work instead of falling into what, for him, is the critical trap of a subjective, characterological study that isolates the protagonist from his dramatic environment. To do otherwise, says Eliot, is to perpetrate a "substitution" of the critic's Hamlet for Shakespeare's.[42] The problem with this approach—and Eliot points the finger directly at Goethe and Samuel Taylor Coleridge, and indirectly at Walter Pater, who would have done similar damage had he fixed his attention there—is that a transference takes place in which the critic, his creativity getting the better of him, takes Hamlet as something like an excuse to invent an object of criticism instead of remaining focused upon what is already there. This allows such a critic to treat Hamlet as plenitudinous and fully formed, a fixed point from which to launch into his own version of subjectivity, character, or whatever subject he wants to work out; hence, as Eliot points out, Goethe's Werther and Coleridge's Coleridge. Eliot seems acutely aware of both the lure of finding in Hamlet an imitable subject from which to start one's own ruminations and the danger of answering such a siren call. His first long poem and major published work, "The Love Song of J. Alfred Prufrock," is, we note, concerned not only with determination and identity generally, but also with Hamlet in particular. The problem, as Eliot puts it in the opening of his essay, is one of avoiding the temptation to use Hamlet as a shibboleth for working out ideas about such things as decision making, the individual's relationship to society, love, and other concerns. And further, the problem is to avoid becoming the histrionic Hamlet in one's own drama. To thus present oneself, while at the same time engaging in criticism, is to violate an essential boundary between two modes of expression. What creeps in at such times, and Eliot is relentless in his reporting of them, is that consciously unconscious self-presentation that the Romantics made, literally, into an art.

Eliot is explicit in his deconstruction of the criticism of Goethe's and Coleridge's approach to *Hamlet*: "For they both possessed unquestionable critical insight, and both make their critical aberrations the more plausible by the substitution—of their own Hamlet for Shakespeare's—which their creative gift effects."[43] At this point, we might conclude that our essayist is on his way to suggesting that these critics are merely performing that dramatic sleight of hand that *Hamlet* itself does when it implicates the audience in producing a Hamlet whose subjectivity is so realistic that it is taken as the model for modern subjectivity itself. But Eliot is still referring to the critic's transforming himself into a Hamlet, a fictive character with the power to allow critics to experience "a vicarious existence for their own artistic realization."[44] The danger in this is that the critic will become too much like the delaying prince; but this, ultimately, is not Eliot's worry. Rather, he wants to insist upon the dangers of the poet's mistake in becoming too much like the ruminating, dilatory figure whose poetic practice becomes dissociated from concrete objects and experiences of the world. In order to emphasize this point, Eliot, as if suddenly remembering that he is supposed to be producing a book review, refers to the two works (putatively) under discussion, and then quotes from one: "they [critics of the seventeenth and eighteenth century] knew less about psychology than more recent Hamlet critics, but they were nearer in spirit to Shakespeare's art; and as they insisted on the importance of the effect of the whole rather than on the importance of the leading character, they were nearer, in their old-fashioned way, to the secret of dramatic art in general."[45] This, again, sounds as if it were a call to look closely at the functioning of the mechanisms of the drama itself instead of laboring to solve the riddle of Hamlet's madness or delay. But neither Elmer Stoll, J. M. Robertson, nor Eliot can quite escape the temptation to take Hamlet as the problem of *Hamlet*, despite assurances to the contrary.

The "secret of dramatic art" to which Stoll refers in this passage is perhaps what leads critics and poets alike to follow a trail that leads them after their "man" (as the object of Scotland Yard's famous dictum goes). What it does *not* lead to is a thorough consideration of the working of the drama itself. Eliot's next point concerns Robertson's insistence that one must have historical facts in one's mind if one is to read a drama such as *Hamlet* with the full knowledge of its structure. This would also seem to point to a consideration of the play's stratification, since Eliot takes us through the various texts that precede the play Shakespeare comes to write *(The Spanish Tragedy, Arden of Faversham)*. At the end of relating these details from Robertson's study, Eliot comes to the conclusion that the professor's examination is "irrefragable: that Shakespeare's *Hamlet,* so far as it is Shakespeare's, is a play dealing with the effect of a mother's guilt upon her son, and that Shakespeare was unable to impose this motive successfully upon the 'intractable' material of the old play."[46]

This raises a number of questions. If it is Shakespeare's intention to write a play concerning "the effect of a mother's guilt upon her son," then why is the effect sufficient to register with the critic, yet its cause, or source, insufficient? After all, the charge of the lack of an objective correlative hinges on something missing that would make Hamlet's reactions proper to some object or set of events. Also, if the problem is a result of some inability by the dramatist to transform his material, why does he not simply alter Gertrude's character?[47] Something is just not right here in this line of reasoning, since it both affirms the play's potency as a consequence of the dramatist's success in getting us to read, study, and analyze it based on its dramatic power, while at the same time lamenting the author's inability to transform his source material. This would be easily and properly dismissed—since Shakespeare, of all dramatists perhaps, is a master of this skill—if it were not so relevant to Eliot's larger purpose in the essay. It is the transformation of pre-existing material—textual, personal, or otherwise—that Eliot is so concerned about here, and that he wants to make certain of when it comes to poetic practice.

He wants to make an argument for poetry as that which connects language to objects and experience in the world, instead of letting it devolve into an onanism of subjective isolation. Eliot's caricatured view of the Romantics as dreamy narcissists who could only write poetry that had to do with their own internal world and not the one people live in hovers over this discussion like a tutor with a switch of willow.[48] We are not to see such poetry as an alternative, and any behavior such as Hamlet's, where nothing can be accomplished due to an overattenuated consciousness, cannot be tolerated.

Eliot's next mode of explication concerns what he identifies as the play's instability in what he calls the poet's "period of crisis."[49] This is in the same paragraph in which he famously tags *Hamlet* "the 'Mona Lisa' of literature."[50] That a play can stand comparison to such an accomplished, though enigmatic work of art is due, suggests Eliot, to its being interesting rather than as fundamentally a work of art.[51] It is conspicuous that as the essay develops, Eliot turns continuously to the figure of Hamlet, as a character who simply will not fit the formulaic needs of the critic who is determined to construct a system out of such an otherwise emblematic literature. There is always here the deft maneuver around criticizing Shakespeare as a faulty dramatist, as one who is unable to master the material properly; it is rather the "intractable" material or the objective conditions of "crisis" under which the playwright labored. What Eliot is not willing to do here—and it is not because the books under review do not suggest it; they do, yet do not follow through either—is to focus upon the manner in which *Hamlet* functions at the highest level and in the most complex fashion to perform "the secret of dramatic art in general." This is a secret only so long as one continues to be implicated by the main character in the production of the play rather than resisting at least long enough to read and listen closely enough to the mechanisms of the play that labor so diligently to produce its multiple levels of meaning and dramatic effects (and affects).[52]

Eliot admits that such affects are made by the drama, since the objective correlative is a formula that first adduces affect before seeking retroactively for objective cause. Yet the criticism of *Hamlet* is that such objective reference is missing: "Both workmanship and thought are in an unstable position."[53] Whose thought? Hamlet's? This might certainly be the case, but the playwright has gotten the critic to look at everything from Hamlet's point of view, which is one of instability to be sure, but of contrived, crafted instability of a most conscious sort. Hamlet offers just such an invitation throughout the play: to come with him, to be on his side, to see things through his eyes, to understand that he must play a role but (just between you and me) he'd rather not, and we are the confidants to that shadow world of Hamlet's coinage that wants to break out of the plot but cannot. It is one thing to argue that Hamlet does not have the proper motivation for behaving as he does, but *behave* he does, acting with considerable skill to pull the audience in and out of the play along with him. On this model, it is not poetic practice that is at risk in contemplating *Hamlet*, since it works to create dramatic tension more successfully than perhaps any other specimen of its kind, but rather Hamlet as a dangerous familiar for poets who choose reflection over direct apprehension, who fail to keep their senses at their fingers' ends.

Eliot next affirms Robertson's assertion that "Hamlet's tone is that of one who has suffered tortures on the score of his mother's degradation . . . The guilt of a mother is an almost intolerable motive for drama, but it had to be maintained and emphasized to supply a psychological solution, or rather a hint of one." But, he is quick to say, "this is by no means the whole story."[54] If it were *only* the guilt of a mother, Shakespeare could easily have handled it as he had so many other difficult subjects. There is, however, something more, something excessive that the playwright's powers are not up to controlling:

> *Hamlet,* like the sonnets, is full of some stuff that the writer could not drag to light, contemplate, or manipulate into art. And when we search for this feeling, we find it, as in the sonnets, very difficult to localize. You cannot point to it in the speeches; indeed, if you examine the two famous soliloquies you see the versification of Shakespeare, but a content which might be claimed by another. We find Shakespeare's Hamlet not in the action, not in any quotations that we might select, so much as in an unmistakable tone which is unmistakably not in the earlier play.[55]

Hamlet escapes from Eliot's criticism of the play with his mystery intact, as does the play, since it lacks the essential element that would correlate it and that the dramatist, because of a psychological deficiency, is unable to provide. Though Eliot was certainly no fan of psychoanalysis, bristling at the idea of Freudian explanations of literature, there is here, perhaps more overtly than anywhere else in the Eliot critical canon, a decided preference for something unconscious at work in the construction of the drama. To equate *Hamlet* at this point with the *Sonnets* is to give it that tincture of the autobiographical and to suggest a homology of protagonist and writer akin to taking the speaker and poet of the *Sonnets* as one and the same person. Though criticism has largely stopped speaking about the intentions of the author—and Eliot is ahead of his time generally in this respect—it has not slowed in its substitution of a character such as Hamlet for the psychological complexities and mental difficulties of his author. The final salvo in this paragraph of Eliot's seems to precisely retreat from the kind of reading of the play that I have been suggesting. That is to say, we can indeed find Shakespeare's Hamlet in the action, as well as in the quotations we might select, since, to sound horribly naïve about the whole thing, there is no other place we might find him but in the complex structure of the play as it works to produce its main character and the dramatic effects that follow. That Shakespeare adds a "tone" that is not in the earlier play stands to reason. But what is this tone? What is it to say that it is "tone" that makes a drama different? Tone is that effect of all of the labor put into producing the play as a drama played before an audience or read by an individual. Tone is not accidental and cannot be said to exist in a play—nor in music, painting, or any other art—by some fluke of chance. It is a product of the play of forces that the dramatist painstakingly creates from a variety of places (other plays, collaborators, experience, events in the world, stock phrases, old ballads, ad libs from actors, and so on).[56] However these bits and pieces find their way into a drama such as *Hamlet,* they are not merely placed there haphazardly as in a collage, like bits of colored string in an otherwise rudimentary nest, but rather in a structure whose intention is to affect an audience, to do the mimetic work that gets attention paid to it and even lures the audience into helping produce the play itself. And though all dramas cannot be said to be as successful as *Hamlet* at doing this, that this play does indeed function in such a way can only be found by looking for it, not throwing up one's hands and putting it all down to "mystery," nor indeed to "insufficiency." Nor to a formula.

It is in the very next paragraph that Eliot introduces the "objective correlative": "The only way of expressing emotion in the form of art is by finding an 'objective correlative'; in other words, a set of objects, a chain of events which shall be the formula of that *particular* emotion; such that when the external facts, which must terminate in sensory experience, are given, the emotion is immediately evoked."[57] This "formula" appears to supplement the tone that the play "unmistakably" has but that cannot be located either within the play's action or language, or in some objective "facts" in either the author's life, mind, or environment. That Eliot resorts to a formula here at all, in order to clear up the missing piece of the puzzle, is not a neutral critical move. Does this formula come from the play or from some other mode of literary analysis? Is this a formula based on poetic praxis and experience? It may well be true that Eliot's insistence upon the exclusivity of this method—"The *only* way of expressing emotion"—makes the formula resonate more forcefully, yet this does not, for all its impudence, make it an accurate hypothesis of artistic functioning. *Hamlet* would seem to offer a difficult test case for this formula in that the play calls into question the ability of external facts, or a chain of events, to evoke a proper emotion. It is precisely this disjointure that *Hamlet* performs over and over, until we begin to see that the object or events that "cause" action are not external, preexisting objects or events. It is how the play gets us to feel as though it is in the wake of concrete things that is an index to its successful mimetic work.

Eliot proceeds to the main point of his argument: "If you examine any of Shakespeare's successful tragedies, you will find this exact equivalence."[58] He then gives *Macbeth* as an example, as the dramatist provides "a skillful accumulation of imagined sensory impressions."[59] In this play, writes Eliot, "The artistic "inevitability" lies in this complete adequacy of the external to the emotion; and this is precisely what is deficient in *Hamlet*."[60] But where is this "inevitability," and how does it get there? What Eliot wants to insist upon as existing outside the drama is that which the drama must prepare for all along *within* the drama itself. In his example from *Macbeth* he refers to scenes in the play that prepare us for the emotion evoked later in the play, while in *Hamlet* this is somehow missing. What Eliot is unwilling to do here is consider carefully Hamlet's dramatic construction, since this mimetic structure is crafted with a subtlety that goes beyond most of his other plays and does, as Eliot suggests, work not unlike the *Sonnets*. So to Eliot we might reply that it is not that *Hamlet* is lacking an objective correlative, but that such an object is in, and produced by, the play itself. Further, it is one of the "meanings" of the play that acting does not always so readily have its cause available but must work to posit that cause in a manner such that acting can take place. This, however, is a reading that cannot occur so long as Hamlet and his myriad, complex problems remain the only subject of critical scrutiny.

Eliot goes on, finally, to suggest that Hamlet cannot objectify his situation, that he cannot find an adequate cause for his reason for feeling to the extent that he does, because Shakespeare could himself not get hold of his material: "And the supposed identity of Hamlet with his author is genuine to this point: that Hamlet's bafflement at the absence of objective equivalent to his feelings is a prolongation of the bafflement of his creator in the face of his artistic problem."[61] Hamlet's bafflement? Shakespeare's bafflement? It is as though Eliot has come upon Shakespeare "striking too short at Greeks," unable in his infirmity even to hold his antique pen. A closer reading of the play that attends to its highly complex representational structure will find neither Hamlet nor Shakespeare baffled. On the contrary, we will find the latter if we attend to the language and structure of the action, preparing the affective potential of the drama in the language of the play as it works to bring the audience to Hamlet's extremity of feeling. There is much going on here, and it is all in service of an intentional, concentrated purpose: bringing the audience into Hamlet's "reality" of being in just this situation at just this time. Such mimetic work in *Hamlet* is indeed demanding and difficult, hard to explain and not readily given to digestible meanings, but this is what keeps this play so forceful and effective over time.

Hamlet manages to do what Eliot most desired in his poetry, to take us along as though there were no boundary in our reading the poem and experiencing it ("Let us go then, you and I"). Eliot's own problem in this essay, mere book review that it is, is that the drama that he was so attuned to in his poetry and the poetry of others cannot be so easily formulated by reference to a principle based on such a dubious premise. Whether we prefer Donne to Swinburne because of the historical evolution of a "dissociation of sensibility" or not, such a criterion cannot be based on a specious assertion (especially one that uses *Hamlet* to prove its point) that locates the emotional force of poetry in its relationship to objects and events that precede the poetry or drama. Eliot is far more eloquent in other places on how poetry does its work, in the way it invents and creates worlds and experiences that do not limit this artistic practice to a slavish copying or mere attempt to capture what exists before it. I have gone to such lengths to discuss this remarkable essay not because I am interested in refuting it or even criticizing Eliot as a reader of *Hamlet;* rather, I wanted to demonstrate the extent to which even a sensitive, knowledgeable critic/poet/dramatist such as T. S. Eliot can be lured into missing the fundamental mimetic work of this play as it relates to representational practice.

NOTES

1. T. S. Eliot, *Elizabethan Essays* (London: Faber and Faber, 1934); T. S. Eliot, *Essays on Elizabethan Drama* (New York: Harcourt, Brace, 1956). Though it does not amount to irony, there is something eyebrow-raising in cutting essays specifically dramatic then adding *Drama* to the title.

2. Quoted in Ronald Schuchard, *Eliot's Dark Angel: Intersections of Life and Art* (Oxford: Oxford University Press, 1999), 215. See the appendix in which this quotation appears for a discussion of the manner in which the publication, and more importantly, the lack thereof, of Eliot's prose writings has done a great disservice to the force and coherence of his thoughts on literature.

3. For a thorough study of Eliot's relationship to Shakespeare criticism of the twentieth century, particularly New Criticism in the English academy, see Richard Halpern, *Shakespeare among the Moderns* (Ithaca, NY: Cornell University Press, 1997). Arguing against critics who assume that a rupture took place that displaced modernism from its position of critical dominance, Halpern explores how our "'postmodern condition' represents a mutation, rather than a cessation, of the modernist paradigm" (2). For a detailed discussion on how this plays out in the context of "the primitive," see his chapter "Shakespeare in the Tropics: From High Modernism to New Historicism," 15–50.

4. A related example of Eliot's self-conscious critical dissonance, in this case positive, occurs in his "Introduction" to Djuna Barnes's *Nightwood* (New York: Harcourt, Brace, 1937). Here, instead of "impudence," Eliot opens his comments by deploying false modesty in his praise of Barnes's book thusly: "When the question is raised, of writing an introduction to a book of a creative order, I always feel that the few books worth introducing are exactly those which it is an impertinence to introduce" (xi). He returns to this word, and the challenge it implies to those who would judge the novel (even positively), without properly understanding its modernist style, at the close of his remarks: "I should have considered the foregoing paragraph impertinent, and perhaps too pretentious for a preface meant to be a

simple recommendation of a book I greatly admire, were it not that one review (at least), intended in praise of the book, has already appeared which would in effect induce the reader to begin with this mistaken attitude . . . As I said in the beginning, I am conscious of impertinence in introducing the book at all . . . What I would leave the reader prepared to find is the great achievement of a style, the beauty of phrasing, the brilliance of wit and characterization, and a quality of horror and doom very nearly related to that of Elizabethan tragedy" (xvi).

5. For a comprehensive treatment of Hamlet and "the modern," see Margreta de Grazia, Hamlet *without Hamlet* (Cambridge: Cambridge University Press, 2007), 7–22.

6. "Hamlet and His Problems," in *The Sacred Wood: Essays on Poetry and Criticism* (1920; London: Methuen, 1960), 95. See note 10 for more on the essay's title and its mutations.

7. We can spot this same mode of analysis in Richard Halpern's otherwise excellent study, cited above, of how modernism "set the tone for [the] twentieth century's reception of Shakespeare" by exploring its relationship with anthropological tropes of "the primitive" (2). He offers the following on Eliot's *Hamlet* essay: "This side of Eliot's formalism comes closer to the surface in his treatment of the 'objective correlative' in the *Hamlet* essay. *Hamlet*'s failure, as described therein, is precisely a problem of form. It is not that the emotions generated by the play are in themselves unacceptable; rather, it is that the play lacks an adequate form—the objective correlative—to *contain* them. Eliot's criticism of the play is entirely consistent with his methodology throughout the *Elizabethan Essays* in focusing on the adequacy and consistency of dramatic convention . . . *Hamlet*'s failure, in one sense merely a formal problem, is more fundamentally that of having released 'ecstatic' and primitive energies without a containing convention. Here literary judgment results from the turning inward of an anthropological and primitivist discourse" (31). In this context, Eliot indeed prefers an anthropological paradigm to a psychoanalytic one in formulating the disposition of the artist, poet, and tragic protagonist. The question of how this comes to bear upon the play's *formal* characteristics is one that Halpern passes over: "It is not that the emotions generated by the play are in themselves unacceptable; rather, it is that the play lacks an adequate form—the objective correlative—to *contain* them." Here, Halpern has followed Eliot in substituting the character's lack for that of the play as a whole. Hamlet's lack of a sufficient object cause, we might say, leads the critic focused on the character to assume that this "fault" is also a "fault," a lack, in the play's formal functioning. What this reasoning ignores is the positive nature of such a lack. The play works hard to elide causes, preferring to present effects. *Hamlet* is a more consuming object of study because of its relentless production of meaning surrounding, emanating from, its main character and his action/inaction. As a meaning-making machine it has few peers, *even though* its protagonist's emotions are not properly objectively correlated—perhaps because they are so.

8. "[B]y showing the aforenamed *Socrates*, *Plato* is saying to us (for, the expert tells us, he is addressing himself to us): you all transfer everything, and everyone, onto *Socrates*. You do not know if this is an order or an affirmation." Jacques Derrida, *The Post Card: From Socrates to Freud and Beyond*, trans. Alan Bass (Chicago: University of Chicago Press, 1987), 218.

9. Not only in the poems coinciding with the *Hamlet* essay ("The Love Song of J. Alfred Prufrock" and "The Waste Land") but also in his lectures, book reviews,

and critical essays. See Timothy Materer, "T. S. Eliot's Critical Program," and Jean-Michel Rabaté, "T. S. Eliot and Tradition," both in *The Cambridge Companion to T. S. Eliot,* A. David Moody, ed. (Cambridge: Cambridge University Press, 1994), 48–59 and 210–222.

10. The title of Eliot's book review/essay (tending as it does toward the peregrinations of the latter rather than the implied responsibility of the former) has undergone some odd alterations, and it is difficult not to detect in these an uncertainty about its intended subject matter. That is, whether it takes as its subject *Hamlet* or Hamlet. It is first published on September 26, 1919, in *The Athenaeum* as "Hamlet and his problems," then reprinted shortly thereafter with the same title, capital letters added, in *The Sacred Wood.* However, in the *Selected Essays: 1917–1932* published in England, the title is simply "Hamlet" (London: Faber and Faber, 1932) without italics or other indication that it refers to the play (the quotation marks here are mine). If it seems clear that despite changes, both titles refer to the character and not the play, Frank Kermode, in his widely used and referenced *Selected Prose of T. S. Eliot* (New York: Harcourt Brace Jovanovich, 1975), uses the title *Hamlet* (in italics in the table of contents and without italics at the head of the essay). If this change has any significance, it is perhaps in toning down the impudence of pointing a critical finger at Hamlet in the title instead of being simply an essay on the play more generally. Both American editions of *Selected Essays: 1917–1932* (New York: Harcourt, Brace, 1932; revised and enlarged, 1950) employ the "Hamlet and His Problems" title. All references hereafter to *Selected Essays: 1917–1932* refer to the 1950 version of this collection, hereafter cited as SE.

11. Hugh Kenner suggests that this stylistic, even substantive quirk is a product of Eliot's writing quick, short review pieces wherein he works his ideas out "ad hoc": "Each review is an occasion to think something out as he goes along, and while the last paragraph remembers the first, the first does not often foresee the last." Kenner sums up such writing of Eliot's as the seizing of "a succession of opportunities for enlightening himself." *The Invisible Poet: T. S. Eliot* (New York: McDowell, Obolensky, 1959), 102. Most of Kenner's book concerns an explication of the influence of F. H. Bradley's philosophy on Eliot's poetic ideas and style, though he is silent about the relationship of Bradley's philosophical thought about subjects and objects to Eliot's objective correlative. Lewis Freed, in his *T. S. Eliot: The Critic as Philosopher* (West Lafayette, IN: Purdue University Press, 1979), 44–84, takes Kenner to task for just this lacuna. See also William Skaff, *The Philosophy of T. S. Eliot* (Philadelphia: University of Pennsylvania Press, 1986), which pushes very hard for a reading of the objective correlative as the culmination of Eliot's philosophical thought as applied to literature.

12. Published as *Knowledge and Experience in the Philosophy of F. H. Bradley* (London: Faber and Faber, 1964).

13. The greatest concentration is from 1919 to 1920, where Eliot publishes the essays collected in *The Sacred Wood.* The emphasis here is on the Elizabethans as well as a critical look at late nineteenth-century poetry. The difference that will be made explicit in "The Metaphysical Poets" in his "dissociation of sensibility" formula is being prepared for here in various ways.

14. This strand is a rather thick one, containing most of the century's poetic output. Eliot's quarrel with the Romantics is well known, and I will not rehearse it here except to point out that this poetry of "rumination" spans the century through, and especially including, Algernon Charles Swinburne.

15. Eliot tends to stretch this period at times to include certain poets that come just a bit later, such as Lord Herbert of Cherbury. The limit cases of the periodization of this canon raise difficult and interesting questions about just where a cutoff can occur, as well as what material reality might have corresponded with such a perceived change in sensibility. One characteristic of the sort of effort revealed here is the retroactive structure of periodization generally. Eliot seems to be much more aware of this in "Tradition and the Individual Talent," where he demonstrates the manner in which present actions rearrange the past and any access we have to it.

16. "Shakespeare and the Stoicism of Seneca," SE, 117.

17. Ibid., 118–119.

18. "Tradition and Talent," SE, 3–11.

19. See, for example, "Imperfect Critics: Swinburne as Critic," *Sacred Wood,* 17. Swinburne here stands as that writer from whom Eliot would most like to distinguish himself as a poet who writes criticism. Eliot reduces Swinburne to merely a commentator on the Elizabethans, which implies that he sees no difference in his practice from what has come before. Eliot wishes us to see that it is only the critic as a maker of difference that can place his poetry in the space made for it by his criticism. The relationship between these two modes of writing is an active one for Eliot, and though it may well be for others, Eliot would rather have us think that it remains outside of their awareness or perhaps ability.

20. See "Swinburne as Poet," SE, 281–285.

21. "Shakespeare and the Stoicism of Seneca," SE, 118.

22. It is telling that *The Sacred Wood,* Eliot's first book of criticism, opens with both Arnold (in the introduction) and Coleridge (in chapter 1, "The Perfect Critic," where Arnold is also present). Both writers are praised for their criticism, but there is a sense that both have failed to leave something useful for the poets who follow. Arnold is "rather a propagandist for criticism than a critic, a popularizer rather than a creator of ideas" (1). There are at least two problems here, and they are as devastating as they are muted: both writers lacked something in their poetry, and both failed to create ideas sufficient for the profitable use of poets who follow. The breakdown Eliot locates here, and that he seeks to remedy in his criticism and poetry, is to create a synthesis wherein the criticism creates ideas that the poetry can already be seen to be practicing. Whether we would judge Eliot's poetry to have overcome the problem of dissociation that his criticism points out, it is difficult not to be influenced by the rhetorical shadow that falls from the critical formula onto the reading of any of his poems.

23. Collected with the Turnbull Lectures by Ronald Schuchard as *The Varieties of Metaphysical Poetry* (Cambridge, MA: Harvard University Press, 1993). These lectures are a much more coherent working through of the liminal ideas set forth in his "The Metaphysical Poets," in which, as we will see, he coins the formula "dissociation of sensibility."

24. Immediately after a retrospective glance at the genesis and providence of "the term 'objective correlative,'" Eliot says: "But I prophesy that if my phrases are given consideration, a century hence, it will be only in their historical context, by scholars interested in the mind of my generation." From "To Criticize the Critic," in the volume of the same name (New York: Farrar, Straus and Giroux, 1965), 19. This was a lecture delivered in July 1961.

25. "The Metaphysical Poets," SE, 241–250.

26. As R. A. Foakes points out, "the term 'Hamletism' was established by 1840, with reference usually to (a) the well-intentioned but ineffectual behaviour of characters in plays and novels (by writers such as Turgenev, Chekov, Thomas Mann, Jules Laforgue and D. H. Lawrence); or (b) to dithering intellectuals in European politics; or (c) the sensitive artist or intellectual who felt out of place in a philistine world" (231). It is curious in an otherwise thorough survey of this subject that Foakes would leave out Eliot, about whose essay he says nothing. If anyone would have shuddered at William Hazlitt's comment that "It is *we* who are Hamlet," and at the prospect of poetry following the lead of these writers, it is Eliot. R. A. Foakes, "The Critical Reception of Shakespeare's Tragedies," in *The Cambridge Companion to Shakespearean Tragedy,* Claire McEachern, ed. (Cambridge: Cambridge University Press, 2002), 224–240. Hazlitt's apothegm, quoted by Foakes (231), is from *The Complete Works of William Hazlitt,* P. P. Howe, ed. (London: J. M. Dent and Sons, 1930), vol. 4, 232.

27. "The Metaphysical Poets," SE, 247.

28. See Louis Menand, *Discovering Modernism: T. S. Eliot and His Context* (Oxford: Oxford University Press, 1987), 134.

29. *The Letters of John Keats: 1814–1821,* vol. 1, ed. Hyder Rollins (Cambridge, MA: Harvard University Press, 1958), 193–194.

30. See "The Romantic Generation, If It Existed," *Athenaeum,* July 18, 1919, 616. This is two months before "Hamlet and His Problems" would come out in the same journal.

31. Eliot, *Selected Essays,* 7. See also "Shelley and Keats," in *T. S. Eliot, The Use of Poetry and the Use of Criticism* (London: Faber and Faber, 1933), 101, where Eliot quotes Keats saying something very similar to Eliot's position in "Tradition and the Individual Talent."

32. "Shelley and Keats," in Eliot, *Use of Poetry,* 87–102. This volume collects Eliot's lectures at Harvard from 1932 to 1933. In a line from the preface, we catch a glimpse of Eliot's sensitivity to the production of the modernist program through dramatizing it: "These lectures, delivered at Harvard University during the winter of 1932–1933, owe much to an audience only too ready to applaud merit and condone defect; but I am aware that such success as they had was largely dramatic, and that they will be still more disappointing to those who heard them than they will be to those who did not" (11). If there is impudence in formulizing through "unqualified assertion," there is another kind of impudence in the feeble modesty here. Suggesting that "the performance is all" invites us, Hamlet-like, to re-create the tension, the atmosphere, in order to participate in the drama.

33. Eliot, *Use of Poetry,* 100. In rereading Eliot's essays, I have been struck by his use of the semicolon. It is not just that he uses it so often and so masterfully and that its use stands out so markedly in a time when it has been all but abandoned. Rather, it is the rhetorical effect of the pauses it introduces in sentences where he wants to slow the reader down before introducing an epigrammatic idea whose sententiousness takes time to digest. This has the effect of taking out the conjunctions that would imply an association of ideas and replacing them with separating, caesura-like pauses, which tend to aggregate (or in Eliot's own phrase, "amalgamate") ideas rather than stringing them out in linear fashion. This is less a strategy for reasoning by argumentative logic than it is an effort to *create ideas.* Such a creative act needs a grammar and a rhetorical style to give it substance, and this

may be one reason that Eliot's formulations have been so readily lifted out of their context.

34. Ibid., 144–145; emphasis in original.

35. "The Metaphysical Poets," SE, 247.

36. In his *The Structure of Complex Words* (Ann Arbor: University of Michigan Press, 1967), William Empson devotes a chapter to "Sense and Sensibility" (250–269), where he is critical of Eliot's rather blithe use of "sensibility." In accusing Eliot of simply "expounding the paradox of the word," while still giving him credit for "going through an independent process of thought with the original machine that formed the words," Empson insists that there is much more to be said. The value of Empson's discussion here is how he forces us to think about the difference between sense—how we apprehend the world and process external stimuli—and sensibility, that far more rarified portion of consciousness that describes a complex mode of feeling that synthesizes the external, internal, and the interrelation that allows consciousness to transcend both (or at least think them at the same time). To Eliot's credit, he is clearer about all of this when read over the oeuvre that composes his thinking on seventeenth-century poetry, including the Clark and Turnbull Lectures as well as the essays on individual poets.

37. See, for example, "Reflections on *Vers Libre*" (first published in the *New Statesman*, March 3, 1917), in which Eliot condemns "free verse" as a mistaken way of describing poetry that lacks regularized meter and rhyme. He characterizes it first in the context of "a lady, renowned in her small circle for the accuracy of her stop-press information of literature," who complains to him of "a growing pococurantism," and responds to Eliot's suggestion of proper reading material that she "could no longer read any verse but *vers libre*." This set piece—with its drawing room atmosphere where one can faintly hear people come and go, talking of Michelangelo—leads to a defense of modernist versification that steadfastly resists the charge that "making it new" involves a dissociation from the history of poetry. This essay, not included in either *The Sacred Wood* or the *Selected Essays,* is an early genealogical move that anticipates Eliot's efforts in the essays of a few years later. That he is developing the same habits of mind evinced in the *Hamlet* and Metaphysical Poets essays is evident in his attempt to come to grips with what *vers libre* actually is: "If *vers libre* is a genuine verse-form it will have a positive definition. And I can define it only in negatives: (1) absence of pattern, (2) absence of rhyme, (3) absence of meter." *Selected Prose of T. S. Eliot,* 32. The essay goes on to demonstrate his point that "it is this contrast between fixity and flux, this unperceived evasion of monotony, which is the very life of verse," by referencing a number of English Renaissance dramatists (John Webster, Thomas Middleton). Eliot is also playing that familiar game in his criticism of affirmation through denial: good unregulated verse is not "free" ("it is a battle-cry of freedom, and there is no freedom in art," 32), but rather *vers libre*. This nominal change performs the liberating function that paradoxically asserts a yoking to a tradition properly perceived, whose end product is good modernist verse. Liberation, he implies, is hardly free. Or as Eliot writes in closing: "we conclude that the division between Conservative Verse and *vers libre* does not exist, for there is only good verse, bad verse, and chaos" (36). See also his comments on Pound's versification in his contemporary essay "Ezra Pound: His Metric and Poetry," *Selected Prose of T. S. Eliot,* 149–150.

38. There are no "shes" in Eliot's dissociated pantheon (nor in his associated one).

39. There is certainly an important question of reference here. Eliot's claim for poetry is that it can render present the referential object such that the word or phrase itself is merely a medium, a transparent yet direct connection between object and feeling. What gets in the way of this connection is language as a differential system of values rather than indexical correspondences. We can agree with Eliot that the language of one poet is more evocative than another without attributing this to a necessary and proper relation between word and object. It seems particularly odd that a poet who holds to such a relation of correspondence between words and feelings, not to mention objects and the modification of sensibility, would write a long poem with such obscurity of reference that he was obliged afterward to provide footnotes and references. Is there in such a modernist archetype an avoidance of the dissociation of sensibility?

40. "The Metaphysical Poets," SE, 247.

41. "Shakespeare and the Stoicism of Seneca," SE, 121.

42. In a letter of September 13, 1930, Eliot writes to Bonamy Dobrée: "I doubt myself whether good philosophy any more than good criticism or any more than good poetry can be written without strong feeling . . . my essay on Machiavelli, for instance, is not good, not because I did not know enough (which I didn't) but because I had not soaked deep enough in Machiavelli to feel intensely—therefore, in so far as there is any good in it, that is because it is not about Machiavelli at all." Quoted in Schuchard, *Eliot's Dark Angel*, 254.

Though I am not sure who this essay might be about, it is indeed at times *very* astute about Machiavelli, especially concerning his relationship with the Elizabethans. In Eliot's description of Machiavelli and his reception, we might also glimpse the manner in which Hamlet is posed in various forms of the histrionic. As Eliot writes: "It is easy to admire Machiavelli in a sentimental way. It is only one of the sentimental and histrionic poses of human nature—and human nature is incorrigibly histrionic—to pose as a 'realist,' a person of 'no nonsense,' to admire the 'brutal frankness' or the 'cynicism' of Machiavelli. This is a form of self-satisfaction and self-deception, which merely propagates the Jew of Malta-Nietzsche myth of Machiavelli. In Elizabethan England the reputation of Machiavelli was merely manipulated unconsciously to feed the perpetually recurring tendency to Manichaean heresy: the desire for a devil to worship. The heretical impulses remain fairly constant; they recur in the Satan of Milton and the Cain of Byron. But with these indulgences of human frailties Machiavelli has no traffic. He had none of the instinct to pose; and therefore human beings, in order to accept him at all, had to make him into a dramatic figure. His reputation is the history of the attempt of humanity to protect itself, by secreting a coating of falsehood, against any statement of the truth." "Niccolo Machiavelli," in *For Lancelot Andrewes* (London: Faber and Gwyer, 1928), 64–65.

43. "Shakespeare and the Stoicism of Seneca," SE, 121.

44. Ibid.

45. Elmer Edgar Stoll, *Hamlet: An Historical and Comparative Study* (New York: Gordian Press, 1919). Eliot steals (I mean borrows) the first line of his essay from Stoll's second chapter: "The only fault that the eighteenth century discovered, was, insofar as the two can be separated, in the play and not in the man." It is worth noting Stoll's use here of "man" for Hamlet instead of "character." Stoll is a critic especially caught between the attempt to set out the manner in which the play creates its main character (without "psychology," he says) and his failure to avoid treating

Hamlet as precisely a real, fully realized and realizable "man." See his revealingly titled "Hamlet the Man," a pamphlet published by the English Association (#91, March 1935). The other book under consideration in Eliot's review is J. M. Robertson, *The Problem of Hamlet* (London: Cobden-Sanderson, 1919).

46. "Shakespeare and the Stoicism of Seneca," SE, 123.

47. Eliot addresses this later in the essay: "To have heightened the criminality of Gertrude would have been to provide the formula for a totally different emotion in Hamlet; it is just because her character is so negative and insignificant that she arouses in Hamlet the feeling which she is incapable of representing" (125). This volte-face concerning the dramatist's constructing of the play is a telling reminder at this late point in the essay that Eliot has not been able to adequately account for the formula he has earlier, perhaps impudently, proposed. For Jacqueline Rose, "the question of femininity clearly underpins this central, if not indeed the central, concept of Eliot's aesthetic theory, and this is confirmed by the fact that Eliot again uses an image of femininity—and by no means one of the most straightforward in its own representation or in the responses it has produced—to give us the measure of the consequent failure of the play." Jacqueline Rose, "*Hamlet*—the Mona Lisa of Literature," in *Sexuality in the Field of Vision* (London: Verso, 1986), 123.

48. But see *Henry VIII*, 5.4.7, for Shakespeare's suggestion that the crabtree provides a more useful and indeed potent source for corrective instruments. In *The Norton Shakespeare*, Stephen Greenblatt, Walter Cohen, Jean E. Howard, and Katherine Eisaman Maus, eds. (New York: Norton, 1997).

49. I will resist the temptation to likewise wonder about Eliot's own "period of crisis" in these very years following "Prufrock" as his difficulties with Vivien became nearly unbearable. Whether or not this results in the poet losing control of his material is the question, and for Eliot it might be said that in the midst of such turmoil, poetry is that place of control and stability otherwise missing in his life.

50. On this idea and Eliot's symptomatic use of "woman as inadequate" as a support for the structuring of fiction, see Rose, "*Hamlet*—the Mona Lisa of Literature," 125–132, 136–139.

51. "And probably more people have thought *Hamlet* a work of art because they have found it interesting, than have found it interesting because it is a work of art" (124). A fabulous piece of rhetoric, in which the crucial question of what makes a work of art—how it performs its function, what criteria are applicable (and missing)—is left out of this equation. Another formulation that works by affirmation through denial.

52. Critics to this day follow Eliot in failing (or perhaps being unwilling) to separate clearly their reading of the character from a reading of the play. This results all too often in taking Hamlet as a reliable index to the play's functioning without the requisite effort of exploring the representational strategy of the play. For example, in his otherwise fascinating essay on Keats, Romantic poetry, Adorno's aesthetic theory, and poetic politics, Robert Kaufman writes: "In Eliot's eyes, nineteenth-century poetry too often mistakes the cause (or at least, artistic carrier) of dissociated sensibility—*Hamlet*—for its cure. You cannot cure *Hamlet* with more *Hamlet*, Eliot believes, not even with a *Hamlet* that's been married to fully objectified form. For Eliot, objective form and *Hamlet* cancel one another out, are incapable of being placed in interesting tension" (377). As I have been trying to demonstrate here, it's not *Hamlet* that Eliot identifies as the problem for poetic practice, but Hamlet's characterological subjectivity. While Eliot's essay does indeed

seem to argue for the play's participation in the dissociation of sensibility, it is rather the main character who bears the burden for failure, despite the feign to the contrary in the essay's opening line. The reason, in other words, that you "cannot cure *Hamlet* with more *Hamlet*," is that the dis-ease in question does not turn out to be in the play's functioning. What's ill is the hyper-reflective subjective state that Hamlet offers to a poetic practice that mistakenly embraces it. As for interesting tension, Keats and Eliot often mimic the dramatic practice of *Hamlet* in their lyrics by understanding intuitively that dramatizing ruminatory subjectivity (sometimes even invoking Hamlet's name or paraphrasing lines from the play) can be very useful in exploring experience through sensibility. Kaufman's essay is "Negatively Capable Dialectics: Keats, Vendler, Adorno, and the Theory of the Avant-Garde," *Critical Inquiry* 27, no. 2 (Winter 2001): 354–384.

53. "Shakespeare and the Stoicism of Seneca," SE, 124.

54. Ibid.

55. Ibid.

56. On the relationship between Eliot's work, especially his poetry, and his historical context (particularly English popular culture of the early twentieth century), see Schuchard's remarkable chapter in *Eliot's Dark Angel,* 102–118. See also Eric Sigg, "Eliot as a Product of America," in *Cambridge Companion to T. S. Eliot,* 14–30.

57. "Shakespeare and the Stoicism of Seneca," SE, 124–125.

58. Ibid., 125.

59. Ibid.

60. Ibid.

61. Ibid.

ACKNOWLEDGMENT

I would like to thank Margreta de Grazia for her comments on an earlier version of this essay.

MARIA DEL SAPIO GARBERO

Translating Hamlet /
Botching up Ophelia's Half Sense

Introduction

There is one point in *Hamlet* where Shakespeare portrays *en abîme* the part the audience is called to perform in the undemanding of the play, and it hints at a transaction which is both frustrating and dangerous: frustrating in the audience's possibility of getting to meaning other than as something made up of patches; dangerous in what could be improperly inferred. This is when Ophelia's madness is first announced to the queen (IV.5.4–13) and hearers at court are said *"to botch"* her words up to make them "fit their own thoughts".

Gent. She speaks much of her father, says she hears

    There's tricks i'th' world, and hems, and beats her heart,

    Spurns enviously at straws, speaks things in doubt

    That carry but half sense. Her speech is nothing,

    Yet the unshaped use of it doth move

    The hearers to collection. They aim at it,

    And botch the words up fit to their own thoughts,

    Which, as her winks and nods and gestures yield them,

    Indeed would make one think there might be thought,

    Though nothing sure, yet much unhappily.[1]

Textus: English Studies in Italy, Volume 20, Number 3 (September–December 2007): pp. 519–538. Copyright © 2007 Maria Del Sapio Garbero.

Soon afterwards, the queen, who had seemed firm at the outset in refusing to talk to Ophelia, yields to Horatio's cautionary suggestion: "for she may strew / Dangerous conjectures in ill-breeding minds" (lines 14–15). Is he prompting talk as an act of piety or as a policing of Ophelia's "half sense"? The verb "to strew" used by Horatio might well serve to capture the disseminative functioning of meaning of the whole play (or even of language in general, for that matter), were it not negatively connoted here to refer to a culturally targeted female excess, something unshaped, and yet dangerous, something to embank and put under control. Significantly, it is Horatio who is here taking on the responsibilities of truth, a role which will be given official status, although for times to come, possibly in another play, when the dying Hamlet asks him to report his "cause aright to the unsatisfied" (V.2.343–344). But, emblematically enough in this scene, being a warrantor of truth can be no unambiguous task. If we follow editions of this scene based on its Folio source, we will find that lines 4–15 (as we as lines 2–3) are all uttered by Horatio. But this may only strengthen the questions we are elicited to ask. Shall we deem him sincerely concerned with Ophelia's truth? And in taking charge of the verb "to botch" should the audience, reader or translator, the "unsatisfied" who are figured out of the play, privilege the sense of "conjecturing", "repairing", or "bungling"?

The relevance of this scene to a hermeneutics of *Hamlet* as such has not been missed by critics, especially by those adopting deconstructive strategies of reading (see Evans 1989: 179–181). It will be the aim of my paper to explore how translation of this scene into a different language[2] can help us further interrogate the range of meanings lurking in its vocabulary; a vocabulary which in my view posits Ophelia's ineffability as a question concerning a poetics, as well as a politics and a policing, of female language. Indeed, through mad Ophelia's "unshaped" and mixed use of speech, (and quite differently from Hamlet's highly shaped articulation of folly), language is given its ultimate exposure as a material inviting and defying the jurisdiction of truth.

In the space available to me in this article, I will also explore how these issues are present and handled in a few European "botched" translations (pastiches/rewritings) of Ophelia's "unhappy" state. I will take examples from Mary Cowden Clarke's tale "The Rose of Elsinore" (1852) and Marina Tsvetaeva's poems (written in the 1920s), but mostly from Alba de Céspedes's novel *Dalla parte di lei* (1949), written in the aftermath of the Second World War. The author, who has only recently started to enjoy the appreciation she deserves among Italian critics,[3] was active in the Resistance against Fascism between 1943 and 1945, a pioneer in the feminist movement, and one of the most translated Italian authors in her time. Her novel (available in a 1952 abridged American edition as *The Best of Husbands*) is vibrant with the story of a protagonist who finds in Shakespeare's tragic heroines, and especially in Ophelia's tragic love, a model (i.e., a poetics and a politics) for a peculiar form of heroism and unheeded resistance to the shallowness not only of the *régime* but of the patriarchal culture as such.

Teasing and Unvoiced: Ophelia's Call for Translation

Hor. 'Twere good she were spoken with, for she may strew
    Dangerous conjectures in ill-breeding minds.

The verb "to strew" used by Horatio (in IV.5.14) aptly comments on the potentially endangering effect of Ophelia's unintelligibility by precautionarily incorporating, as it were, Ophelia's disquieting language of flowers; even the very disseminating gesture with which in a while we will see her administering flowers alongside words and snatches of old songs.

Horatio's "to strew" also retrieves the hearers' collection of Ophelia's unshaped speech by driving that term, *collection*, within the same semantic field of scattering/piecing together, or else gathering by inference. Etymologically in fact "collection" is an interesting conflation in English of the Latin *col-ligĕre* (to gather), plus *col-ligāre* (to tie up/to connect), plus *legĕre* (to read as well as literally to pluck/to pick up, and hence figuratively, to gather with one's ears or eyes); a set of connotations which in Italian the poet Eugenio Montale underscores by simply sticking to the letter of the verb *to collect* ("Il suo parlare senza forma muove però gli ascoltatori / a raccoglierlo"). "Strewing" and "collecting" also refer us (and I am grateful to Manfred Pfister for this further suggestion) to the notion of "anthology", literally a gathering of flowers, a "florilegium".

But, while stressing gathering and "botching up" as the hearer's or reader's task, all seems to contribute in scene 5 to align images of uncontrollable seeds and breeding with ideas of random production of meaning (or else, an improper florilegium) which can be as disturbing and infective as, for Hamlet, Gertrude's sexualized "un-weeded garden" (1.2.135).[4]

Through Ophelia meaning is in fact given a disruptive hermeneutic model based on a botanical trope, the more so for being at the same time preventively encased within Horatio's cautionary frame.

The botanical trope has been given full resonance in French by the verb *semer* used by both Georges Roth (1952) and André Gide (1959) to translate Horatio's "to strew": "Il serait bon qu'on lui parlât, car elle risque de semer chez les malveillants de dangereux soupcons" (Gide). Others in their translations (Yves Bonnefoy, 1988; François Mauguin, 1995) will resort to the similar, but less immediately metaphoric, *répandre*.

The rhetorical economy of scene 5 is important when we consider that from the outset it is one with the conceptual space opened by mad Ophelia's disseminative poetics. In Italian it is kept alive by those translators who, like Agostino Lombardo in his rendering of lines 10–11, present us with an image of Ophelia who *porge* ("hands") her words ("con ammiccamenti, gesti, cenni del capo"). Alessandro Serpieri, who has resorted to the verb *rendere* to translate "to yield" (thus: "parole che, per come sono rese dal suoi ammicchi / e cenni e gesti"), emphasizes the part played by the body in the uttering of words, or rather the excess of sense which remains tied to it, expressed and unvoiced, more than the Flora-like act of yielding/proffering it.

Needless to say that in Shakespeare one has everything. Or at least so it seems. Perhaps because of an effect of mutual illumination, of the language past and of our own language or languages, which one experiences through translation, comparing translations. This can be best illustrated by Benjamin's metaphor of the never-ending reconstitution of the *amphora*, a becoming of tongues towards a possible reconciliated whole; an "impossible possibility" in the comment of Derrida, the presentiment or announcement of a language which in the translating process can appear as being greater than both the original and the target-text (see Benjamin 1996: 260 and Derrida 1985b: 123). This is of course the more so in the case of *Hamlet*, a ghost text to every Western literature, a philological object and a ventriloquist body, origin and palimpsest par excellence, and to whose growing reverberation, translations paradoxically contribute by facing their own limit, when one is making space for the impropriety/foreignness of other words: a *complementarity* for the Benjamin expounded by Derrida (1985a: 201).

The call for translation (and/or interpretation) as both a complement and a way for the "original" to deploy its irreducible "position of demand or debt" (Derrida) is itself epitomized, I think, in scene 5, so strongly marked from the outset by verbs like "to strew", "to aim at", "to botch up", before finding in Ophelia's ambiguous distribution of flowers an objectivation and a metaphor.

"Elie risque de semer" (Gide). "Elie pourrait semer" (Roth). (And with an eye more alert to infection) "Potrebbe spargere pericolosi germi" / "She might strew dangerous germs" (Baldini). The cooperation of languages help us highlight the overturning, in scene 5, of Ophelia's passivity into an ambiguity which sweeps over the very symbols—flowers /plants—with which women's main virtue, innocence (namely a lack of virtue), is traditionally associated. But it is not by relying on translation as such (a traditional male territory in the case of such a classical repertory as Shakespeare) that I will try to comply with Ophelia's elusiveness and/or demand for interpretation, but rather by "complementing" it with a few examples of female pastiches or rewritings which positively appropriate "botching up" as an empowering transgression of boundaries: the law of genre, a normative practice of reading, the jurisdiction of truth.

Collecting Ophelia's Story: An Improper Florilegium

In discussing the fascination of poets and philosophers with the language of botany, and in linking it with the feminine, the unconscious, sexuality, the nonlinear, Claudette Sartiliot has written:

> It should [. . .] be no surprise if Derrida is interested in the botanical discourse or in the worlds of plants, from which he had already borrowed the term *dissemination*. The word *dissemination* implies that meaning does not happen in a linear and teleological fashion but according to an alliance of rule and chance. Production of meaning, or survival of the species, happens in the botanical or linguistic world through a scattering of seeds or semen. Thus in the world of flowers, reproduction, survival, fecundation is the rule, however, this telos is achieved through chance and intermediaries (insects, water, air, animals, humans).[5]

What Ophelia's "half sense" explicitly calls for is just this: intermediaries who will eventually gather and remake her words, but with no assurance as to either purity or destination, all their "aiming at" meaning leading to misreadings ("conjectures"), the result of a "rattoppo", or else a "pasticcio", as "to botch up" (to patch or stitch together, to mend imperfectly, to bungle, according to the *OED*) has been respectively rendered in Italian by Serpieri and Lombardo.

As to Gertrude, in the interval of the dozen lines reporting Ophelia's untranslatable unhappy state, she has been invaded by her guilt: "To my sick soul, as sin's true nature is, / Each toy seems prologue to some great amiss. / So full of artless jealousy is guilt, / It spills itself on fearing to be spilt" (lines 19–20). But what guilt? When Ophelia is let in before the queen, and as from the stage direction, she *sings* (does not "spill" also mean "to sing" in the sense of "to divulge"?), it is to chant of love's deceptive signs (*"How should I your true love know / From another one?"*, lines 23–24). We do not know whether Horatio would consider Gertrude's sense of guilt a partial result. But the language of the play has at this point accomplished Hamlet's conflation of the two women. More than bringing them together to exchange understanding, it has made them share the same predicament of wretchedness and unavoidable disaster. In the process Horatio's call for piety has unawares shifted from Gertrude to the audience, the frustration at the first appearance of Ophelia being thus, if not superseded, assuaged by a more sustainable piteous feeling for the fate which awaits the two women, whatever its meaning or cause.[6]

There is a desire to heal and make good Ophelia's fragmented speech, in women's *re-collection* of her story, as well as a drive to make sense of Gertrude's "sin". Marina Tsvetaeva reunites Ophelia's voice to her own poetical *persona* and makes her speak on behalf of Gertrude, as her indignant advocate. In her poem "Ophelia. In Defence of Gertrude" (1923), the two figures are no longer aligned on the basis of a prohibited female knowledge, the one the mirror of the other's guilt or wretchedness, but on the basis of a defence of passion as opposed to a misogynist idea of chastity.

> Prince Hamlet, you defile the Queen's
> Womb. Enough. A virgin cannot
> Judge passion. Don't you know Phaedra
> Was more guilty, yet men sing of her,
>
> And will go on singing. You, with your blend
> Of chalk and rot, you bony
> Scandalmonger, how can you ever
> Understand a fever in the blood? (Tsvetaeva 1984: ll. 5–12)

The poem's reference to Phaedra indirectly likens Hamlet, who is paranoically obsessed by "wormy flower-beds", to Hyppolite, Phaedra's unresponsive stepson, the devotee of the cult of the chaste Artemis in the myth, and the "pleasure's enemy" in Tsvetaeva's poem "Epistle".

As virginal as Hyppolite, Tsvetaeva's bloodless and cold reasoning prince, a skeletal body all pallor and dust in her vision, is ousted from his position of judge and summoned as a defiler of his mother's womb, a scandalmonger. With a man like this Tsvetaeva's love subject will never arrive at the appointment, "much too high" the curve of both his sky and hers ("Appointment"). So, either as a reminder of Hamlet's guilt ("Ophelia to Hamlet", "Hamlet's Dialogue with His Conscience"), or as a cherished unnamed kinship with an unfulfilled and ever craving passionate self ("The Poem of the End"), or as a premonition of the suicidal poet herself, the drowning Ophelia always returns, "between the grasses bordering every stream", the one who "gulped at love, and filled her mouth / with silt" ("Appointment", lines 12–15).

Tsvetaeva never accepted confinement within the conventions of the gender role divide, or being listed under prejudicial categorizations of anything like "feminine writing". Nevertheless, as such, as a poet committed to nothing else but women's "limited" horizon, she was, with others, the object in the revolutionary Russia of disdainful attacks at the hands of male critics, and most famously by Trockij, whose book *Literature and Revolution*, published in 1923 and translated into many languages, was widely known abroad.[7] Tsvetaeva, who had chosen to leave her country the previous year, was then an *émigré* in Prague, where she wrote her poems on Ophelia, an articulated accusing creature from the land of the dead who comes to stand, to my mind, as a figure of exile, the expression of a marginalized cause in a world of abstract if not destructive virile truths and dogmas.

If Tsvetaeva rescues Shakespeare's Ophelia from her deranged speech by translating her into a figure "capable" and not "incapable of her own distress" (*Hamlet* IV.7.177), thus disseminating what in her "half sense" lies censored in a state of living-dead knowledge, others similarly intrigued by Ophelia's banned truth have made conjectures as to what, well before her madness, has made her into that poor creature, "divided from herself", pitied by Claudius (IV.5.86). To the Victorian Mary Cowden Clarke, Ophelia's deranged behaviour gestures beyond Shakespeare's plot towards an antecedent story, the story of an intimidated and silenced body which comes to stand for a common female destiny. In her fictional envisioning of "the girlhood of Shakespeare's heroines" (published in three volumes between 1850 and 1852), as if anticipating the psychoanalytic angle adopted by feminist thought in its critique of the cultural formation of the female gender, *ce sexe qui n'est pas un* in the terms of Irigaray (1977), Ophelia's *Bildungsroman* is imagined as a gradual construction of her main Shakespearean trait: "nothingness". Brought up in the countryside by a couple of peasants to whom the child Ophelia has been entrusted during her parents' long diplomatic mission at the court of France, and where she is actually raised as by a mother by the elder peasants' daughter Jutha, her growth is perceptively narrated as a story of separations and alienation: from her mother, from an identifying maternal language, from the fable of romantic love, but even from nature, and from flowers as unequivocal symbols of the feminine. Which is another way of addressing the much debated, exploded relation between things and signs, a problem that in Shakespeare haunts the whole play and which, in Act 4, scene 5, appears strongly as the problem of the feminine.

Nature in fact, the context of Ophelia's growth, is seen as being at the same time the site of possible identifying images and of gradual estrangement, an estrangement which is parallel to Jutha's seduction in the wood by a deceitful knight, and parallel to Ophelia being harassed by Ulf, the peasants' idiot younger boy who "appeared to take a ferocious delight in ripping and destroying flowers" (1851: 198).[8] Ophelia's flora undergoes a gradual reification: flowers lose their innocence, roses can metamorphosize into wild-roses, into wintry, skeletal, thorny flowers.

Marked as it is by the intimidating phallic scenario of seduction, nature will be the context of an apprenticeship to sexual identity as a story of fear and of cancellation, a story which has its traumatic climax for the little Ophelia fantasized by Cowden Clarke, when coming down to the parlour one night, she finds on the table the dead body of Jutha and of her child. "Naturally gentle she became timid. She shrank about, scared, and trembling; fearful of she hardly knew what, but feeling unassured, doubtful, full of a vague uneasiness and alarm" (1851: 215), writes Cowden Clarke, thus furnishing with a set of primal scenes Laertes' policing warning to her sister: "Be wary then. Best safety lies in fear" (1.3.43). It is with such a tremulous body that she enters the sunny court of Elsinore, only to be present at (and before starting her romance with Hamlet) other stories of seduction and betrayal, and another death, that of her now aristocratic friend Tyra. In a word, what we are asked to confront in Cowden Clarke's story is a depressed more than an innocent body, a body unconsciously but traumatically bound to silence and to nothingness.

"A body devoid of signification," Kristeva has observed, "is a depressed body prone to suicide" (1989: 89). It is precisely this psychoanalytic insight which seems to be precociously at work in Cowden Clarke's re-vision of Shakespeare's Ophelia. She gathers the melancholic objects[9] of Ophelia's disordering mad pose (her orticant flora, her scraps of songs and speech) and makes them produce a sense in the imagined context of her growth, a pre-text. In that light they appear as the alien objects of a history culturally inscribed in the very fibres of the feminine, a history which in time has become body, posture, Unconscious, destiny: a repetitive destiny of death, as in Ophelia's last feverish dream which reconsigns her to Shakespeare's play:

> "Those figures—those women. It was down by the brook—among the reeds—beneath the willow [...]. It was there she sat,—the first figure I saw; the moon's light struggled feebly through them; there was a veil of haze upon tree, and shrub, and brooks; but I saw her plainly, and knew her at once, though her long hair fell drooping over her knees as she sat [...] It was Jutha, mother!
>
> [...] But there were two others I saw. One was my poor Thyra. I knew her by a terrible token [...] her livid throat, mother, [...]!"
>
> A moment's pause; and then Ophelia went on.
>
> [...] "The wind sighed amid the reeds. The heads of nettles and long-purples were stirred by the night breeze, as it swept on mournfully. [...] Then I saw one approach whose face I could not see, and whose figure I knew not. She was clothed in white, all hung about with weeds and wild flowers [...] and then the white figure moved on, impelled towards the water. I saw her glide on, floating its surface; I saw her dimly, among the silver-leaved branches of the drooping willow, as they waved around and above her, up-buoyed by her spreading white garments." (1851: 248–250)

Multiplied into a procession of silent denouncing female ghosts, the intimidated body of Ophelia becomes to Ophelia's gaze itself a phantom of

History, its hidden guilt, its true guilty memory. One is induced to think of *Hamletmachine* (1977) by Heiner Müller, who, in twentieth century East Germany, will resort to a strikingly similar serialization of Ophelia's death to make her express the world's sorrow: "I am Ophelia. The one the river didn't keep. The woman dangling from the rope. The woman with her arteries cut open. The woman with the overdose [. . .] The woman with her head in the gas stove . . ." (1984: 54).

But is there any way out of this suicidal script? In her novel *Dalla parte di lei* (1949) the Italian writer Alba de Céspedes explores the extent to which women can share an Ophelia-like poetics of the feminine. She also figures out a provocative exit from a fatherly imprisoning text.

Alba de Céspedes's Crime News

If one glances at the crime news of the Roman paper *Il Messaggero* in the immediate aftermath of the Second World War, one is surprised to find that the death toll remained high. History was still having its considerable amount of deaths although on a different battle field: "Alle 22 di ieri sera una giovane donna, dall'apparente età di 35 anni, si toglieva improvvisamente la giacchetta che indossava e scavalcato il paraperro del Ponte Mazzini si gettava nel Tevere. Gli astanti udirono il suo urlo: 'Oreste!'" (June 25th, 1947). "Certa Isolina Mazzitelli di 18 anni, é stata ieri trasportata all'ospedale di San Giovanni dove quei sanitari le riallacciavano le vene ch'erano state segate con una lametta" (July 2nd, 1947). "Beve benzina per un diverbio col marito" (July 29th, 1947). "Tentato suicidio all'inchiostro di china" (February 17th, 1948).[10] War did not end with the defeat of Fascism and the liberation of 1945. In *The Messaggero*, the paper where the novelist Alba de Céspedes had started a career as a journalist in the thirties, suicides of both sexes were reported as a daily occurrence. Women did it for love, a betrayed or opposed love, or to escape a grim conjugal tie. Many of them killed themselves by gulping down or melting into Ophelia's "element", a liquid, a vortex or gush turned evil, chlorine bleach, petrol, ink, water, blood. Many of them in Rome drowned in the Tiber.

There is an Ophelia-like drowned woman in de Céspedes's novel *Dalla parte di lei*.[11] This is Alessandra's mother, the protagonist and narrator of a story set in Rome in the years going from the late thirties—from pre-war Fascist Italy to the reorganization of a free parliamentary life in 1945. She was named Eleonora—after Ibsen's famous heroine—by Alessandra's grandmother, an actress who had renounced the stage for the family, and from whom she has also inherited a highly symbolic box with the theatrical veils of Juliet, Desdemona, and Ophelia. The life of Alessandra's mother is suffused from the start with colours the protagonist wants to reverberate on her own. The aura of a longing literary figure that Eleonora is given in the novel (by Ibsen's Nora, Shakespeare's heroines, and especially Ophelia as a representation of tragic unfulfilled desire) is the way by which Alessandra, the daughter, forcefully validates a female lineage which escapes the confinement of the feminine within the maternal reproductive function assigned to it by patriarchy, a function which in Irigaray's terms "de/subjectivizes" women (see 1991: 42–46), in so far as they are denied a symbolic identitarian system of their own, and which was reinforced even more in Italy during Fascism. This is clearly evidenced in the depersonalizing role women were called upon to play in a patriotic policy of population increase, even without considering the ideology which forced upon them the requirement of continually posing before the strongly masculine gaze of that culture.

So, what about Eleonora, and why Ophelia? A piano teacher who contributes with her private lessons to the poor budget of her shabby middle-class family, a person in love with literature, art, and love, Alessandra's mother is the poetic creature of an ill-matched couple, her father, a white-collar employee, inferior to his wife in background and sensitivity, being depicted as very prosaic and unintellectual. Like all the men in the huge grey apartment house in Prati where they live, he is away most of the day, and not only during office hours. This strengthens an exclusive mother-daughter bond and a silent sense of intimacy for Alessandra with the other women of the neighbourhood, during those moments when men's jurisdictional gaze wanes and they can give up the "good" pose. Hers is an intimacy with their solitude and prohibited discontent ("Yes, we were a gentle and unfortunate race", 1952: 31), but also with their secret loves whose tales to Alessandra's eyes defy anonymity and enrich them with a narrative of their own.

Still, it was outrageous in a novel published in 1949 Italy, when women (in accordance with the fascist penal code) could still be jailed for adultery, that the protagonist might side unconditionally with her mother when she falls in love with Hervey Pierce, an artist, the gentle ephebic brother of the English aristocratic girl she is giving music lessons to in their villa on the Gianicolo. Her cherishing an adulterous feeling doesn't disqualify her as a suitable mother. Quite the opposite. She is given a sacral aura. She is a mystic, a saint. "The sight of my mother in love was the sweetest I had ever seen" (1952: 51). When her mother realizes there is nothing in her poor wardrobe for her momentous concert at Villa Peirce, the adolescent Alessandra euphorically presides over the making of a new dress from the veils preserved in her grandmother's box. "We must make my mother a dress with the veils of Ophelia," she says to their friends Fulvia and Lydia (1952: 52); an endeavour which turns out to be the staging of a joyful bridal rite. And when her mother, regretting that she cannot take her daughter with her, drowns herself in the Tiber, she defiantly appropriates both the mourning space and the *post mortem* monumentalizing intention which in Shakespeare's play are litigiously held by Hamlet and Laertes. In a burial with maimed rites as in Shakespeare, but which, in my view, is a radical reworking of the cemetery scene, she visualizes one's gender location as that of an army in front of another; thus pointing at a war within the War which was approaching, and which is doomed to go on unperceived by men, were it not for the erratic intermittence of disturbing crime news.

> Since my mother had taken her own life she could not be admitted to the basilica itself. The priest came out in black vestments and eyed us half with compassion and half with suspicion, perhaps because he knew my mother had thrown herself into the river. A black cloth was draped over the coffin, and the blanket of roses was replaced on it. I found myself between Lydia and Fulvia; for we had instinctively fallen into two separate groups, of men and of women [. . .].
>
> Indifferent to what [the priest] was saying, I stared at the group of men on the other side of the coffin. They seemed more shamefaced than sorry, shocked by the fact that a woman could have made so rash a gesture, one that obscurely reflected on them a large part of the blame. [. . .] I stated intensely at [them] and had an urge to tell them to go away and leave us alone. We were divided like two armies preparing to join combat, and between us, in the coffin, lay the body of one of our dead.
>
> My mother was buried in unconsecrated ground; but to me her presence made it holy. The gravediggers draped the blanket of roses over the coffin, tucking it in all around. And my father looked on without showing anger or scorn; his jurisdiction over her was finished. (1952: 96–97)

By making her Ophelia take the field in defence of Gertrude, Tsvetaeva forcefully enacts in her poems the political project later advocated by Irigaray of recognizing "the woman in every mother" (1991: 42). Alba de Céspedes never hints overtly at Gertrude in her novel, but her protagonist similarly releases the banned desire of a mother figure, thus constructing the maternal not as a disabling mirror of guilt, or abjection, one might say borrowing from Kristeva (1980), but as a site of resistance and as an engendering matrix of an alternative female iconography: "In verità ella m'aveva dato la vita" ("In truth, she had brought me to the world"), "coi nostri colloqui accanto alla finestra, con la sua voce morbida che leggeva le poesie, raccontava le favole, mi pre-sentava le eroine delle tragedie d'amore" (1949: 116).[12] It is not a coincidence that in re-using Shakespeare's Ophelia the author presents us with a narrative

which stealthily patches together in the single character of the innocently
adulterous Eleonora the traits of Gertrude and Ophelia.

Through the oppositional function assigned in this way to Shakespeare's
tragic heroines, the protagonist of *Dalla parte di lei* passionately claims for
her mother the role of a language-giving figure, not just a dispenser of life
but of signs, like the daisies she scatters in the Tiber, in an Ophelia-like
manner, a few days before drowning in it, and which is the means for the
daughter to conceptualize differently her life and desires, however destructive all that may be in the patriarchal censoring culture of the *régime* and of
the post-war period.

What I have not said so far, and what is kept secret from the reader
until the last of the 549 pages that make up the novel, is that Alessandra's life
story is born out of a memoir she has written in prison after she has killed
her much-loved husband, "the best of husbands", with the intention of setting her "cause aright" in front of a jury, obviously a purely male one in the
historical context of the novel, but actually with the intention of disputing, as
Tsvetaeva had also done with Hamlet, men's jurisdiction over truth and over
her truth as a woman. "In my opinion no man has the right to judge a woman
without knowing of what totally different stuff she is made. Why should a
jury composed entirely of men decide whether or not she is guilty?" (1952:
55), she says in the course of the novel, when the reader doesn't yet know she
is referring to a real jury. And then at the very end, thus underlining the elusiveness of her truth, unless one were willing to piece it together from a report
as slow, digressive, and decentring as the life of a woman: "Now that I am in
prison, waiting for my lawyer to present an appeal, I want to tell the whole
tragic story from my point of view. I don't know if the judge of the higher
court will have time to read my account. It is a long one, I admit—as long,
hour by hour and day by day, as the life of a woman. Seldom can one pick
out one simple cause for her sudden rebellion" (1952: 342). Shall we imagine a suspicious Horatio-like figure reading Alessandra's improbable appeal?
Or perhaps, hope for more persevering interpreters (than those imagined by
Shakespeare) in "botching up" a meaning out of a woman's story? Alba de
Céspedes wrote her novel in the aftermath of Fascist Italy, and before the
higher court Alessandra has no extenuating circumstance to allege as a justification on her behalf ("dalla parte di lei"), if not the ordinary disseminated
circumstances of a woman's life.

In fact, hers is a very long account in the confessional mode, in which
the narrative retrospective e of her mother's unique legacy ("La mia storia era
nella scatola dove la mamma conservava gelosamente i veli di Giulietta e di
Desdemona", 1949: 210)[13] is interwoven with the detailed narrative of the
events subsequent to her mother's death: her studies at the University and her
living on a part-time job as a secretary, her becoming increasingly aware of

the existence of a differently policed discontentment, of other "scontenti" who in a whisper are called "communists" and who are occasionally arrested, her falling in love with Francesco, an academic and an opponent of the *régime*, his being fascinated by the "young girl whose mother had killed herself for love" (1952: 334), their marriage, his imprisonment, her siding (like a courageous Desdemona) with her husband's cause in the Resistance during his absence, her hardships during the war, Francesco's return home after the defeat of Fascism, her competing with politics for Francesco's love, his ethos, her mystics of passion, the sense of having been betrayed in the sacral idea of love she has inherited from her mother, the endless wall of Francesco's back every night, her mute invocation, her deluded quest for absoluteness, her emptying the revolver into his back.

What is still necessary to say is that Alessandra's gesture has been obsessively fantasized in the previous pages as a combat between the image of her mother, "graziosamente atteggiata", "graciously posing" (1949: 541), wavering on her green bed from beneath the transparent water, and that of herself as an unsatiated mad dog living on scraps of food, a *hydro*phobic animal antagonist to Ophelia's element, water. "Non sentivo più il fiume scorrere come un fluido legame tra mia madre e me" (1949: 323),[14] she obliquely warns pages earlier at the first dawning of delusion, as if to say that her unanswered craving self, although empowered by her mother's Shakespearean identifying images, can no longer be contained by them. Alba de Céspedes heroine is going to get rid of her mother's box.

In fact, while bringing to light, like Tsvetaeva and Cowden Clarke, Ophelia's distress, thus complementing with a gender angle and from yet another different geography her dangerous "half sense", de Céspedes renounces, with a final unexpected flick of the tail, the beauty of her suicidal watery image.

Her heroine uncannily claws at and destroys her own poetics in order to say like Müller's Ophelia, a few decades later: "Yesterday I stopped killing myself". Which at the very end of the novel and from a newly invalidating space, that of a real prison, problematically reopens the question of both the Shakespearean maternal legacy and of Ophelia's difficult demand for understanding. And truth, perhaps.

NOTES

1. All quotations from *Hamlet* are taken from the Arden Shakespeare edition, ed. H. Jenkins (1982).

2. In my paper I will be referring to the following translations: Eugenio Montale (1949), Georges Roth (1952), Yves Bonnefoy (1957), André Gide (1959), Gabriele Baldini (1963). Agostino Lombardo (1995), François Mauguin (1995). Alessandro Serpieri (1997).

3. See Zancan (2005). For the author's success in English-speaking countries, see Gallucci and Nerenberg (eds) (2000). The monograph *Esperienza e narrazione nella scrittura di Alba de Céspedes* (1993) was written by an Italian scholar working in Australia, Piera Carroli.

4. For the relevance of this metaphor from *Hamlet* onwards, see Adelman (1992: 16–18).

5. C. Sartiliot. "Verbarium: The Discourse of Flowers" (1988: 79). I owe to S. Carotenuto (1999: 257) the quotation of this essay in relation to Ophelia.

6. For a comment on similar dramatic devices in *King Lear,* and on how they work in positioning "the audience as a coherent whole, comfortably situated *vis-à-vis* the text", see McLuskie (1994: 102).

7. Cf. Karlinsy (1989: 154–157). Of related interest are Filonov Gove (1977: 231–255) and Taubman (1994: 77–90). On the poet's cycle on Ophelia see Hasty (1993: 56–82).

8. For a more extensive discussion of Cowden Clarke's Ophelia, see Del Sapio Garbero (2002: 109–139).

9. My adjective is reminiscent of the connotations inherent in the disseminated objects of Dürer's *Melancholia*.

10. "At 10 o'clock last night, a young woman apparently aged 35, suddenly took off the jacket she was wearing and jumping over the parapet of the Mazzini Bridge threw herself into the Tiber. The onlookers heard her crying: 'Oreste!'". "A certain Isolina Mazzitelli, aged 18, was taken yesterday to the San Giovanni hospital where the local surgeons reconnected the veins she had slit with a razor blade". "A woman swallows gasoline after a row with her husband". "Attempted suicide with Indian ink" (my transl.).

11. References to the novel in the text are to the only available version in English (*The Best of Husbands,* New York 1952, trans. Frances Frenaye), especially abridged by the author herself for the American translation. When necessary (and with my translation), I refer to the 1949 original Mondadori edition.

12. "In truth, she had brought me to the world with our talks near the window, while she read me poetry with her soft voice, told me fables, introduced me to the love tragedies's heroines" (my transl.).

13. "My story was all in the box where my mother preciously kept Juliet's and Desdemona's veils" (my transl.).

14. "I no longer felt the river run like a fluid bond between my mother and me" (my transl.).

Works Cited

Adelman J., 1992, *Suffocating Mothers. Fantasies of Maternal Origin in Shakespeare's Plays.* Hamlet *to* The Tempest, Routledge, New York and London.

Benjamin W., 1996, "The Task of the Translator", in M. Bullock and M. W. Jennings (eds), *Selected Writings*, Belknap Press, Cambridge (MA).

Carotenuto S., 1999, *Ellissi di senso*, Belzoni, Roma.

Carroll P., 1993, *Esperienza e narrazione nella scrittura di Alba de Céspedes*, Longo Editore, Ravenna.

Cowden Clarke M., 1851, "The Rose of Elsinore", in *The Girlhood of Shakespeare's Heroines*, 3 vols, W. H. Smith, London, 1850–1852, vol. II.

de Céspedes A., 1949, *Dalla parte di lei*, Mondadori, Milano.

de Céspedes A., 1952, *The Best of Husbands*, Macmillan, New York.

Del Sapio Garbero M., 2002, "Reinvenzione di Ofelia", in Id. (ed.), *La traduzione di Amleto nella cultura europea*, Marsilio, Venezia.

Del Sapio Garbero M., 2005, *Il bene ritrovato. Le figlie di Shakespeare dal* King Lear *ai romances*, Belzoni, Roma.

Derrida J., 1985a, "De Tours de Babel", in J. F. Graham (ed.), *Difference in Translation*, Cornell University Press, Ithaca and London.

Derrida J., 1985b, "Roundtable on Translation", in *The Ear of the Other: Otobioghraphy, Transference, Translation*, Schocken Books, New York.

Evans M., 1989, *Signifying Nothing. Truth's True Contents in Shakespeare's Text*, Harvester Wheatsheaf, New York and London.

Filonov Gove A., 1977, "The Feminine Stereotype and Beyond: Role Conflict and Resolution in the Poetics of Marina Tsvetaeva". *Slavonic Review*, 1977, 36.

Gallucci C. G. and E. Nerenberg (eds), 2000, *Writing Beyond Fascism. Cultural Resistance in the Life and Works of Alba de Céspedes*, Associated University Presses, Cranbury (NJ) and London.

Hasty O. P., 1993, *Tsvetaeva's Orphic Journey in the Worlds of the Word*, Northwestern University Press, Evanston.

Irigaray L, 1977, *Ce sexe qui n'est pas un*, Les Éditions de Minuit, Paris.

Irigaray L, 1991, "The Bodily Encounter with the Mother", in M. Whitford (ed.), Blackwell, Cambridge (MA).

Karlinsy S., 1989, *Marina Cvetaeva*, Guida Editori, Napoli.

Kristeva J., 1980, *Pouvoirs de l'horreur. Essai sur l'abjection*, Éditions du Seuil, Paris.

Kristeva J., 1989, *Sole Nero (Soleil noir. Dépression et mélancolie)*, Feltrinelli, Milano.

McLuskie K., 1994, "The Patriarchal Bard: Feminist Criticism and Shakespeare: *King Lear* and *Measure for Measure*", in J. Dollimore and A. Sinfield (eds), *Political Shakespeare. Essays in Cultural Materialism*, Manchester University Press, Manchester.

Müller H., 1984, *Hamletmachine and Other Texts for the Stage*, trans. Carl Weber, Performing Arts Journal Publications, New York.

Sartiliot C., 1988, "Verbarium: The Discourse of Flowers", *Diacritics*, 4, Winter.

Shakespeare W., 1949/2006, *Amleto* (transl. by Eugenio Montale), Mondadori, Milano.

Shakespeare W., 1952, *Hamlet* (transl. by Georges Roth), Larousse, Paris.

Shakespeare W., 1957/1988, *Hamlet* (transl. by Yves Bonnefoy), Mercure de France, Paris.

Shakespeare W., 1959, *Hamlet* (transl, by André Gide), Gallimard, Paris.

Shakespeare W., 1963/2006, *Amleto* (transl. by Gabriele Baldini), Rizzoli, Milano.

Shakespeare W., 1982, *Hamlet*, H. Jenkins (ed.), Arden Edition, Routledge, London and New York.

Shakespeare W., 1995, *Hamlet* (transl. by François Mauguin), Flammarion, Paris.

Shakespeare W., 1995/2000, *Amleto* (transl. by Agostino Lombardo), Feltrinelli, Milano.

Shakespeare W., 1997, *Amleto* (transl. by Alessandro Serpieri), Manilio, Venezia.

Showalter E., 1991, "Representing Ophelia: Women, Madness, and the Responsibilities of Feminist Criticism", in P. Parker and G. Hartman (eds), *Shakespeare and the Question of Theory*, Routledge, London.

Taubman, J. A. 1994, "Tsvetaeva and the Feminine Tradition in Russian Poetry", in V. Schweitzer *et al* (eds), *Marina Tsvetaeva: One Hundred Years*, Berkley Slavic Specialties, Oakland.

Tsvetaeva M., 1984, *Selected Poems* (transl. by E. Feinstein), Penguin, New York.

Zancan M. (ed.), 2005, *Alba de Céspedes*, Il Saggiatore, Milano.

ACKNOWLEDGMENTS

I would like to thank Janet Adelman for offering friendship and constructive criticism of this essay.

SAYRE N. GREENFIELD

Quoting Hamlet *in the Early Seventeenth Century*

In the early eighteenth century, the philosophic mind began to find sustenance in *Hamlet*. In 1710, the Earl of Shaftesbury writes that the play of *Hamlet*, "which appears to have most affected *English* Hearts, and has perhaps been oftnest acted of any which have come upon our Stage, is almost one continu'd *Moral*."[1] In 1713, an English translation of André François Boureau-Deslandes's *Reflexions sur les Grands Hommes qui sont morts en Plaisantant* brings *Hamlet* to a discussion of dying "with ease":

> For DEATH in it self has nothing dismal; 'tis like the Moment we fall asleep, Why then, so much ado about so common a Thing?
> I am not unacquainted with the Celebrated Passage of the *English Sophocles,* the Immortal *Shakespear,* who makes his Prince *Hamlet* discourse in this manner about DEATH, and a future State.[2]

It is no innovation that the translator of the philosophical treatise quotes the "Celebrated" soliloquy as a speech on "a future State," for the first anthology of English literary quotations to include the "To be, or not to be" soliloquy, Edward Bysshe's 1702 *The Art of English Poetry,* reprinted the entire passage under the heading of "Futurity."[3]

Modern Philology, Volume 105, Number 3 (February 2008): pp. 510–534. Copyright © 2008 The University of Chicago Press.

151

Such philosophical use of the play, however, is the reaction of a later age. Before William Shakespeare wrote his version of *Hamlet*, Thomas Lodge, in 1596, described "y[e] ghost which cried so miserally at y[e] Theator like an oisterwife, *Hamlet, revenge*."[4] Shakespeare's play, coming a few years later, around 1600, seems designed to counter this clearly histrionic presentation of the Hamlet material with a more cerebral version. Nonetheless, for the first half of the seventeenth century, the response to the new, presumably improved and more thoughtful Shakespearean *Hamlet* was surprisingly close to Lodge's reaction to the earlier drama: a sensationalistic one. While the theme of revenge attracted some attention in the initial fifty years, it was the ghost scenes, the grave scene, and the behavior occasioned by pretended and real madness in the play that were the focal points of popular and literary response. Yet the more serious reapplications of phrases from the play, even in the early period, locate that sensationalism in the very issue that leads the philosophical emergence of the play: the "future state" of the individual, physical and metaphysical. So while both periods appropriate Hamlet in relation to this topic of futurity, in the eighteenth century, the play seems capable of elevating the mind on this theme; in the first half of the seventeenth century, it holds more promise of raising the hairs.

Hamlet leaves a larger trail of early seventeenth-century references than almost any other play by Shakespeare, but this record indicates not an ongoing, full-blown cultural conversation about the play so much as a confluence of the uses to which the play could be put. *The Shakspere Allusion-Book*, whence many passages cited in this article derive, judges that "Of his early plays, those which most struck his contemporaries were *Romeo* and *Richard III*. After 1600 these gave place to *Hamlet* and the Falstaff plays, which, having taken the chief place in popular favour, have held it ever since."[5] The collection notes, however, that the question of *Hamlet*'s renown is actually more complicated: "After this [1605] for some years there is a curious dearth of references to the play itself; and yet no play of Shakspere's (except, perhaps, that Hamlet gives place to Falstaff) gained more attention. The evidences of the play's profound influence are to be seen, not in the ordinary verbal allusions, but in the many imitations and plagiarisings to which it was subjected" (*SAB*, 1:xxxv–xxxvi). What this means is that many of the "borrowings" are not explicit or even implied references to *Hamlet*. The act of quotation itself in early modern England says little about the popularity of particular lines. Clive Hart explains, "Copying and adaptation of other men's phrases and ideas was the normal literary practice in Jacobean England."[6] The "early modern playwrights," says Douglas Bruster, "quoted with remarkable frequency, weaving their plays from many other 'texts.'" The description of their texts as bricolage, which "puts together things already produced (even used) and circulating in a culture,"[7] seems quite appropriate for many writers who frequently employ Shakespeare's words, like John Marston, John Webster, Philip Massinger, and Sir John Suckling. With such cultural practices, the quotations do not prove that the source lines were well known or that they circulated among the literary members of society as what Richard Dawkins calls a "meme," a "replicator" in "the soup of human culture."[8]

However, the play as a whole, and certainly the lead character, were quite famous. The 1604 poem *Daiphantus*, by "An. Sc. Gentleman," indicates the popularity of "Friendly Shake-speares" tragedy when, referring to his own preface, the author says, "Faith it should please all, like Prince *Hamlet*." Much of this popularity links the play to the theme of madness. Indeed, the Gentleman-poet immediately continues, undercutting his praise, "But in sadnesse, then it were to be feared, he would runne mad: Insooth I will not be moone-sicke, to please: nor out of my wits though I displeased all."[9] There seems to be a hint in this comment that the displaying of a madman is an easy but effective trick to court popularity, a trick in which the poet himself will not indulge—although he promptly does. *Daiphantus* additionally makes two other references to Hamlet's madness, for instance by describing the insane lover: "his shirt he onely weares, / Much like mad-*Hamlet*" (sig. E4v).

Thomas Dekker has a more interesting connection of Hamlet to madness in his 1608 *Lanthorne and Candle-light*, where the allusion invokes an ill-advised desire to expose the truth. This work contains the following passage concerning gypsy women stealing and killing farm animals:

> The Stage is some large Heath, or a Firre-bush Common, far from any houses; Upon which casting them-selues into a Ring, they inclose the Murderers, till the Massacre be finished. If any passenger come by, and wondring to see such a coniuring circle kept by Hel-houndes, demaund what spirits they raise ther? one of the Murderers steps to him poysons him with sweete wordes and shifts him off, with this lye, that one of the women is falne in labour. But if any mad *Hamlet* hearing this, smell villanie, and rush in by violence to see what the tawny Diuels are dooing; then they excuse the fact. (Sig. G3v; noted in *SAB*, 1:156)

Dekker picks up other aspects of Hamlet's character here, such as ineffectual truth-seeking, but he expects his audience to recognize the appropriateness of the label "mad *Hamlet*."

Although the character of Hamlet thus seems to have circulated as cultural currency on the basis of his supposed madness, specific lines connected with Hamlet's (pretense of) insanity are rare in the surviving record. The most notable insanity allusion suggesting some sort of audience recognition points to Ophelia and comes soon after the play's release in print. In *Eastward*

Ho (1605), Ophelia's mad song about her father is sung in a mangled form by young Girtred (Gertrude), who is neither insane like Ophelia nor a queen like Hamlet's mother (her possible namesake). She is merely an aspiring gold-smith's daughter, now married to a knight and annoyed at her father:

> *His head as white as milke, All flaxen was his haire:*
> *But now he is dead, And laid in his Bed,*
> *And neuer will come againe. God be at your labour.*
>   (Sig. D2r; noted in *SAB*, 1:152)

The echo of Ophelia's "And will he not come againe" song is unmistakable: "His beard as white as snowe: / All flaxen was his pole, / He is dead, he is gone" (first quarto, lines 1712–1714).[10] Given how little sense this song makes in its new comic context, beyond being a jibe at Gertrude's very-much-alive father, it seems thrown into *Eastward Ho* as a cheap joke, one that depends on the listeners' recognition of the song. Another cheap joke, completely unnecessary to the action, is the creation of a footman named Hamlet in the play, present apparently only to occasion the line, "Sfoote *Hamlet;* are you madde?" (sig. D1r).[11]

Eastward Ho was in the immediate wake of *Hamlet*'s early success on the stage and so could use it as the basis for a blatant allusion. When John Webster in *The White Devil* (published 1612)[12] converts Ophelia's mad scene into Cornelia's, there seems to be no need to create a recognizable parody:

> This rosemarie is wither'd, pray get fresh;
> I would haue these herbes grow vp in his graue
> When I am dead and rotten. . . .
>
>   . . .
>
> There's Rosemarie for you, and Rue for you,
> Hearts-ease for you. I pray make much of it.
> I haue left more for my selfe.
>   (Sigs. L1r–L1v; noted in *SAB*, 1:116)

Probably the years between *Eastward Ho* and *The White Devil* diminished the capacity for recognition in the imagined audiences, and what must be a joke in the first instance might well be simply recirculation in the second. However, making the distinction between a clever allusion and a more neutral recirculation in Webster's case suggests a unity in the audience that probably never existed. Webster himself insists in his printed preface that the original performance lacked "a full and understanding Auditory" (sig. A2r). Whether he was expecting some elite section of the audience to see Ophelia under Cornelia cannot be determined. Some may have understood the echo, most not; but the scene does not depend on that recognition. In any case, whether Shakespeare's depiction of Ophelia's insanity was exploited overtly or subtly, comically or seriously, the power of that "document in madnesse" attracted the emulation of other authors and, in *Eastward Ho*, relied on popular recognition of the scene.

The reproducibility of Ophelia's mad scenes lodges not only in such precise details as hair and flowers, but in her contemplation of death or, rather, her contemplation of the earthly future after death. Such a concern reappears as the "never will come again" in *Eastward Ho*, and as the flowers growing on the grave versus the rottenness of a corpse in the passage from Webster. Concern about the physical state beyond life also drew early seventeenth-century writers toward the beginning of act 5 and Hamlet's contemplation of the skulls. The image is hardly a new one, but Shakespeare's words, as David Frost notes, become a particular source for subsequent memento mori scenes.[13] "Now get you," says Hamlet to the skull of Yorick, "to my Ladies table, & tell her, let her paint an inch thicke, to this fauour she must come, make her laugh at that" (second quarto, 5.1.193–195). This passage apparently inspired imitation soon after *Hamlet*'s release. Dekker and Middleton's *The Honest Whore, Part 1* (1604) has a scene that places a skull upon a table next to the portrait of a lady, though it is the painting rather than the skull that inspires comments such as "fond women loue to buy / Adulterate complexion: here 'tis read, / False coulours last after the true be dead" (sig. G1r). John Reynolds, in his poem *Dolarnys Primerose* (published 1606),[14] has a hermit holding a skull, who comments on ladies' decorations:

> And might it not, a Lady somtimes ioye,
> T'haue deckt, and trim'd, this now rainbeaten face,
> With many a trick, and new-found pleasing toye?
> Which if that now, she did behold her case.
> > Although on earth, she were for to remaine,
> > She would not paint, nor trimme it vp againe.
> > > > > (Sig. E1r; noted in *SAB*, 1:160–161)

Neither of those passages have clear verbal echoes of *Hamlet*, though the staged situations are similar enough to suggest possible Shakespearean derivation.

At a slightly greater temporal remove from the play one can find a sharper echo near the end of *"A memento for mortalitie*. Taken from the view of Sepulchers of so many Kings and Nobles, as lye interred in the Abbey of Westminster," appearing in the 1619 *A Helpe to Discourse*, by W. B. and E. P., a miscellany *"of wittie, Philosophicall and Astronomicall Questions and Answers"*:

Bid her paint till day of doome,
To this fauour she must come.

(Sig. I11r)[15]

Whether this "Memento" is "philosophicall" or merely "wittie," is debatable, but the moralistic commonplace reiterated throughout the poem adopts, in this couplet, the image and language of *Hamlet*.[16]

Also imitated were the slightly earlier lines of skull study, those where Hamlet remarks on the remains of men of worldly shrewdness and knowledge:

Why, mai't not be the scull of some Lawyer?
Me thinkes he should indite that fellow
Of an action of Batterie, for knocking
Him about the pate with's shouel: now where is your
Quirkes and quillets now, your vouchers and
Double vouchers, your leases and free-holde,
And tenements?

(First quarto, lines 1947–1953)[17]

The Honest Whore follows its remarks upon ladies' face-painting with commentary upon a skull itself. "Perhaps this shrewd pate was mine enemies; / Las! say it were: I need not feare him now" (sig. G1r; noted in *SAB*, 1:65). More certainly under Shakespeare's influence, Reynolds's hermit follows his hypothetical dead lady with:

Why might not this, haue beene some lawiers pate,
The which sometimes, brib'd, brawl'd, and tooke a fee,
And lawe exacted, to the highest rate?
Why might not this, be such a one as he?
    Your quirks, and quillets, now sir where be they,
    Now he is mute, and not a word can say.

(Sig. E1r)

Though it is an idiomatic expression that runs at least from John Lyly's *Euphues* (1578) to Butler's *Hudibras* (1677), "quirks and quillets" applied in a context similar to that in Q1 *Hamlet*, strongly suggests that text as Reynolds's source.[18]

Terms and images from Shakespeare's version of skull contemplation also reappear in Thomas Randolph's *The Jealous Lovers* (Cambridge, 1632),[19] where Asotus speaks to a poet's skull:

Where be thy querks and tricks? show me again
The strange conundrums of thy frisking brain,
Thou Poets skull, and say, What's rime to chimney?

and, a little later, a Sexton says,

It had been a mighty favour once, to have kiss'd these lips that
grin so. . . .
Paint Ladies while you live, and plaister fair,
But when the house is fallne 'tis past repair.

(Sigs. H2v–H3r)

Randolph's passage does not presume audience knowledge of *Hamlet*'s grave
scene, but the ideas are similar, and "querks," "tricks," "favour" (in a different
sense), "paint," and "fallne" are all traceable to that source. And Randolph's
next scene has the Sexton discuss grave robbing in these terms:

Look here: This is a Lawyers skull. There was a tongue in't once, a
damnable eloquent tongue, that would almost have perswaded any
man to the gallows. This was a turbulent busie fellow, till death gave
him his *Quietus est*. And yet I ventured to rob him of his gown. . . .
Now a man may clappe you o'th' coxcombe with his spade, and
never stand in fear of an action of batterie. . . . Come, we must
strip you Gallants, the worms care not for having the dishes serv'd
up to their table cover'd. (Sigs. H3v–H4r)[20]

Randolph's lines certainly derive from Shakespeare, but they do not necessarily suggest any widespread cultural familiarity with *Hamlet*. What they
do suggest is that *Hamlet*'s graveside humor found a receptive audience and
encouraged imitation.

Focusing upon the remains of the body is only one way of looking beyond the moment of death. *Hamlet* also provides a more metaphysical after-
death experience in the ghost of Hamlet's father. These episodes can allow,
in their imitations, either more spirituality or more histrionics. These scenes
are closest to what little we know of the *Ur-Hamlet* (see the quotation from
Thomas Lodge), but the melodramatic wildness of Hamlet's response to the
ghost is what wins the attention of subsequent authors.

As with *Eastward Ho*'s comic twist on Ophelia's madness, some of the earliest references to the ghost in *Hamlet* are parodic. Francis Beaumont's *The Woman
Hater* (first played 1606, published 1607) starts off parodying the even-more-
recent *Measure for Measure*, for the prologue states, "A Duke there is, and the

Scene lyes in Italy, as those two thinges lightly wee neuer misse" (sigs. A2r–A2v), and there is a character called Lucio, as well, who says, in the opening scene, "I thinke your grace intendes to walke the publique streetes disguised, to see the streetes disorders" (sig. A3v). In the second act, however, glances at *Hamlet* start to accumulate. One finds an exchange where the Count is giving his sister sexual advice, as Laertes does to Ophelia, and a passage where Lazarello tries to speak in courtly manner to the Duke in verse modeled on the opening of *The Mousetrap:*

> Full eight and twenty seuerall Almanackes
> Hath been compyled, all for seuerall yeares,
>
> . . .
>
> And eight and twenty times hath Phoebus carre
> Runne out his yearely course since.
>
> (Sig. D1r)

Then comes a line obviously making fun of *Hamlet*'s histrionics. Lazarello, who is an epicure hunting an exotic fish's head and is being sent from one nobleman to another, receives bad news about his much-anticipated dish:

> *Laza[rello]* . . . speake I am bound to heare.
> *Count.*　　　　　　So art thou to reuenge, when thou shalt heare
> the fish head is gone, and we know not whither.
>
> (Sig. D2r; noted in *SAB*, 1:180)

The lines follow word for word those of the second quarto (the lines are absent from the first):

> *Ham.*　　　　　　Speake, I am bound to heare.
> *Ghost.*　　　　So art thou to reuenge, when thou shalt heare.
>
> (1.5.6–7)

Of course, the addition of the fish head provides the bathos, and the lines can serve no purpose but to parody Shakespeare's play. This is a rare instance where another seventeenth-century writer plays with the theme of revenge in Shakespeare's *Hamlet,* but audience's recent memories of the ghost scene allow Beaumont his incongruous comic effect.

　　An even earlier appropriation of lines from the scene comes in John Marston's *The Malcontent* (1602-1604) and again relies on the humor of recognition, in this case particularly the recall of Hamlet's wilder and more whirling words. The hero, Malevole, greets the chief villain of the play, Mendoza, with "*Illo, ho ho ho,* art there, old true peny, Where hast thou spent thy selfe this morning?" (sig. E2v; noted in *SAB*, 1:129–131).[21] Neither the halloo nor the appellation "old true peny" are exclusive to *Hamlet*,[22] but the possibility of allusion is strengthened by the fact that Malevole was acted by Richard Burbage, who would have uttered those phrases very recently in *Hamlet*.[23] The point of the allusion is less easily defined, beyond turning the phrase "true peny" into a pun on "spent," highlighting Mendoza's sexual appetite. Bernard Harris finds Marston's play full of "deliberately disjunctive contrivances,"[21] So, if we are to take these as overt references to *Hamlet*, like those in *Eastward Ho*, perhaps Marston here momentarily switches from concerns with plot to a parody of revenge tragedy, a form at which *The Malcontent* seems to aim but which it ultimately avoids. On closer inspection, the scene is full of *Hamlet*. A few lines on, Mendoza says, "*Maleuole*, thou art an arrant knaue" (sig. E2v), and Malevole later says the two of them will agree "As Lent and Fishmongers, come *a cap a pe*, how informe?" (sig. E3r). Certainly, there are parallels in position and personality between Malevole and Hamlet, so Marston, through such allusions to madness and the ghost, may mock his apparent and ultimately subverted genre of revenge tragedy. One can imagine the initial "*Illo, ho ho ho*, art there, old true peny" spoken with a wink and a nod as Burbage adopts his pose from *Hamlet*. As Thomas Lodge poked fun at the overdone quality of the pre-Shakespearean *Hamlet*, Marston may similarly be mocking Shakespeare's version.[25]

Most reuses of the major ghost scene in *Hamlet* are not comic but collectively reveal how the scene was mined for phrases by other authors, even when the possibilities of parody would have receded after the initial seasons of performance (which probably were only a few).[26] In *A Mad World, my Masters* (written ca. 1605; published 1608), Thomas Middleton has "Shield me you ministers of faith and grace" at the entrance of a spirit (this a succubus) (sig. F2r; noted in *SAB*, 1:142), recalling "Angels and Ministers of grace defend vs" (first quarto, line 428). Casual uses of phrases from the major ghost scene continue to appear in later decades. In John Kirke's *The Seven Champions of Christendome* (1638), at the summoning of ghosts, we find, "Defend me all you ministers of grace," this with an "Illo ho, ho Illo" earlier in the scene (sigs. C1r and B2v). Henry Glapthorne's play *The Lady Mother* (1635) refers to "the glowewormes vneffectuall fire,"[27] and Nathanael Richards's "The Jesuite," from *The Celestiall Publican* (1630), contains "He that dares awe his Countrey, King and State, / Smile, and yet be a villaine, all men hate" (sig. H7v).[28] Although these instances are convincing enough as Shakespearean echoes, none shows an expectation that the audience will identify the lines as allusions.

In an equally large part, however, the 1623–1640 ghost-scene borrowings take Shakespeare's *Hamlet* as an established literary source for explicit reference. John Gee, in *New Shreds of the old Snare* (1624), using the idea of exposing Catholic miracles by linking them with stagecraft,[29] identifies "the

Iesuites [as] being or having *Actors* of such dexteritie" that they might as well set up their own theater company. Nonetheless, "Representations and Apparitions from the dead might be seene farre cheaper at other Play-houses. As for example, the *Ghost in Hamblet, Don Andreas Ghost in Hieronimo*. As for flashes of light, we might see very cheape in the Comedie of *Piramus* and *Thisbe*, where one comes in with a Lanthorne and Acts *Mooneshine*" (sigs. D2r, D3v; noted in *SAB*, 1:327). These plays, all between twenty-four and thirty-five years old, contain classic examples of stage effects. Again taking Shakespeare's play as an established reference point come two passages that refer to the same phrase from the ghost scene: *"Hic & vbique"* (1.5.156). The words occur, naturally enough, in Latin passages predating *Hamlet*, such as in Gabriel Harvey's letter to Spenser in *Three Proper, and wittie, familiar Letters*, 1580 (sig. E2r). They also exist in otherwise English sentences, for example in the dedication to Thomas Nash's *Lenten Stuffe* (159.9): "To his worthie good patron, Lustie Humfrey . . . King of the Tobacconists *hic & vbique*" (sig. A2r).[30] But two later works associate the phrase or idea with Shakespeare's play in particular. In 1623, Edward Sutton's *Anthropophagus: or, a Caution for the Credulous*, speaks of flatterers: "they are like *Hamlets ghost, hic & vbique*, here and there, and euery where, for their owne occasion" (sig. B4v; noted in *SAB*, 1:326). Eight years later, Wye Saltonstall's *Picturae Loquentes* (1631) describes a chamberlain: "Hee's as nimble as *Hamlets* ghost heere and everywhere" (sig. E4r; noted in *SAB*, 1:351). These two references require in their fit readers some fairly specific familiarity with the scene, and they demonstrate how *Hamlet* could, even in the early seventeenth century, appropriate preexisting phrases as its own. The play has developed into a cultural site for the supernatural.

Many of the borrowings spring from the immediate description of or reaction to the ghost. While the borrowings do not necessarily link the ghostly references to a future life after death, the most commonly quoted line from the scene does concern itself with the ability to look into the future. Of all the borrowed phrases from *Hamlet* in the seventeenth century, the words the hero utters upon learning that his uncle is the murderer of his father, "O my Propheticke soule" (1.5.41), had the greatest cultural success. Whether readers or listeners identified it as a phrase from *Hamlet* is another matter. The central word pair reappears, after all, in Shakespeare's own sonnet 107:

Not mine own feares, nor the prophetick soule,
Of the wide world, dreaming on things to come,
Can yet the lease of my true loue controule,
Supposde as forfeit to a confin'd doome.
The mortall Moone hath her eclipse indur'de.
                                   (1609 ed., sonnet 107, lines 1–5)[31]

Assuming that the reference of the fifth line is to Queen Elizabeth's death, dating the sonnet to 1603 or soon after, Shakespeare, nervous about political alterations underway with the regime change, would be reusing the essence of his own phrase from *Hamlet*. But Shakespeare was not the first to find his expression worth repeating. Thomas Dekker and John Webster, in *The Famous History of Sir Thomas Wyat* (staged 1602, published 1607) place "O propheticke soule" in the mouth of Guil[d]ford Dudley, Lady Jane Grey's husband, (sig. A4r; noted in *SAB*, 1:183). The words may have been picked up from an oral performance of Shakespeare's play (all early texts of *Hamlet* have the phrase), but there is no call for audience recognition of the words here.[32]

However, these two duplications of the phrase are succeeded by at least twenty-eight other uses of it by about 1650, and at least thirteen more in the second half of the century, as searches in Chadwyck-Healey's EEBO and LION databases reveal. A survey of these sources using the phrase "prophet* soul*" (the * catches variations in endings) brings up no instances before *Hamlet*, but many afterwards, and mainly in the drama. The next datable instance after the *Wyat* reference is John Hind's *Eliosto Libidinoso* (1606): "his propheticke soule layd downe before him, both the enormitie of the fact, and the condigne punishment" (sig. E2v). Six of the later 1619–1650 references revert to a more definitively Hamletian form, "O my prophetic soul," from Thomas Goffe's circa 1618 *Tragedy of Orestes* to Jasper Mayne's 1648 *The Amorous Warre*. These more exact echoes lead one to suspect that those authors are consciously quoting Shakespeare. Whether they expected audience recognition is doubtful, but the phrase has become literarily well established.

The record for that phrase—present in the first decade; quoted by only one author in the second; and coming back strongly, sometimes in a more consciously quoted way, in the third through fifth decades—may be suggestive of a larger pattern. Were we not prejudiced by our modern sense of Hamlet's importance, we might not have expected the play to achieve cultural prominence quickly. The play crossed the stage of one acting company for perhaps only a few years; the casual use of scraps from it apparently diminishes after 1611 for about a decade. Staged performance and quarto publication are one sort of cultural presence; publication in a folio edition is another. The folio of 1623 may have had an effect on the cultural manifestations of *Hamlet* in the new kinds of references to the ghost scene that emerge. The play's lines, as we have seen, have become a literary resource. As to why "O my Propheticke soule" seemed so especially appropriable, Shakespeare perhaps suggests the reason in sonnet 107: the soul of the world in this period, or at least of the English culture that Shakespeare knew, was "dreaming, on things to come," fixated on fantasies or hopes or nightmares of the future. Such a fascination might explain why madness or sanity that contemplates the state of being dead, why scenes with ghosts that come back to hint at "secrets" of the after-life, and why a sudden proclamation of heretofore unknown prophetic power might appear in the record again and again.

Surely, if such a cultural enthrallment were the case, one would think that the now most famous embodiment of these concerns in *Hamlet*, the "To be, or not to be" soliloquy, would have been repeatedly plundered. But it was not. Yet this relative lack of reference may speak not to a lack of interest in the theme but to the unhistrionic nature of this soliloquy. A modern actor in the role, David Rintoul, comments "I grew to love playing the cooler, more rational 'To be' so soon after the emotional 'O, what a rogue'" soliloquy, and Mary Z. Maher, interviewing Rintoul, places "To be or not to be" among the "reflective soliloquies."[33] The subject matter was in accord with the cultural fascinations of the early seventeenth century, but writers of this period went to Shakespeare for dramatics, not philosophy.

Throughout the entire century, that soliloquy was not "celebrated" and certainly not for its opening line. Searches through the EEBO database for "to be or not to be" and "that is the question" reveal how common these phrases were, but they were not yet culturally Shakespeare's. They are both non-Shakespearean and pre-Shakespearean. A search for "to be or not to be," even without spelling variations, produces fifty-three texts, while "that is the question" exposes 118 records in the sixteenth and seventeenth centuries.[34] The two halves of the line are idioms common in theological, philosophi-cal, and legal treatises, dating back, in both cases, to well before *Hamlet*. We can see that Shakespeare composed his now most memorable line out of abstract or space-filling idioms from nonliterary texts: intellectual, academic, and controversial.

The first idiom, in the form "to be or nat to be," appears as early as Thomas Usk's *The Testament of Love* from 1384–1387 (in *The Workes of Gef-fray Chaucer* [1532], sigs. Ppp6r and Qqq5v). A fairly typical use is found in William Perkins's *A Discourse of Conscience; Wherein is Set Downe the Nature, Properties, and Differences Thereof* (Cambridge, 1596): "Conscience is distin-guished from all other gifts of the minde, as intelligence, opinion, science, faith, prudence. Intelligence simply conceiues a thing to be or not to be: sci-ence iudgeth it to be certen and sure" (sig. A2v). A legal example comes from Abraham Fraunce, *The Lawiers Logike exemplifying the Praecepts of Logike by the Practise of the Common Lawe* (1588): "An Axiome or proposition is a dis-position of one argument with an other, whereby wée iudge a thing to bée, or not to bée" (sig. Aa3v). From 1601 we find John Deacon's and John Walker's confutation of an exorcist, *A Summarie Ansvvere to al the Material Points in any of Master Darel his Bookes*, which has the following: "For, would you not (in good sooth) imagine vs all to be out of our *wits:* if you could make vs beleeue, that the *maister diuell* himselfe with all his adherents, were able to make a thing *essentiallie existing in nature,* eyther *to be,* or *not to be,* whe~ it pleaseth himselfe?" (sig. D8r). And the uses of the phrase continue through-out the seventeenth century. Sometimes it arises out of mere grammatical convenience, as in John Dryden's "'tis free for every man to write, or not to write, in verse, as he judges it to be, or not to be his Tallent."[35] Sometimes the phrase comes close to the philosophical meaning it has in the soliloquy, as in John Norris's *An Idea of Happiness, in a Letter to a Friend: Enquiring Wherein the Greatest Happiness attainable by Man in this Life does consist* (1683):

> For if the Good and the Evil be equal-balanc'd, it must needs be indifferent to that man either to be or not to be, there being not the least *Grain* of good to determine his Choice: So that he can no more be said to be happy in that Condition, than he could before he was born. And much less, if the Evil exceeds the Good. . . . And when 'tis once come to this (whatever some Mens *Metaphysicks* may perswade them) I am very well satisfied, that 'tis better not to be than to be. (Sigs. A2v–A3r)

Even at that late date in the century, it needed no prince come from Den-mark to produce that philosophical reflection.

One does encounter "to be or not to be" in more literary contexts throughout the seventeenth century, but only one of these clearly derives from *Hamlet*. William Hemings's *Jewes Tragedy* (possibly as early as 1624–1628 but published 1662) has Eleazer, contemplating patricide, begin a soliloquy:

> To be, or not to be, I there's the doubt,
> For to be Sovereign by unlawful means,
> Is but to be a slave to base desire,
> And where's my honour then?
>
> (Sig. E1r; noted in *SAB*, 2:121)

Hemings sounds most Shakespearean if one knows the first quarto text of the soliloquy, which begins "To be, nor not to be, I there's the point" (836). It helps if one is aware that the author is the son of Shakespeare's co-actor and editor John Heminge,[36] and if one notices that the play also echoes *Henry IV, Part 1,* and *Much Ado About Nothing.* Joseph Quincy Adams Jr. points out numerous Shakespearean parallels in Flemings's circa 1637 *The Fatall Contract* (published 1653). Besides a character named Aphelia, there are lines reminiscent of *Othello, Romeo and Juliet, King Lear, Richard III, Richard II, Coriolanus, As You Like It, Julius Caesar,* and *Twelfth Night,* and thirty-two passages seemingly derived from *Hamlet.* Adams (later seconded by David Frost) asserts that the Shakespearean influence came from "Heminge's closet study of Shakespeare's collected works as issued in the First Folio," since Hemings echoes plays never printed in quarto.[37] They may be right, and it may be simple coincidence that Hemings took a phrase ("I there's the _____") from nine lines later in the folio version to match with the opening phrase, but Hemings's special connections to the play may have placed a version of the first quarto in his hands.

Other literary instances of the opening phrase do not seem Shakespearean when one is acquainted with the longer tradition of its use. George Wither, in *Wither's Motto Nec habeo, nec Careo, nec Curo* (1621), writes in a confession of his own weakness, "*I haue not* of my selfe the powre, or grace, / To be, or not to be; one minute-space" (sig. A8r). This might sound Hamlet-like in its sense of uncertainty, but as the poem develops, it becomes clear that the real subject here is closer to that of some religious treatises than it is to Shakespeare's play. Thomas Heywood, a fellow playwright, seems likely to adopt phrases from Shakespeare, but his use of this phrase occurs in *The Hierarchie of the blessed Angells* (1635). In a section of book I called *The Seraphim*, Heywood writes about the Atheist: "Tell me, (ô thou of Mankind most accurst) / Whether to be, or not to be, was first?" (sig. A6r). Again, no evidence of influence from *Hamlet* shines through, and the long tradition of the idiom in religious and philosophical discourse gives us a more likely alternative source.[38]

As to the second half of the soliloquy's opening line, the instances of "that is the question" in EEBO date as early as 1572–1573 in John Whitgift's *An ansvvere to a certen Libel intituled, An admonition to the Parliament:* "you should rather haue proued, that women may not in time of necessitie minister baptisme, for that is the question, and not the other" (sig. Cc2r). As with the first phrase, the idiom appears consistently amid theological and legal disputations, the sort of texts to which one might much more reasonably go for one's religious, philosophical, and legal needs than to a play. Both idioms are well established before *Hamlet*, though Shakespeare's combination of them is unprecedented—and unechoed in the seventeenth century. It is clear that, in using the phrases for an especially theological and philosophical speech in the play, Shakespeare was applying them within their normal contexts and signaling the nature of this particular soliloquy.

The initial performance of *Hamlet* at the turn of the century had no visible influence on the use of the two idioms, and the publications of the play in the seventeenth century had no immediate effect on uses of the phrases in print. However, the soliloquy beginning with these phrases is not so free from rhetorical flourishes that it was completely ignored by Shakespeare's immediate literary successors. *The Shakspere Allusion-Book* gives Beaumont's and Fletcher's *The Scornful Ladie* (performed ca. 1610–1611, published 1616) as an instance of borrowing from Hamlet's "To dye to sleepe, / To sleepe, per-chance to Dreame" (3.1.63–64). The play has one Sir Roger wittily remark, "Haue patience Sir, vntill our fellowe *Nicholas* bee deceast, that is, a sleepe: for so the word is taken; to sleepe to die, to die to sleepe: a very Figure Sir" (sig. C4r; noted in *SAB,* 1:229). The joke here improves if the audience un-derstands that this figure should identify death with sleep, not the other way around. Sir Roger reverses the sense, calls falling asleep dying, and Sir Roger explicitly identifies the phrase as a "figure" taken from elsewhere. The phrase "to die, to sleep" appears twice in Hamlet's soliloquy, and not only is the brief echo precise, but the four-word phrase appears nowhere in a search through the EEBO database except in *Hamlet* and in *The Scornful Ladie.* The rhetori-cal figure in this form does not appear to be a commonplace, which suggests that Beaumont's source is indeed Shakespeare.[39]

Philip Massinger, a decade and a half on, uses the same comparison more seriously in *The Roman Actor* (1626, published 1629), apparently taking the words from a later line in the soliloquy, "For in that sleepe of death, what dreames may come" (3.1.65). Massinger has "Tremble to thinke how terrible the dreame is / After this sleepe of death" (sig. F2v; noted in *SAB,* 1:302). A search through the EEBO database for "Sleep* of death:" however, receives over one hundred hits in the sixteenth and seventeenth centuries, dating back to 1578. The widespread idiom even appears in Psalm 13, verse 3, in the King James Version of the Bible.[40] One must rely on the reference to a dream and on the sense of dread to see Massinger's line as Shakespearean. Massinger also uses the figure in *The Maid of Honour* (1621–1622, published 1632), referring to "the horrid dreame / To be suffer'd in the other world" (sig. E3r; noted in *SAB,* 1:359). These apparently Shakespearean sleep-and-death allusions may or may not be such, though Massinger's instances share considerable meaning with the phrases as employed in Hamlet's soliloquy.

Caution should attend pronouncements of Shakespearean influence when those identifications derive from brief phrases or single words. The EEBO and LION databases can expose cases of apparent borrowing as being more probably mutual participation by Shakespeare and other writers in the same idiom. An example would be the passage from Thomas Randolph's *The Jealous Lovers* cited earlier. While the influence of *Hamlet*'s later skull scene on Randolph is clear, Randolph's phrase, "death gave him his *Quietus est*" might seem a borrowing from "To be, or not to be." Yet recourse to EEBO calls that impression into question. A simple search for "quietus," pre-1600, shows that, even before *Hamlet,* half the vernacular uses of *"quietus"* or *"quietus est"* as the object of any verb exhibit the pattern that Randolph follows in making the term the object of the particular verb "to give." Randolph is primarily echoing an established idiom and not Shakespeare's "he may his full *Quietus* make."

Of course, Randolph may have had the standard idiomatic formulation called into his mind by the soliloquy, but that is not demonstrable.

Two other instances in the first half of the seventeenth century, however, show the language of Hamlet's soliloquy proving irresistible on the topic of futurity. Robert Dent describes "A Short and necessary Treatise, entituled: Deaths welcome" by Samuel Garey, bound in a volume called *Two Treatises* (1605), which contains this passage: "VVho would endure the mockes and scornes of the world . . . vnlesse they hoped, that after the vessel of theyr bodies were seasoned in the wombe of the earth, they should arriue at that blessed vndiscouered country, where is no mediocritie of ioy, no end of pleasure" (sig. A3v).[41] Dent is cautious in relating this to the first quarto, although the first quarto is much more upbeat than the second about the possibilities in the afterlife; Q1 refers to:

> The vndiscouered country, at whose sight
> The happy smile, and the accursed damn'd.
> But for this, the ioyfull hope of this,
> Whol'd beare the scornes and flattery of the world.
>
> (Lines 842–845)

A few lines further on, the first quarto invokes the "hope of something after death" (853), instead of the later texts' "dread of something after death" (3.1.77). The first quarto also has "the scornes and flattery of the world" not "the Whips and Scornes of time."[42] The influence of Q1 on Garey shines through plainly.

The other echo of this part of the soliloquy, one listed in *The Shakspere Allusion Book,* also considers the afterlife and the attitude of the living to it. *The London Post,* January 14, 1644/1645, reported on Archbishop Laud's execution: "although he came with confidence to the Scaffold, atnd [*sic*] the blood wrought lively in his cheeke, yet when he did lye down upon the block, he trembled every ioint of him, the sence of somthing after death, and the undiscovered Country, unto which his soul was wandring, startling his resolution, and possessing every part of him with an universall Palsey of feare" (sig. T1v; noted in *SAB*, 1:488). The phrase "something after death" predates *Hamlet* in John King's *Lectures upon Jonas delivered at Yorke In the year of our Lorde 1594* (printed in Oxford, 1597): "because they feare not death, they shoulde feare somethinge after death" (sig. M7r); nonetheless, the conjunction in the *London Post* of this phrase with a metaphorical "undiscovered Country" confirms *Hamlet*'s Q2 or Folio soliloquy as the source. The tenors of Garey's and the *Post*'s appropriations of the speech oppose each other, one hopeful and one horrified, as they imitate different texts of the soliloquy, but both of the appropriations concentrate upon the mind's contemplation of the afterlife—not in theoretical but in emotional ways.

Gabriel Harvey judged that Shakespeare's "tragedie of Hamlet, Prince of Denmarke, [and *The Rape of Lucrece*] haue it in them, to please the wiser sort,"[43] but the record on *Hamlet* bears out that prophecy in complicated ways. *Hamlet* was much admired by other writers in the first half of the seventeenth century—if theft is admiration—yet those who borrowed from the play did not always use the material reverently. In the first decade or so of the play's life, allusions more often are humorous, sometimes relying upon a public awareness of Shakespeare's scenes, characters, and lines. If the references diminish after 1611 and return more strongly in the 1620s, 1630s, and 1640s, that may be the effect of either the folio publication or of temporal distance. This later lack of theatrical familiarity may also account for the more serious nature of the references: few would get the theatrical jokes, and, besides, the play had become literature. The writers who first adapted lines from the play to serious concerns were struck by the play's language of emotional response to death and to the supernatural. When these stimuli tipped their characters into real or counterfeit lunacy, the *Hamlet* passages became all the more attractive. Even as these writers drew upon the more histrionic scenes, however, they were often inspired to visions of the individual's postmortem future, the very theme that would lead to the philosophical conception of the play in the eighteenth century. The early seventeenth century, however, was more attuned to the play's power to harrow up the soul and freeze the blood.

Notes

1. Anthony Ashley Cooper, Earl of Shaftesbury, "Soliloquy: or Advice to an Author," in *Characteristicks of Men, Manners, Opinions, Times* (1711), 1:275–276, noted as "Printed first" in 1710. The place of publication for sixteenth-, seventeenth-, and eighteenth-century texts cited throughout this article is London unless otherwise noted.

2. André François Boureau-Deslandes, *A Philological Essay: or, Reflections on the Death of Free-Thinkers* (1713), 59. The translator is merely noted as "Mr. B——." In the French original from 1712, a quotation from Clément Marot appears at the same spot.

3. Bysshe's text has a second edition in 1705, a third in 1708, a fourth in 1710, and many later editions.

4. Thomas Lodge, *Wits Miserie, and the World's Madness* (1596), sig. H4v.

5. John Munro, ed., *The Shakspere Allusion-Book: A Collection of Allusions to Shakspere from 1591 to 1700* (originally compiled by C. M. Ingleby, L. Toulmin Smith, and F. J. Furnivall), 2 vols. (London: Chatto and Windus, 1909); reissued with a preface by Edmund Chambers (London: Oxford University Press, 1909), 1:xxxv. Hereafter *SAB*, with references in the text. Echoes of *Romeo and Juliet* often concentrate on fine metaphoric passages, but among the histrionic lines from *Richard III* and the plays involving Falstaff, *Richard III*'s final call for a horse achieved early

prominence. John Marston was especially enamored of the cry, starting Satyre 7 of his 1598 *Scourge of Villanie* with a cynic despairingly calling aloud, "A Man, a man, a kingdome for a man" (sig. F1v; noted in *SAB*, 1:54). Among other of his allusions to the phrase, Marston has a character in his 1607 *What You Will* declare, "A horse, a horse, my kingdom for a horse, / Looke the[e] I speake play scrappes" (sigs. C1r–C1v; noted in *SAB*, 1:176). It is clear that Marston expects the line to be recognized. The same "play scrap" appears in other writers, significantly in a poem from between 1618 and 1621 by Richard Corbet, Bishop of Oxford and Norwich, where Corbet tells a tale of a host showing him around the battlefield sites, who confuses the historical royal figure with the actor: "For when he would have said, King *Richard* dy'd, / And call'd a Horse, a Horse, he *Burbage* cry'd" ("Iter Boreale," in *Certain Elegant Poems, written by Dr. Corbet* [1647], sig. B6v; noted and dated in *SAB*, 1:271). Among the many references to Falstaff, his verbal defense of his valor in *1 Henry IV* inspired many allusions. As early as 1598, Francis Meres (in praise of Michael Drayton), comments on "these declining and corrupt times, when there is nothing but rogery in villanous man" (*Palladis Tamia*, sig. Oo1v; noted in *SAB*, 1:49). The same phrase persists referentially in 1634 when James Shirley writes, "Falstaffe I will beleeve thee, / Thee is noe faith in vilanous man" (*The Example* [1637], sig. C4v; noted in *SAB*, 1:391). An instance demonstrating how thoroughly familiar Falstaff and his lines were in the civil war period appears in a poem by Henry Bold from 1648: "On *Oxford* Visitors, setting up their Commissions on the Colledge Gates, &c":

> Why what's the matter *Friends*? I hope that all's safe!
> D'ye run away, b'*instinct*, like Sir *John Falstaffe*,
> And *stare*, and *huffe*, and *puff*, as if y'had been
> Mauld, by th'*unluckie Rogues* in *Kendall Green*;
> The *Women*, in such *tirrits*, and *frights* do goe,
> Dame *Quickly*, near fear'd *swagg'ring Pistol*, so.

This reference would seem to be from memory, as the "rogues" are originally in buckram and the "misbegotten knaves" are the ones in Kendal green (in *Poems Lyrique, Macaronique, Heroique, &c.* [1664], sig. M2v; noted in John Munro, "More Shakspere Allusions," *Modern Philology* 13 [1916]: 150).

6. Clive Hart, ed., introduction to *The White Devil*, by John Webster (Berkeley: University of California Press, 1970), 7.

7. Douglas Bruster, *Quoting Shakespeare: Form and Culture in Early Modern Drama* (Lincoln: University of Nebraska Press, 2000), 25, 22–23.

8. Richard Dawkins, *The Selfish Gene*, 2nd ed. (Oxford University Press, 1989), 192.

9. *Diaphantus* (1604), sig. A2r; noted in *SAB*, 1:133. The poem is often attributed to Anthony Scoloker, as it is in *SAB*, but Josephine A. Roberts ("*Daiphantus* [1604]: a Jacobean Perspective on Hamlet's Madness," *Library Chronicle* 42 [1978]: 128–137), suggests there is no foundation for that attribution beyond the ambiguous initials on the title page (136–137, n. 12). Roberts finds many echoes of *Hamlet* in this poem, some more convincing than others, but overall she sees the poem linking, as Polonius does, Hamlet's madness to disappointed love. For another indication of the play's popularity, see *Ratseis Ghost* (1605), a pamphlet alluding to Burbage's performance in the title role (sig. B1r).

10. As one would expect, given the date of *Eastward Ho,* the song there more closely parodies the first quarto text of *Hamlet.* The second quarto has "His beard was as white as snow, / Flaxen was his pole, / He is gone, he is gone." Quotations from *Hamlet* are from Bernice Kliman and Paul Bertram, eds., *The Three-Text Hamlet: Parallel Texts of the First and Second Quartos and the First Folio,* 2nd ed. (New York: AMS, 2003). If no earlier edition is specified, quotations are from the first folio. Act, scene, and line numbers are given for the folio and the second quarto; consecutive line numbers are given for the first quarto.

11. For other early parodic allusions to *Hamlet,* see Charles Cathcart, "*Hamlet:* Date and Early Afterlife," *Review of English Studies* 52 (2001): 355–356, and "*Histriomastix, Hamlet,* and the 'Quintessence of Duckes,'" *Notes and Queries* 50 (2003): 427–430.

12. Hart says that the play "cannot have been written before 1610" (Hart, *The White Devil,* 1).

13. David L. Frost comments, "Outside the Revenge tradition, memorable episodes from *Hamlet* were imitated in several plays. The graveyard scene, and Hamlet's speech on the skull, were favorites" (*The School of Shakespeare: The Influence of Shakespeare on English Drama, 1600–1642* [Cambridge University Press, 1968], 206).

14. Reynolds spelled his name Raynolds, of which the first word in his title is an anagram.

15. Although the second line of the couplet copies the Shakespearean original, "Bid" appears here in *Hamlet* only as part of the first quarto's lines: "bid her paint her self an inch thicke, to this she must come." The poem uses a series of three "bids" at the end as a structuring device, though this word need not be inspired by any Shakespearean text. The authorship of the poem in question is a puzzle, as E. A. J. Honigmann explains, and it may be by John Weever or William Basse, both of Shakespeare's circle. See Honigmann *John Weever: A Biography of a Literary Associate of Shakespeare and Jonson, Together with a Photographic Facsimile of Weever's Epigrammes* (1599) (Manchester University Press, 1987), 65–67.

16. For detailed discussion of attitudes toward makeup, see Annette Drew-Bear, *Painted Faces on the Renaissance Stage: The Moral Significance of Face-Painting Conventions* (Lewisburg, PA: Bucknell University Press, 1994), esp. 71–73 on *The Honest Whore, Part 1;* and Frances E. Dolan, "Taking the Pencil Out of God's Hand: Art, Nature, and the Face-Painting Debate in Early Modern England," *PMLA* 108 (1993): 224–239.

17. Compare the second quarto: "this might be the pate of a pollitician. . . . There's another, why may not that be the skull of a Lawyer, where be his quiddities now, his quillites, his cases, his tenurs, and his tricks? why dooes he suffer this madde knaue now to knocke him about the sconce with a durtie shouell, and will not tell him of his action of battery?" (5.1.79–104).

18. Lyly's *Euphues* (1578) has the following: "It behoueth youth with all industry to serch not onely the harde questions of the Philosophers, but also the fine cases of the Lawiers, not only the quirks and quillyties of the *Logicians,* but also to haue a sight in the numbers of the *Arithmetricians*" (sig. L3v). Philemon Holland's translation of Ammianus Marcellinus's *The Roman Historie* (1609) has "entangling causes with insoluble quirkes and quillits" (sig. Dddlv). Samuel Butler's *Hudibras, The Third and Last Part* (1677), has "Ply her with *Love-letters,* and *Billets,* / And Bait

'em well, for *Quirks,* and *Quillets*" (*Hudibras,* ed. John Wilders [Oxford: Clarendon, 1967], canto-3, lines 747–748).

19. The play is described on the title page as "A Comedie presented to their gracious Majesties at Cambridge, by the Students of Trinity-Colledge," dating the play to the visit of Charles I and Henrietta Maria in March 1632. F. S. Boas notes the "imitation of the gravedigger's scene in *Hamlet*" ("University Plays," in *The Cambridge History of English and American Literature,* ed. A. W. Ward and A. R. Waller [New York: Putnam's Sons, 1910], 6:366).

20. This passage confirms that the first quarto was not the source. The Lawyer's skull with a tongue cannot come from the first quarto, as "that skull had a tongue in it" appears only in subsequent texts; perhaps "turbulent, busie fellow" echoes the description of Yorick as a "whoreson mad fellow" (also in the second quarto and folio but not in the first quarto); while the "action of batterie" is in all *Hamlet* texts, the second quarto replaces the first quarto's "two dishes to one messe" with "two dishes but to one table" at 4.3.24–25.

21. Here and throughout this section, I quote from the facsimile of the first of the three 1604 editions of *The Malcontent,* STC 17479. In "The Date of *The Malcontent* Once More" (*Philological Quarterly* 39 [1960]: 106), Gustav Cross notes some of the Hamletian phrases I mention and points out echoes of "What peece of worke is a man" (second quarto 2.2.304), "looke where sadly the poore wretch comes reading" (2.2.168), and "springs to catch wood-cockes" (1.3.115).

22. The name "Truepenie" goes back to a character in *Ralph Roister Doister* (ca. 1552).

23. Whether the part was originally written for Burbage is another matter, as the play seems to have been composed originally for the Children of the Queen's Revels; see Bernard Harris, ed., introduction to *The Malcontent,* by John Marston (New York: Hill & Wang, 1967), xiv.

24. Ibid., xix.

25. How much John Marston in particular falls under Shakespeare's verbal influence can be seen by Marston's appropriation of "the front of loue" from 3.4.56 in *Hamlet,* at least if one accepts that *Antonio's Revenge* comes after *Hamlet* in about 1601, for which see Frost, *School of Shakespeare,* 7–9, and Cathcart, "*Hamlet:* Date and Early Afterlife," 342. Harold Jenkins argues that "the front of Jove," though having hyperbolic descriptive force in *Hamlet,* has, in *Antonio's Revenge,* "become no more than a vague cliché for heaven" (Jenkins, ed., *Hamlet* [New York: Methuen, 1982], 12). But the phrase does not seem to be a cliché. A scan through the Literature Online (LION) and Early English Books Online (EEBO) databases produces only four uses in the first half of the seventeenth century, all by Marston: twice in *Antonio's Revenge* (sigs. F2r and I4v); in the 1601 (published 1607) *What You Will* (sig. F4v); and in the 1600–1608 (published 1613) John Marston, William Barksted, and Lewis Mackin, *Insatiate Countess.* The last of these texts has: "A donatiue he hath of euery God; / *Apollo* gaue him lockes, *Ioue* his high front" (sig. A3r). There is even one instance of "High fronted *Iuno*" from Marston, in the 1606 *The Wonder of Women* (sig. B1v). When one aligns this multiple borrowing with Marston's fourfold parodying of "A horse! A horse! My kingdom for a horse!" in various works (see n. 5 above), one can see that a fixation upon Shakespeare's phrases characterizes this author.

26. Although the modern devotee might like to believe that *Hamlet* held the boards for many seasons after its opening, there is no surviving direct evidence of

any London performance between the publication of the second quarto of the play (1604–1605) and 1630. See Andrew Gurr, *The Shakespearean Playing Companies* (Oxford: Clarendon, 1996), 302-5, 388–393; and Roslyn L. Knutson, *The Repertory of Shakespeare's Company, 1594–1613* (Fayetteville: University of Arkansas Press, 1991), 186.

27. Quoted from Chadwyck-Healey's *English Drama* database, in act 4, scene 1, line 321; noted in *SAB*, 1:392.

28. Noted in Munro, "More Shakspere Allusions," 143–144.

29. See Stephen Greenblatt, "Shakespeare and the Exorcists," in *Shakespeare and the Question of Theory*, ed. Patricia Parker and Geoffrey Hartman (London: Methuen, 1985), 163–187, and his *Shakespearean Negotiations: The Circulation of Social Energy in Renaissance England* (Berkeley: University of California Press, 1988), 94–128.

30. The phrase appears again in Robert Armin's *The History of the two Maids of More-clacke* (1609): "I am tutch right, *hic & vbique*, euery where" (sig. H1r).

31. *Shakespeares Sonnets* (1609), sig. G3r.

32. Another possibility for the first appropriation of the phrase can be found in Sir Francis Hubert's long poem *The Deplorable Life and Death of Edward the Second* (sig. H8v). This was not published until 1628, but, according to the *Oxford Dictionary of National Biography*, "Hubert originally composed it between 1597 and 1600."

33. Mary Z. Maher, *Modern Hamlets and Their Soliloquies* (Iowa City: University of Iowa Press, 1992), 139, 145.

34. Searches for sixteenth- and seventeenth-century phrases from *Hamlet* in this essay were conducted or updated in October and November of 2007. The three LION databases combined (English Poetry, Early English Prose Fiction, and English Drama) produce, for the dates 1500–1700, only five hits on "to be or, not to be," including *Hamlet*, while "that is the question" garners no hits in any of these three databases except for *Hamlet* itself. The LION databases' exclusion of nonfictional prose accounts for the entirely different statistics. Peter Stallybrass, in "Against Thinking" (*PMLA* 122 [2007]: 1581), notes, without considering the contexts, a few pre-Shakespearean uses of phrases from the "To be or not to be" soliloquy: both halves of the opening line; "mind to suffer"; "sea of troubles"; and "sleep of death."

35. John Dryden, "Of Heroique Playes. An Essay," in *The Conquest of Granada by the Spaniards: In Two Parts* (1672), sig. a2v.

36. There is no established spelling of William Hemings's name. The English Short-Title Catalogue (ESTC), for example, has him under both Heming and Hemings, mainly the latter, but not Heminge. He emerges only as Hemings in searches of EEBO, and he appears thus on the title pages of the two plays I mention. However, the edition of his works by Carol A. Morley, *The Plays and Poems of William Heminge* (Madison, NJ: Fairleigh Dickinson University Press, 2005), spells his name to match that of his father, John.

37. Joseph Quincy Adams Jr., "William Heminge and Shakespeare," *Modern Philology* 12 (1914): 51; Frost adds the *Twelfth Night* reference (*School of Shakespeare*, 205).

38. Both of these writers have other seeming echoes of the soliloquy. George Wither's 1628 *Britain's Remembrancer Containing a Narration of the Plague lately past*, has, in its fifth canto, "although thou hast / The *Sea* of Troubles, without

ship wrack, past," and the eighth canto has "A sea of troubles, all thy hopes shall swallow" (sigs. O1r, Y8v). Thomas Heywood, in *The Hierarchie*, has "So the fift step in a New Creature, is, To line and reioyce in a sea of Troubles, and fly by Prayer and Contemplation towards Heauen" (sig. Hh6v), a passage itself taken from John Lightfoot's 1629 *Erubhin or Miscellanies Christian and Judaicall* (sig. L3r). But "sea of troubles" constitutes another common idiom, producing thirty-two pre-1700 texts in EEBO (and another eleven with a singular "trouble") and going back at least to William Painter's *Palace of Pleasure* from 1566 (sig. Ff3v).

39. For the attribution of act 2, scene 1 to Beaumont in particular, see Cyrus Hoy, "The Shares of Fletcher and His Collaborators in the Beaumont and Fletcher Canon (III)," *Studies in Bibliography* 11 (1958): 96.

40. Earlier English bibles generally do not have this exact phrase: the Bishops' Bible of 1568 has "sleepe in death," for instance.

41. Each treatise has separate signatures. See Robert Dent, "An Early *Hamlet* Echo?" *Shakespeare Quarterly* 14 (1963): 87–89.

42. Dent considers other possibilities for the source of Garey's passage: the phrases may derive from some work other than *Hamlet* ("the *Ur-Hamlet* or whatever"), or the "undiscovered country" phrase may be an "unrecognized commonplace," although, he says, "I know of no other instance." The EEBO database does not indicate commonplace status for this phrase, exposing only a few other uses of "undiscovered Country" prior to 1700, and those are usually in the plural and always merely literal.

43. Gabriel Harvey, quoted in Jenkins's edition of *Hamlet*, 573.

RICHARD LEVIN

Gertrude's Elusive Libido
and Shakespeare's Unreliable Narrators

I would like to begin by examining the striking differences that appear in the three statements we are given in *Hamlet* about Gertrude's sexuality—differences that I believe, in the words of what used to be the standard opening gambit of articles in our field, deserve more critical attention than they have yet received. In the first statement, which is located in the center of his first soliloquy, Hamlet presents a vivid picture of his parents' marital relationship as he recalls it. He says that his father was

> So excellent a king, that was to this
> Hyperion to a satyr, so loving to my mother
> That he might not beteem the winds of heaven
> Visit her face too roughly. Heaven and earth,
> Must I remember? Why, she should hang on him
> As if increase of appetite had grown
> By what it fed on, and yet, within a month—
> Let me not think on't! Frailty, thy name is woman!—
> A little month, or ere those shoes were old
> With which she followed my poor father's body,
> Like Niobe, all tears—why, she, even she—
> O God, a beast that wants discourse of reason

SEL: Studies in English Literature, 1500–1900, Volume 48, Number 2 (Spring 2008): pp. 305–326. Copyright © 2008 William Marsh Rice University. Reprinted by permission of The Johns Hopkins University Press.

Would have mourn'd longer—married with my uncle,
My father's brother, but no more like my father
Than I to Hercules.[1]

It is clear that their relationship, as described here, was asymmetrical, and
that this asymmetry was gendered, but not in the conventional patriarchal
pattern. His father's attitude toward Gertrude was protective—almost
absurdly overprotective—and did not seem to have any sexual component.
Therefore, when Hamlet says that she would "hang on him," we probably
expect to hear that she clung to his protection in a reciprocal dependency,
but instead we are told that her hanging expressed her "appetite," and we do
not usually think of people having an appetite for being protected, especially
one that grows by what it feeds on. It certainly sounds like a sexual appetite,
similar to those that Enobarbus refers to in *Antony and Cleopatra* when he
tries to explain Cleopatra's extraordinary hold on men: "Other women cloy
/ The appetites they feed, but she makes hungry / Where most she satisfies"
(II.ii.235–237). The difference, of course, is that Enobarbus is saying that
the appetites of Cleopatra's lovers are insatiable, whereas Hamlet says this
about Gertrude's appetite.

   The second statement appears in the passage in which the Ghost tells
Hamlet that Claudius

   With witchcraft of his wits, with traitorous gifts—
   O wicked wit and gifts that have the power
   So to seduce!—won to his shameful lust
   The will of my most seeming virtuous queen.
   O Hamlet, what a falling-off was there
   From me, whose love was of that dignity
   That it went hand in hand even with the vow
   I made to her in marriage, and to decline
   Upon a wretch whose natural gifts were poor
   To those of mine!
   But virtue, as it never will be moved,
   Though lewdness court it in a shape of heaven,
   So lust, though to a radiant angel link'd,
   Will sate itself in a celestial bed
   And prey on garbage.

                                             (I.v.43–57)

The Ghost's account of his love for Gertrude is more detailed than, but
consistent with, Hamlet's recollection of it in the first soliloquy: it was
governed by his sense of "dignity"; it was viewed by him as the fulfillment

of his religious obligation ("the vow / I made to her"); and it was consummated in "a celestial bed," which does not sound very sexy. But his account of Gertrude's love directly contradicts Hamlet's. Hamlet described her insatiable sexual appetite for her husband, whereas the Ghost asserts that her appetite—which he calls "lust"—had sated itself on him and therefore sought out ("decline / Upon" and especially "prey on" imply that she did some of the initiating, or at least was robustly proactive in this enterprise) the gross carnal love of Claudius. The Ghost also calls this carnal love "lust," which, he later adds, was consummated in "A couch for luxury" (I.v.83), very different from the "celestial bed" that he provided for her.

The third statement appears in the closet scene, where Hamlet berates Gertrude for preferring Claudius to his father:

> You cannot call it love, for at your age
> The heyday in the blood is tame, it's humble,
> And waits upon the judgment, and what judgment
> Would step from this to this? . . .
> . . . .
>   O shame, where is thy blush?
> Rebellious hell,
> If thou canst mutine in a matron's bones,
> To flaming youth let virtue be as wax
> And melt in her own fire. Proclaim no shame
> When the compulsive ardure gives the charge,
> Since frost itself as actively doth burn,
> And reason panders will. . . .
> . . . .
>   Nay, but to live
> In the rank sweat of an enseamed bed,
> Stew'd in corruption, honeying and making love
> Over the nasty sty!
>   (III.iv.68–94)

In the first excerpt from this statement she has outgrown the "heyday" of her libido, signified here by "blood," which is regarded as the seat or symbol of erotic energy, and which has become "tame" and "humble" (Quarto 1 reads, "Why appetite with you is in the waine, / Your blood runnes backeward now from whence it came.").[2] The insatiable sexual drive attributed to her by Hamlet and the Ghost in the first two statements is now explicitly denied (in fact, the Hamlet of Q1 says that the same "appetite" that waxed in his first soliloquy is now "in the waine"). And the explanation cannot be that she has actually grown older, because only a few months have elapsed since the time when, according to Hamlet, she hung upon his father, or when, according to the Ghost, she preyed upon his brother. But this abruptly changes in the second and third excerpts, where her sexual blood mutinies and actively burns, and impels her to honey and make love with Claudius.

Which of these conflicting accounts of Gertrude's sexuality is correct? The answer, I will argue, is that there is no answer. None of them can be considered objective, since they come from her son and her late husband, both of whom believe that they have been wronged by her, and each account is generated by and serves a specific agenda that is directly related to that wrong. I am not suggesting that this involves any conscious deception on their parts. Hamlet and the Ghost do not deliberately distort their memories or perceptions of Gertrude in order to further their agendas; rather, their memories and perceptions of her have already been filtered through and colored by those agendas. Moreover, I think that the first two accounts are influenced by some negative stereotypes of women that circulated in this period.

Hamlet's principal grievance in the first soliloquy is Gertrude's hasty remarriage, which he feels has made his life unbearable. (He is also distressed that her second husband is so inferior to his father, but he devotes only four half-lines to this, and, of course, he does not yet know of her adultery.) His agenda, therefore, is to make the timing of her remarriage even more shocking and reprehensible, and this is served by his memory of the relationship between her and his father. He has apparently idealized their relationship since he magnifies his father's protective concern for his mother, as I noted, and her attachment to him, and also her grief at his funeral ("Like Niobe, all tears"). It seems to me that this description draws upon and invokes the popular stereotype of the "wanton widow"—a woman who overprotests her eternal devotion to her husband, often vowing that she will never remarry, and then, shortly after his death, takes on a second husband or a lover.[3] We are not told that Gertrude made such a vow, but her excessive hanging upon her husband during his lifetime and her excessive weeping during his funeral are presented here as a form of overprotestation and a nonverbal commitment to remain faithful to him after his death. This casts an ironic light on her later response to the performance of *The Murther of Gonzago*, where she protests that the Player Queen, who turns out to be another wanton widow, "doth protest too much" that she will never have another husband (III.ii.230). It is also significant that Hamlet attributes Gertrude's second marriage to the "frailty" of women, which calls up another popular stereotype that had even attained proverbial status.[4] The greater her attachment to her first husband, therefore, the greater the gendered frailty that she exhibited in her subsequent behavior, and thus her sexual appetite for his father that Hamlet describes in this soliloquy becomes further evidence to support and augment his grievance against her and against her remarriage.

The Ghost's grievance obviously is Gertrude's adultery, and his agenda is to explain and condemn it—or, more precisely, to explain it in a way that will completely condemn her role and Claudius's and valorize his own. He begins by accusing Claudius of seducing her "With witchcraft of his wits, with traitorous gifts" (I.v.43), but that will not work. Brabantio, similarly, tries to explain his daughter's marriage by telling the Duke that Othello employed "witchcraft" to win her (*Othello*, I.iii.60–64), but both he and the Duke take this literally ("spells and medicines bought of mountebanks" [I.iii.61]), whereas here it is only a metaphor for cleverness; and while proverbial wisdom had it that women are tempted by gifts, it is hard to imagine any gift that could tempt the Queen of Denmark, who presumably did not suffer from a dearth of worldly goods.[5] His main explanation, which more directly serves his agenda, is the elaborate contrast he develops between the pure, dignified, religious love that he offered Gertrude and the carnal "lust" that Claudius offered her and that appealed to her own "lust." This also seems to draw upon and to invoke yet another popular stereotype of the period, the stereotype of upper-class ladies who are sexually attracted to lower-class men (often horse keepers or stable grooms) because they are supposed to be more physical, more primitive, more animal-like, and therefore more virile than the men of their own class.[6] The underlying idea here is explained in Thomas Heywood's *Loues Mistris,* where Apuleius distinguishes between the two basic forms of "Desire," the true spiritual love that "Doates on the Soules sweete beauty" and seeks "Celestiall pleasur," and the "intemperate lust" that "inflame[s] the soule / With some base groome."[7] In another common version, the man is a member, not of a lower class, but of a lower race, usually a Moor or Turk, since they were also supposed to be more physical, primitive, etc., than upper-class European men, which is the idea behind Tamora's infatuation with Aaron in *Titus Andronicus,* and Iago's comments to Brabantio, in the opening scene of *Othello,* about Desdemona's marriage: "an old black ram / Is tupping your white ewe" (I.i.88–89), "your daughter [is] cover'd with a Barbary horse" (I.i.111–112), she "and the Moor are now making the beast with two backs" (I.i.116–117), and she sought "the gross clasps of a lascivious Moor" (I.i.126).[8] Claudius is not a "base groome," of course, and belongs to the same class (and race) as Gertrude and her husband, but in the Ghost's account he possesses, and tempts her with, a base, groomlike erotic power. Moreover, even though the word is not used by the Ghost, his account enlarges the female "frailty" that Hamlet attributed to Gertrude in his first soliloquy because she is not only a wanton widow, which was Hamlet's grievance there, but was also a wanton wife.

In the third statement, Hamlet's principal grievance is that Gertrude chose Claudius over his father, and his agenda, again, is to explain and condemn her choice, although this takes a surprising turn. The condemnation is based on Claudius's manifest inferiority to his father, which Hamlet only touched on briefly in his first soliloquy, but which now becomes his major concern, centering on the portraits of the two men that he shows Gertrude. As we would expect, his description of them in III.iv.53–67, which precedes the statement I quote above, closely corresponds to the Ghost's description of the two kinds of love they offered Gertrude, according to the law that external, physical traits reflect and therefore reveal internal, mental traits. His father's face exhibits "grace," with "Hyperion's curls," "the front of Jove," "An eye like Mars," and "A station like the herald Mercury," so that it combines the virtues of "every god," suiting his dignified and "celestial" love in the Ghost's account (III.iv.55–58, 61), while Claudius's face looks "like a mildewed ear, / Blasting his wholesome brother" (III.iv.64–65), which suits his coarse, bestial love. In fact, this physical contrast seems to be another version or an extension of the stereotype of the lady and the stable groom that the Ghost drew upon, since here the man's sexual prowess and allure are associated with his ugliness instead of, or in addition to, his debased social status or race, which the Ghost relates to "garbage."[9] Thus in Heywood's *Loues Mistris,* just before the speech of Apuleius quoted above, Menetius asks him why a woman's lust is drawn to "some base groome mis-shapen, and deform'd."[10] This idea appears in the stories of "The Beauty and the Beast," for example, and in the mythical figure of the satyr, which is introduced in Hamlet's first soliloquy when he says that his father was to Claudius as "Hyperion to a satyr" (I.ii.140), and may be recalled here when he gives his father "Hyperion's curls" (III.iv.56). The satyr, of course, was very ugly and was not merely animalistic but was part animal, and possessed prodigious sexual equipment and energy, as numerous nymphs could testify. Thus Hamlet's emphasis on the stark physical contrast between the "mildewed," beastlike Claudius whom Gertrude preferred and the handsome, godlike husband whom she betrayed is just what we would expect.

However, Hamlet's attempt to explain Gertrude's preference in the first excerpt I quote from this statement, which follows immediately after his comparison of the two portraits, is certainly *not* what we would expect, because he insists that she is too old to be impelled by lust, which directly contradicts the explicit account in the Ghost's speech and the assumption in the stereotype, and, as I pointed out, even contradicts Hamlet's own description, in his first soliloquy, of her sexual appetite for his father. How are we to understand this? We could, of course, descend into Hamlet's Freudian unconscious to discover that he does not want his mother to have erotic feelings for anyone but his father, although that is not authorized in Sigmund Freud's Oedipal paradigm. But I do not believe that we need to go beyond or below his conscious agendas in order to reconcile these conflicting assertions about Gertrude's sexuality. In the first soliloquy, his agenda is simply to condemn her hasty remarriage, so he recalls (and exaggerates?) her sexual attachment to his father, which makes this haste seem even worse. But now he knows about her adultery, and his agenda is to condemn her choice of Claudius over his father, so he does not want to allow her a sexual motive, which would serve to extenuate her conduct. If she has no excuse, then her preference will seem even worse, and therefore his explanation of it is that it is inexplicable.

All this changes suddenly and completely in the second excerpt, which is still part of the same speech, and in the third, which is only separated from the second by a brief response of Gertrude's. Now Hamlet insists that her motive is lust, just as the Ghost told him, and his vision of her making love to Claudius on "an enseamed bed, / . . . Over the nasty sty" (III.iv.92–94) is very similar to the Ghost's vision of her seeking out a "couch of luxury" to "prey on garbage" (I.v.83, 57). The reason for this change must be found, therefore, in the portion of his speech between the first and second excerpts, because that portion is the logical development of his assertion that her choice of Claudius's face over his father's is inexplicable. Since her choice was an error of "judgment," and since judgment is informed by the senses, he then proceeds through the senses in sequence, from "eyes" to "feeling" to "ears" to "smelling" (I assume that he omits the fifth sense because one does not usually taste faces), and demonstrates that not even "a sickly part of one true sense" (III.iv.80) could have made her mistake. But this leaves him with only one other possibility, that her judgment was distorted by lust, and therefore he finally has to acknowledge this in the agonized question that marks the turning point of his speech: "O shame, where is thy blush?" (III. iv.81). Thus he is reluctantly forced to this conclusion by his two commitments: his commitment to the belief that his father's face, and hence his character, are so obviously superior to Claudius's that there is no other way to explain Gertrude's preference, and, more basically, his commitment to logical inquiry—or, more precisely, to the belief that he is being logical—that is such an essential aspect of his personality.

Even though he finally agrees with the Ghost about Gertrude's lust, however, his complaint about it is quite different. The Ghost's grievance was that it made her disloyal to him and to his "celestial" love, whereas Hamlet's grievance is that she is too old to feel lust, which he emphasizes now by describing it mutinying "in a matron's bones" and burning "frost itself," an image of the sexual frigidity that presumably comes—or ought to come—with age.[11] Therefore he is brought back to his opening accusation, but with a significant emendation: there he told Gertrude that "at your age / The heyday in the blood is tame . . . / And waits upon the judgment" (III.iv.68–70), while now he is saying that at her age the heyday of the blood *should* be tame and *should* wait upon her judgment. But he is still very concerned with the problem of extenuation because he concludes that Gertrude's choice makes the similar mistakes caused by the "compulsive ardure" of "flaming youth" much more excusable and therefore much less shameful, which, of course, makes her own choice much less excusable and therefore much more shameful, and so he is still able to condemn it.

The preceding discussion of the statements about Gertrude's sexuality has been based on the assumption that dramatic characters, including the ones who give us these statements, should be regarded as representations of real individuals who possess personalities and what we now call interiority, which involves agendas, emotions, and even internal conflicts that can affect the reliability of the statements they make. I would now like to examine this assumption, but first I must introduce some much more real individuals who have a crucial role in it—namely, the playwrights and the audiences they had in mind. For the question here is not whether these characters actually possess this interiority, which would not make any sense, but whether the playwrights who created them intended to endow them with interiority, and intended to have their audiences be aware of this factor and take it into account in judging the reliability of the characters' speeches.

The answer to this question, again, is that there is no answer, or rather, that the answer necessarily depends on which speeches and which charac-ters and which playwrights are involved. Even if we limit ourselves to the speeches of Shakespeare's characters, it is clear that they vary widely in this respect. In fact, they can be placed on a scale in terms of the kind or degree of reliability that we attribute to the persons who speak them. At one pole are the speeches of the prologues, epilogues, and choruses in *Romeo and Juliet, 2 Henry IV, Henry V, Troilus and Cressida, Pericles, The Winter's Tale, Henry VIII,* and *The Two Noble Kinsmen,* whom we regard, not as individuals, but as spokespersons for the playwright (indeed, the epilogues in *2 Henry IV* and *Henry V* state explicitly that they speak for "our humble author" [Epi. 27] or "Our bending author" [Epi. 2]).[12] They are therefore authoritative in both senses, which means that we assume that the speakers have no personalities or motives of their own, and that their only purpose is to give us the informa-tion that the author wants us to have about the preceding or following action and, sometimes, to indicate how we should react to it. It follows, then, that the audiences were expected to rely on them completely.

I must point out, however, that not all critics do rely on them, because critics (including what used to be called "the present author") can also have agendas of their own, just like the characters. This, again, does not imply any conscious deception on their parts. They do not deliberately distort the evi-dence in the play in order to further their agendas; rather, that evidence has already been filtered through and colored by those agendas. Thus some critics who do not approve of Henry V, and therefore do not want Shakespeare to approve of him, have to engage in some strenuous filtering of the chorus to that play (which calls him, among other things, "the mirror of all Christian kings" [Cho., II.6] and "This star of England" [Epi. 6]) so that they can tell us that it cannot be relied on and must be ironical.[13] But they do not tell us how the audience would realize this, especially since the reliability of the chorus was a well-established dramatic convention, or how the playwright could rely on their realizing this. That is crucial, because if they did not realize this they would misunderstand the meaning of the chorus and therefore the larger meaning of the play as a whole, which the playwright certainly could not have intended. And that brings me to my basic assumption underlying this examination of the reliability of dramatic speeches—the assumption that the playwright wanted his audience to understand the play that he is writing for them. That would be his major artistic agenda, and one that we can always rely on.

At the same pole would be the speeches of characters such as the bleeding Sergeant in *Macbeth*, I.ii, who describes Macbeth's victory over the rebel Macdonald to Duncan and his attendants. Once again, we rely on him completely, and I think it will be helpful to spell out the reasons for this. Although the Sergeant is a "real" individual, unlike the choruses and prologues, his role here is also defined by another well-established dramatic convention, the convention of the *nuntius*. The sole purpose of a *nuntius* is to inform the other characters and hence the audience about events that took place off stage. We therefore regard him as a reliable narrator, since he cannot have some personal motive (such as a desire to curry favor with Macbeth) to mislead his onstage auditors by falsifying his report.[14] More importantly, Shakespeare could not have any artistic motive to mislead his offstage auditors by making the Sergeant falsify his report because it contains essential information about what Hamlet calls "some necessary question of the play" (III.ii.42–43) that we need to know if we are to follow the ensuing action, which brings me back to my basic assumption about the playwright's agenda—his desire to have his audience understand his play.

This also applies to the speech of Rosse, immediately following this one, where he tells Duncan about the victory over the rebel Cawdor and the Norsemen. Rosse, unlike the Sergeant, is not simply a *nuntius*, since he appears in some later scenes, but here he functions as one, and we rely on his report for the same reasons that we rely on the Sergeant's. There is also another reason that we rely on both of their speeches, because they come at the beginning of the play and therefore are part of the necessary exposition of preceding events that the audience must know before the action proper begins. In this respect, then, they are like an expository prologue, who we saw is by definition a reliable narrator. Indeed, the information they convey could have just as easily (but not as effectively) been rewritten as the prologue to *Macbeth*.

I would also place in the same general category the prologuelike expositions of the preceding action presented in Egeon's long, tedious speech at the beginning of *The Comedy of Errors* and in Prospero's long, tedious speech at the beginning of *The Tempest*. Although both speeches are ostensibly addressed to another character (Duke Solinus and Miranda, respectively), they are obviously intended for the audience, and are therefore supposed to be reliable.[15] This is also true of the expository conversations of the two unnamed Gentlemen about Posthumus and Imogen at the beginning of *Cymbeline* and of Camillo and Archidamus about Leontes and Polixenes at the beginning of *The Winter's Tale*, which function like prologues. Just as reliable, and just as awkward, are Orlando's complaint to Adam about his mistreatment by Oliver (which Adam certainly knows) at the beginning of *As You Like It* and Horatio's explanation to Marcellus and Barnardo of the conflict between Denmark and Norway (which they would probably know) at the beginning of *Hamlet*.

This category would also include the *nuntius*-like speeches that are presented later in the play but have the same purpose of informing other characters and the audience about some offstage action. In terms of their reliability, it does not seem to matter if their speakers are nonentities who are limited to this role (such as the First Lord, who describes Jaques's reaction to the sight of the wounded deer in *As You Like It* [II.i.25–63], and Jaques de Boys, who describes the conversion of Duke Frederick [V.iv.151–166]), or more fully developed individuals.[16] In *Hamlet*, three of these speeches come from major characters: Ophelia's report to Polonius of Hamlet's behavior in her closet (II.i.74–97), Gertrude's report to Claudius and Laertes of Ophelia's death (IV.vii.166–183), and Hamlet's report to Horatio of his exchange of letters on the sea voyage (V.ii.4–55). The reports of Ophelia and Hamlet, unlike those of a simple *nuntius* (or of the First Lord and Jaques de Boys in *As You Like It*), are "in character," as we would now say, since their emotional coloring and even their diction and cadences clearly reflect the personality and mood of the speaker (this is not true of Gertrude's report, which is much more like a self-contained poetic set piece),[17] but they must be reliable because we must rely on the information they convey, and therefore can rely on the playwright's desire to satisfy what we now call our "need to know" a necessary question of the play. This desire, in fact, is an essential corollary of my basic assumption that he wants his audience to understand the play he is writing for them.

All the speeches I have examined so far can be considered special cases in that their reliability is guaranteed by the conventions of Shakespeare's theater, which is why they are all at one pole of the scale I am constructing. At the opposite pole are the speeches of characters who obviously intend to deceive someone, and it is obvious because Shakespeare has them reveal their intention in advance so that they will not deceive the audience. Thus at the beginning of *Richard III*, Richard is given a long, prologuelike soliloquy in which he reveals his basic agenda to "prove a villain" (I.i.30) and his specific "plots" to deceive King Edward and Clarence; and similar soliloquies are given, usually quite early in the play, to most of Shakespeare's other villains, including Aaron in *Titus Andronicus* (II.i.1–25), Iago in *Othello* (I.iii.383–404), and Edmund in *King Lear* (I.ii.1–22), where they declare their evil intentions and plan their deceptions. (Indeed, this itself was a dramatic convention going back to the Vice characters in the Moralities, such as Covetous in W. Wager's *Enough Is as Good as a Feast* and Nichol Newfangle in Ulpian Fulwell's *Like Will to Like*, who on their first appearance took the audience into their confidence.) We can be certain, therefore, that Iago is lying when he tells Othello about Cassio's sleep-talking (III.iii.413–426), and that Edmund is lying when he tells Gloucester about Edgar's remarks on "declin'd" fathers (I.ii.71–74), and so we might say that these villains are really reliable after all, because we can rely on their soliloquies of self-revelation, and these soliloquies assure us that we can rely on the unreliability of their later statements to other characters.

Unlike these soliloquizing villains, Goneril and Regan do not announce in advance that they plan to deceive their father in the love contest at the beginning of *King Lear*, but Shakespeare does not allow them to deceive us. Their protestations of love for Lear are so excessive that we immediately suspect, like Gertrude reacting to the Player Queen in *The Murther of Gonzago*, that they "protest too much" (Lear does not suspect this, which shows that he is much less astute than she is in discerning the playwright's intention, although we saw that her comment reflects ironically on her own overprotestations of devotion to Hamlet's father). We are also told that they are dissembling by Cordelia immediately after their speeches (lines 99–104) and then by Kent later in the scene (lines 151–154). Moreover, there was a well-known dramatic convention, which Lear apparently does not know, that in any contest the first two contestants always get it wrong and the third always gets it right, as we can see in the casket contest in acts II and III of *The Merchant of Venice* and the obedience contest in the closing episode of *The Taming of the Shrew*.[18] Finally, the two sisters dispel any possible doubt at the end of this scene when they reveal their contempt for Lear and decide to act against him, and from then on they are just as reliably unreliable as Richard, Aaron, Iago, and Edmund.

Most of the important speeches in Shakespeare, however, belong somewhere in the middle of this scale because we are expected to believe that the characters who utter them, unlike the prologues, choruses, and *nuntii*, possess an interior dimension, including personal agendas, attitudes, and feelings, that can influence the statements they make and can therefore affect their reliability, although, unlike the outright villains, their dramatic careers are not based upon deliberate deception. This would seem to apply to the speeches of Hamlet and the Ghost examined earlier that deal with Gertrude's sexuality, and I would now like to return to these two characters and these speeches.

Although I am arguing that we are expected to believe that most of Shakespeare's characters possess an interior dimension, which is simply another way of saying that we should regard them as representations of real individuals, we are not always aware of this interiority, just as we are not always aware of the interiority of the really real individuals that we observe every day. We usually become aware of it, in the drama and in life, when these individuals exhibit some signs of internal stress or conflict, and Shakespeare, at least in his mature work, usually provides us with these signs in the more emotional speeches of the characters and especially in their asides and soliloquies, which often give us an insight into the intense, and often submerged, feelings and attitudes underlying the personas that they present to other people and sometimes even to themselves.

There cannot be any question that this applies to the portrayal of Hamlet. Indeed, many critics over many years have recognized that he is the most interiorized of all Shakespeare's characters, with the most complexly layered consciousness and personality.[19] Some of this layering can in fact be seen in the excerpt from his first soliloquy quoted at the outset, since at several points in it he interrupts himself ("Heaven and earth, / Must I remember" [I.ii.142–143], "Let me not think on't" [I.ii.146], and "O God, a beast that wants discourse of reason / Would have mourn'd longer" [I.ii.150–151]), as if powerful emotional pressures are breaking through his conscious train of thought against his conscious will and so reveal an internal struggle between different parts or aspects of his mind. This, of course, is one of the devices employed to create the illusion that Hamlet is a real person, to whom we attribute different levels of consciousness, and it marks one of Shakespeare's major improvements over the soliloquies in the plays of his predecessors and in his own earlier plays (Richard's first soliloquy in *Richard III*, cited above, is a good example) that were usually limited to the straightforward expression or elaboration of a single idea or emotion. And further evidence of Hamlet's multiple layers of consciousness can be found in the excerpt I quoted from his speech to Gertrude in the closet scene, where we saw that he can express— and presumably believe—two contradictory views of her sexuality.

Since Hamlet clearly is supposed to possess such a complex, multileveled interiority, we must ask if we are supposed to regard him as a reliable narrator in his statements about Gertrude. The question, I must repeat, is not whether he is engaged in a deliberate deception. We know that he can be deceptive in his dealings with Claudius, Polonius, Rosencrantz, and Guildenstern, whom he regards as his enemies, although he seems to take more pleasure in playing mind games with them, but he cannot be deliberately deceiving Gertrude in his speech to her, or himself in his first soliloquy. Indeed, it is impossible to deceive oneself deliberately. But we know that self-deception is possible in real people, because of their real interiority with its separate levels of

consciousness, and we can see a striking example of it in Hamlet's long soliloquy in II.ii.549–605 ("O, what a rogue and peasant slave am I"), where he
shifts his focus and his line of thought several times, first attacking himself
for his cowardice in failing to avenge his father by killing Claudius, then attacking Claudius for killing his father, then attacking himself for indulging
in this verbal attack on Claudius instead of acting against him, and then seizing upon the plan to stage *The Murther of Gonzago* to see if the Ghost was
telling the truth about Claudius killing his father.[20] Surely we are supposed
to realize that Hamlet has never doubted the Ghost's words before this (in
fact, when he called Claudius a murderer a few lines earlier, he must have
believed what the Ghost told him), and that this new plan will not bring him
any closer to his revenge than he is now. Perhaps self-deception is too strong
a term to apply to this process, since the plan is perfectly logical—and, as I
noted earlier, Hamlet's commitment to the belief that he is being logical is
an essential aspect of his personality. Yet it obviously serves his agenda here
by letting him off the hook, or rather two hooks: it justifies his delay, since
now he cannot proceed against Claudius without first verifying the Ghost's
accusation (which means that this delay was the result not of his cowardice
but of a rational investigation), and it provides him with an action that he can
easily undertake and that has now become a necessary step in his revenge, so
that the soliloquy that began with him feeling disgusted at himself because he
is doing nothing to further his revenge can end with him feeling very pleased
with himself (indicated in the triumphant closing couplet about catching "the
conscience of the King" [II.ii.605]) because he is doing something to further
it. And it seems equally clear that his statements about Gertrude, Claudius,
and his father in his first soliloquy and his speech in the closet scene also serve
an agenda by condemning her and Claudius and commending his father, so
that we cannot assume that they must be reliable, even though they are not
deliberately deceptive.

The Ghost's statement poses this same problem, but it also involves two
prior problems that do not apply to Hamlet. One is the question of whether
he really is a ghost. Several critics have tried to prove, often by citing evidence from Elizabethan treatises on pneumatology, that he is not the ghost
of Hamlet's father but a devil pretending to be the ghost of Hamlet's father
in order to entrap Hamlet.[21] This is a very serious charge because, if it were
true, it would mean that he is like the deceptive villains in Shakespeare's
other plays, and so his statement to Hamlet would be completely unreliable.
Shakespeare, however, eliminates this possibility by voicing it twice during
the early part of the play and rejecting it both times. Horatio warns Hamlet
not to follow the Ghost because it may "assume some other horrible form"
to drive him mad (I.iv.69–74), but this does not happen and Hamlet returns
from his encounter to assure Horatio and Marcellus that "It is an honest

ghost, that let me tell you" (I.v.138). Then, near the end of the soliloquy that I just discussed, Hamlet himself wonders if the Ghost "May be a devil" who lied about Claudius's crime in order to "damn me" (II.ii.598–603), but when he sees how Claudius reacts to *The Murther of Gonzago,* he tells Horatio, "I'll take the ghost's word for a thousand pound" (III.ii.286–287), which was a lot of money in those days; and after that we hear no more doubts about a demonic ghost. In terms of my basic assumption, therefore, we can be confident that the Ghost is not a devil because, if he were, Shakespeare would have been sure to satisfy his audience's "need to know" this essential fact or "necessary question of the play" because he wanted them to understand this play.

There is another problem with this character, for while it is clear that he is supposed to be a real ghost, it is not clear what a real ghost is supposed to be. Are we to regard him as a human being who just happens to be dead but is otherwise unchanged, so that he retains the same personality, feelings, and limitations that he had in life, or are we to believe that after death he was transformed into a different kind of being? The difficulty can be seen in our uncertainty about whether to refer to the Ghost as "he" or "it," and in some of the awkward locutions that I had to resort to earlier. Thus when I suggested that the Ghost is invoking the stereotype of the lady and her horse keeper in order to explain why Gertrude was sexually attracted to Claudius, I felt that I should say that Claudius belongs to the same social class as "Gertrude and her husband" instead of "Gertrude and the Ghost," even though the Ghost is obviously talking about himself here (that is, about his preghostly self), because it did not seem appropriate to attribute social class to ghosts.

The problem goes well beyond these niceties of stylistic decorum, however, because the Ghost functions as a prologuelike *nuntius* by informing Hamlet, and therefore the audience, of two crucial actions that occurred before the play begins: he says that Claudius poisoned him and that Gertrude committed adultery with Claudius. But Hamlet's father was poisoned while he was sleeping, and the adultery must have been concealed from him while he was alive, so how then did "he" (that is, the Ghost) find out about them? I am not aware that any critic has asked this question, but I believe that in itself gives us the answer, because it shows that we feel that this is, as Falstaff says, "a question not to be ask'd" (*1 Henry IV,* II.iv.408–409), and therefore that asking it would be "to consider too curiously" (V.i.205), as Horatio says, by "thinking too precisely on th' event" (IV.iv.41), as Hamlet says. After all, we do not ask how Jaques de Boys knows about the private conversation between Duke Frederick and the old religious man in the skirts of the Forest of Arden, or how Gertrude knows that Ophelia was making fantastic garlands of crow-flowers, nettles, daisies, and long purples (also given a grosser name) when she fell into the weeping brook. Because of what I called the convention of the reliability of a *nuntius's* report, we simply assume that the *nuntius* actually has the information conveyed in the report, and therefore we do not question how he or she could have acquired it. Perhaps this also applies to the Ghost's two accusations since he is serving here as a kind of *nuntius*. However, the actions that Jaques de Boys and Gertrude report did not happen to them in the same way that the poisoning and cuckolding happened to the Ghost—or rather, happened to him before he became the Ghost—so perhaps we are in the presence of another convention that grants ghosts a kind of omniscience about the events that occurred during their former lives, which means, again, that we should adopt the policy of "don't ask." But it does not really matter in this case because both of the Ghost's accusations are later confirmed by the guilty parties themselves—Claudius explicitly admits to the murder in his aside in III.i.48–53 and again in the prayer scene (III.iii), and Gertrude tacitly admits to the adultery in the closet scene (III.iv) and again in her aside in IV.v.17–20. Therefore we can be confident that, at least on this factual level, he is supposed to be regarded as a reliable narrator.

The Ghost does not limit himself to this factual level, however, because we saw in the passage quoted at the beginning that he also interprets and judges the motivation of the adultery when he asserts that Claudius won Gertrude "to his shameful lust" (I.v.45), and that Gertrude's "lust" was attracted to and preyed on Claudius's, which she preferred to his own pure and dignified love. I argued that this account seems to have been filtered through and affected by his agenda because it makes him look as good as possible and makes Gertrude and Claudius look as bad as possible (which is much the same as Hamlet's agenda in the passages quoted from his first soliloquy and from his speech in the closet scene). Consequently, it has the appearance of a self-serving account, which led me to suggest that it could be regarded as the expression of his human—indeed, all too human—interiority. The difficulty, however, is that we do not know if we are expected to attribute an interior dimension to the Ghost. He speaks to Hamlet in long, sonorous, periodic sentences (in contrast to Hamlet's brief, nervous responses), but we cannot tell if this is supposed to be "in character" for the man when he was alive, or is supposed to indicate his new otherworldly status. Whatever the cause, the result is that the steady flow of his verse is not interrupted by sudden outbursts of feeling or abrupt shifts of focus or any of the other signs that we found in Hamlet's soliloquies and his speech to Gertrude that exposed his internal tensions. But even if the Ghost has also been given a human interiority and a human agenda that is expressed in his account of Gertrude's sexuality, this does not mean that the account must be false, any more than the fact that it comes from a ghost means that it must be true. All this means is that we cannot rely upon its reliability and therefore should try to test it by looking for other evidence within the play that might confirm or refute it.

The most obvious place to look for this evidence is in the words and actions of Gertrude, the central character of this investigation, who has been conspicuously absent from it so far. There is a good reason for this absence, however, because she does not provide an answer to the problem we are investigating. Many years ago, in one of the early feminist readings of Shakespeare, Rebecca Smith pointed out that, while many (male) critics have accepted without question Hamlet's and the Ghost's statements about Gertrude's lustful nature, she herself never gives us any sign of it.[22] Of course, this does not prove that the critics are wrong. Most of her appearances are in public scenes with other members of the Court, where she has no opportunity to say anything lustful, even if she feels it; and her one long speech in the play, her description of Ophelia's death, is another public performance that, we found, is presented as an impersonal set piece. The only speeches where she could reveal her hidden inner feelings are her responses to Hamlet in the closet scene and her one brief aside in IV.v.17–20, and while in both of them she tacitly admits her adultery with Claudius, as I just noted, she never suggests that it was driven by lust. In fact, when she tells Hamlet that "thou hast cleft my heart in twain" (III.iv.156), this implies that she really loves Claudius, just as she really loves Hamlet, and is now forced to choose between them.[23] And the only two episodes where she and Claudius are alone together (IV.i.5–32 and IV.v.75–96) are utterly sexless—we seem, rather, to be hearing the intimate conversation of a long-married couple who are sharing their problems. It should also be pointed out that Claudius never shows any sign that he is driven by lust in his relationship with Gertrude, or that he regards her as a sexual object—indeed, in his prayer scene he says that one of the reasons that he killed his brother was to be "possess'd" of Gertrude, which cannot refer to his sexual possession of her since that predated the murder; and he later tells Laertes that one of the reasons that he cannot proceed against Hamlet is that Gertrude "Lives almost by his looks," and "She is so conjunctive to my life and soul" (IV.vii.12–14) that he could not exist without her. Nor does Gertrude do anything in the play that could be attributed to her lustful nature—in fact, she does not initiate any action except to drink the poisoned wine at the end.[24] Therefore we have no way to determine if what Hamlet and the Ghost say about her lust is true.

This brings me back, finally, to my basic assumption about Shakespeare's desire to have his audience understand the play he is writing for them. How are we to reconcile this with his failure to settle the problem of Gertrude's sexuality? It is possible that he simply did not think that this was something they needed to know, or, more likely, that he did not think that it would pose a problem for them because her adultery occurred before the play begins and therefore should be regarded as a donnée that we are supposed to accept, so that any inquiry into its causes would be another "question not to be ask'd."

We do not ask why Julia fell in love with Proteus before the beginning of *The Two Gentlemen of Verona,* or Hermia with Lysander, or Helena with Bertram, or Imogen with Posthumus before the beginning of *A Midsummer Night's Dream, All's Well that Ends Well,* and *Cymbeline,* or why any of Shakespeare's other heroines fall in love during the course of their plays. That is quite different, however, because a marriageable young woman falling in love with a marriageable young man (and vice versa) was considered "natural," which I place in scare quotes to show that I know it is no longer considered "natural" and has become socially constructed (not in scare quotes). It is just what they were supposed to do, especially if they were characters in a comedy or romance. But we feel that adultery is another matter and that it requires some special explanation, such as the lady/horse keeper stereotype invoked by the Ghost and Hamlet. Shakespeare could have easily settled the question by adding a brief scene between Gertrude and Claudius similar to the one cited earlier in *Titus Andronicus,* II.iii, where Tamora eagerly solicits the carnal attentions of Aaron. But he does not do anything like this, and, consequently, Gertrude's sexuality seems to be an unresolvable problem. Of course, directors of productions of *Hamlet* and actors who take the role of Gertrude do not leave it this way, since they usually feel that they should give her a coherent (and interesting) personality and a clear motivation, so many of them have opted for a sensual or even a lascivious Gertrude. I have seen productions of the play in which she crawls all over Claudius (and sometimes all over Hamlet as well).[25] There is no warrant for this in the text, as we saw, but there is no warrant against it either. Unfortunately for her, Gertrude is the victim of a bad press, not only on the stage and screen and in the critical arena, but also within Shakespeare's text, since she and her libido are constructed for us by the two men who have grievances against her and so must be considered hostile and therefore unreliable witnesses, while she herself is given no opportunity to testify on her own behalf.

Notes

1. Shakespeare, *Hamlet,* I.ii.139–153. All quotations of Shakespeare, except for Quarto 1 *Hamlet,* follow *The Riverside Shakespeare,* ed. G. Blakemore Evans et al. (Boston: Houghton Mifflin, 1974). All subsequent references, apart from the Q1 *Hamlet,* will be cited parenthetically in the text by act, scene, and line number for plays, and line numbers for poetry.

2. Compare the references to Angelo's sexual "blood" in *Measure for Measure:* the Duke says that he "scarce confesses / That his blood flows" (I.iii.51–52); Lucio says that his "blood / Is very snow-broth" (I.iv.57–58); and when his lust is aroused by Isabella, he himself is forced to acknowledge that "Blood, thou art blood" (II. iv.15). *The Three-Text Hamlet: Parallel Texts of the First and Second Quartos and First Folio,* 2d rev. edn., ed. Bernice W. Kliman and Paul Bertram (New York: AMS Press, 2003), lines 1544–1545.

3. In George Chapman's *The Widow's Tears*, I.i.84–86, II.i.11–13, II.iii.50–52, II.iv.20–31, and III.i.119, we learn that both Eudora and Cynthia have taken these vows, which they promptly break (ed. Ethel M. Smeak, Regents Renaissance Drama [Lincoln: University of Nebraska Press, 1966]). Cynthia's actions derive from Petronius's tale of the Ephesian matron, which may be our earliest account of a wanton widow—see *The Satyricon*, trans. William Arrowsmith (New York: Mentor, 1960), pp. 117–120. I discuss these and other examples in "Protesting Too Much in Shakespeare and Elsewhere, and the Invention/ Construction of the Mind," *ELR* 37, 3 (Summer 2007): 337–359, esp. 337–339.

4. See R. W. Dent, *Proverbial Language in English Drama Exclusive of Shakespeare, 1495–1616: An Index* (Berkeley: University of California Press, 1984), W700.1; *The Merry Wives of Windsor*, II.i.233–234; *Twelfth Night*, II.ii.31; *Measure for Measure*, II.iv.124–128; and *Cymbeline*, I.iv.91–96. The word is specifically applied to widows who remarry in Chapman's *The Widow's Tears*, I.ii.204, 207, III.i.184–185, and IV.i.139.

5. In *A Midsummer Night's Dream*, Egeus complains that Lysander "bewitch'd" Hermia, but this simply means that he used "cunning" (I.i.27, 36), while Titania really is bewitched by the magical potion that makes her fall in love with Bottom. On the alleged susceptibility of women to gifts, see Dent, W704; *The Two Gentlemen of Verona*, III.i.89–91; and Dorothy Kehler, "The First Quarto of Hamlet: Reforming Widow Gertred," *SQ* 46, 4 (Winter 1995): 398–413, esp. 407. The description of the dumb show introducing *The Murther of Gonzago* states that *"The pois'ner woos the Queen with gifts"* (III.ii.133–135), but that is after the murder.

6. The stereotype is evoked in the speeches in which Tarquin threatens Lucrece (*The Rape of Lucrece*, lines 515–518, 670–672, 1632–1637, 1644–1645), Boult threatens Marina (*Pericles*, IV.vi.190–191), Beatrice attacks Margaret (*Much Ado about Nothing*, III.iv.44–51), and Antigonus defends Hermione (*The Winter's Tale*, II.i.133–139).

7. Thomas Heywood, *Loues Mistris*, *The Dramatic Works of Thomas Heywood*, ed. R. H. Shepherd, 6 vols. (New York: Russell and Russell, 1964), 5:81–160, pp. 106–107. Note that this distinction assumes that the desirer is a woman.

8. In *Titus Andronicus*, see especially II.iii.10–29, where Tamora eagerly invites Aaron to engage in their sexual "pastimes" and he coldly puts her off, and compare the similar exchanges in the anonymous *Lust's Dominion, or The Lascivious Queen* (ed. Fredson Bowers, *The Dramatic Works of Thomas Dekker*, 4 vols. [Cambridge: Cambridge University Press, 1953–1961], 4), I.i, between Eugenia, the titular queen, and Eleazar the Moor, and in John Mason's *The Turk* (ed. Joseph Q. Adams, *Materialien zur Kunde des Älteren Englischen Dramas* [Louvain: Librairie Universitaire, 1913]), III.iv and IV.i, between Timoclea, another lascivious queen, and Mulleases, the titular Turk. Stallions ("stone-horses") were symbols of unbridled lust, which presumably rubbed off on the men who handled them and made these men so attractive to ladies. The idea survives today: in both Robinson Jeffers's "Roan Stallion" and D. H. Lawrence's "St. Mawr," a horse comes to represent true masculinity, and in "St. Mawr" the horse's grooms, Phoenix and Morgan Lewis, arouse the sexual interest of their upper-class employers, Lady Carrington and Mrs. Witt.

9. Compare Jachimo's account of "satiate yet unsatisfied desire" that "ravening first the lamb, / Longs after for the garbage" (*Cymbeline*, I.vi.48–50). These three categories could be combined in various ways. The early chapters of *The Arabian*

Nights include stories about the adultery of three lovely queens, the wives of Shah Zaman, King Shahryar, and the Prince of the Black Islands, with men who are slaves, black, and hideous (*The Arabian Nights*, trans. Richard Burton [Garden City NY: De Luxe Editions, n.d.], pp. 1–4, 31–33). And in *A Midsummer Night's Dream*, Titania, the delicate fairy queen, falls in love with Bottom, who is not only a laborer but also has an ass's head, although she is compelled by a magical potion and he seems to be asexual, since he is only interested in having her fairies feed and scratch him, and then in taking a nap (IV.i.5–39).

10. Heywood, I.ii, p. 106.

11. The same image is applied by Lear to the "simp'ring dame" who acts as if she has snow between her legs (*King Lear*, IV.vi.118–119), and in *Measure for Measure* Lucio says that Angelo's blood "Is very snow-broth" (I.iv.58) and "his urine is congeal'd ice" (III.ii.110–111). Compare the proverbial expression that "butter would not melt in his (her) mouth" (*The Oxford Dictionary of English Proverbs*, 3d edn., ed. F. P. Wilson [Oxford: Oxford University Press, 1970], 177a), and the Ward's comment on Isabella, another simpering dame, in Thomas Middleton's *Women Beware Women:* "See how she simpers it—as if marmalade would not melt in her mouth" (ed. Roma Gill, New Mermaids [London: Ernest Benn, 1968], III. ii.73–74). Hamlet's attitude may be related to the wishful fantasy of some children that after they were born their parents outgrew sex.

12. The chorus in *Pericles* is an individual, John Gower, but since he is supposed to be the real author of the story, his statements about it are supposed to be authoritative and reliable.

13. For a recent example, see Donald Hedrick, "Advantage, Affect, History, Henry V," *PMLA* 118, 3 (May 2003): 470–487. Roy Battenhouse even tells us that we should not rely on the prologue of Romeo and Juliet and must "decipher" its real meaning because he does not approve of the two lovers (Shakespearean Tragedy: Its Art and Its Christian Premises [Bloomington: Indiana University Press, 1969], p. 127).

14. I borrow the term "reliable narrator" from Wayne C. Booth, *The Rhetoric of Fiction* (Chicago: University of Chicago Press, 1961), chaps. 6, 10, pp. 149–168 and 271–310.

15. There are a few critics who dislike Prospero (much fewer than those noted earlier who dislike Henry V) and so have to explain away this speech. Thus John Cutts seizes on its length as evidence that it is unreliable: "Prospero is tediously striving to justify his actions to himself, to Miranda, and to the audience, and in so doing he metaphorically puts us to sleep. His oration would cure deafness if it were really persuasive" (*Rich and Strange: A Study of Shakespeare's Last Plays* [Pullman: Washington State University Press, 1968], p. 88).

16. The First Lord knows Jaques's reaction because of the dramatic convention that in a soliloquy a character is literally "thinking out loud" and so can be overheard—see James E. Hirsh, *Shakespeare and the History of Soliloquies* (Madison NJ: Fairleigh Dickinson University Press, 2003).

17. This may be related to the fact that Gertrude, unlike Ophelia and Hamlet, did not witness the event she describes. In fact, we are never told how she could have acquired such a detailed knowledge of it, which contributes to the impression that she is functioning here as an impersonal *nuntius*.

18. Compare the folk tales of the shoe-fitting contest of Cinderella and her two stepsisters, and the house-building contest of the Three Little Pigs.

19. There are exceptions. In one of the more amusing early episodes in the new historical turn in Shakespeare criticism, Francis Barker asserted that Hamlet is trying to achieve "interiority" but fails because of its "historical prematurity," since it only came into existence when the bourgeoisie came into power some eighty years later, and therefore "[a]t the centre of Hamlet, in the interior of his mystery, there is, in short, nothing," although this is "doubtless unknown to him" (*The Tremulous Private Body: Essays in Subjection* [London: Methuen, 1984], pp. 36–37).

20. I examine these shifts in greater detail in "Hamlet's Dramatic Soliloquies," in *Style: Essays on Renaissance and Restoration Literature and Culture in Memory of Harriett Hawkins,* ed. Allen Michie and Eric Buckley (Newark: University of Delaware Press), pp. 113–134, esp. 124–126.

21. See, for example, Eleanor Prosser, *Hamlet and Revenge* (Stanford: Stanford University Press, 1967), chaps. 4–5, and Battenhouse, chap. 4.

22. See Rebecca Smith, "A Heart Cleft in Twain: The Dilemma of Shakespeare's Gertrude," in *The Woman's Part: Feminist Criticism of Shakespeare,* ed. Carolyn Ruth Swift Lenz, Gayle Greene, and Carol Thomas Neely (Urbana: University of Illinois Press, 1980), pp. 194–210, esp. 200–201. She also tries to prove that Gertrude did not commit adultery (pp. 202–203), but that is not convincing.

23. The heart was supposed to be the seat of love (compare Claudius's reference to his soul, quoted later in this essay), just as the blood, we saw, was supposed to be the seat of sexual passion.

24. In the closet scene in Q1, unlike Q2 and F1, she agrees to help Hamlet in "What stratagem soe're thou shalt deuise" (lines 1596–1597), but nothing comes of this.

25. There are also productions of *A Midsummer Night's Dream* that indicate that Titania and Bottom have intercourse, even though, according to the text, he shows no interest in sex (see note 9). For two notable examples, see Glenn Loney, *Peter Brook's Production of William Shakespeare's "A Midsummer Night's Dream" for the Royal Shakespeare Company* (Chicago: Dramatic Publishing, 1974), p.61a, and the 1999 movie directed by Michael Hoffman.

Chronology

1564	William Shakespeare born at Stratford-on-Avon to John Shakespeare, a butcher, and Mary Arden. He is baptized on April 26.
1582	Marries Anne Hathaway in November.
1583	Daughter Susanna born, baptized on May 26.
1585	Twins Hamnet and Judith born, baptized on February 2.
1588–1589	First plays are performed in London.
1588–1590	Sometime during these years, Shakespeare goes to London, without family.
1590–1592	*The Comedy of Errors,* the three parts of *Henry VI.*
1593–1594	Publication of *Venus and Adonis* and *The Rape of Lucrece,* both dedicated to the Earl of Southampton. Shakespeare becomes a sharer in the Lord Chamberlain's company of actors. *The Taming of the Shrew, Two Gentlemen of Verona, Richard III.*
1595–1597	*Romeo and Juliet, Richard II, King John, A Midsummer Night's Dream, Love's Labor's Lost.*
1596	Son Hamnet dies. Grant of arms to father.

1597	*The Merchant of Venice, Henry IV* Part I. Purchases New Place in Stratford.
1598–1600	*Henry IV* Part II, *As You Like It, Much Ado About Nothing, Twelfth Night, The Merry Wives of Windsor, Henry V, Julius Caesar.* Moves his company to the new Globe Theatre.
1601	*Hamlet.* Shakespeare's father dies, buried on September 8.
1603	Death of Queen Elizabeth; James VI of Scotland becomes James I of England; Shakespeare's company becomes the King's Men.
1603–1604	*All's Well That Ends Well, Measure for Measure, Othello.*
1605–1606	*King Lear, Macbeth.*
1607	Marriage of daughter Susanna on June 5.
1607–1608	*Timon of Athens, Antony and Cleopatra, Pericles.*
1608	Death of Shakespeare's mother. Buried on September 9.
1609	*Cymbeline,* publication of sonnets. Shakespeare's company purchases Blackfriars Theatre.
1610–1611	*The Winter's Tale, The Tempest.* Shakespeare retires to Stratford.
1616	Marriage of daughter Judith on February 10. William Shakespeare dies at Stratford on April 23.
1623	Publication of the Folio edition of Shakespeare's plays.

Contributors

HAROLD BLOOM is Sterling Professor of the Humanities at Yale University. He is the author of 30 books, including *Shelley's Mythmaking* (1959), *The Visionary Company* (1961), *Blake's Apocalypse* (1963), *Yeats* (1970), *A Map of Misreading* (1975), *Kabbalah and Criticism* (1975), *Agon: Toward a Theory of Revisionism* (1982), *The American Religion* (1992), *The Western Canon* (1994), and *Omens of Millennium: The Gnosis of Angels, Dreams, and Resurrection* (1996). *The Anxiety of Influence* (1973) sets forth Professor Bloom's provocative theory of the literary relationships between the great writers and their predecessors. His most recent books include *Shakespeare: The Invention of the Human* (1998), a 1998 National Book Award finalist; *How to Read and Why* (2000); *Genius: A Mosaic of One Hundred Exemplary Creative Minds* (2002); *Hamlet: Poem Unlimited* (2003); *Where Shall Wisdom Be Found?* (2004); and *Jesus and Yahweh: The Names Divine* (2005). In 1999, Professor Bloom received the prestigious American Academy of Arts and Letters Gold Medal for Criticism. He has also received the International Prize of Catalonia, the Alfonso Reyes Prize of Mexico, and the Hans Christian Andersen Bicentennial Prize of Denmark.

DARYL W. PALMER is associate professor of English and department chair at Regis University. He is the author of *Hospitable Performances: Dramatic Genre and Cultural Practices in Early Modern England* (1992).

CAROLYN SALE is assistant professor of English at the University of Alberta, Edmonton. She has written on early modern jurisprudence, with particular reference to women, and Shakespearean drama.

AMY COOK is assistant professor of English at Indiana University, specializing in theatre history and cognitive approaches to drama. Her 2006 dissertation at the University of California, San Diego, was "Shakespeare, the Illusion of Depth, and the Science of Parts: An Integration of Cognitive Science and Performance Studies."

LINGUI YANG is a professor at Northeast Normal University, Changchun, People's Republic of China. His 2003 dissertation at Texas A&M University was "Materialist Shakespeare and Modern China." He annotated an edition of *King Richard III* (1997) and has written about Chinese approaches to Shakespeare's plays.

PAUL MENZER teaches English at the University of North Texas. His 2002 dissertation at the University of Virginia was "Crowd Control: The Corporate Body on the Renaissance Stage." He has written on theatre history, performance bibliography, early modern acting, and the material conditions of performance on the English Renaissance stage.

BRADLEY GREENBURG is assistant professor of English at Northeastern Illinois University. His 2001 dissertation at State University of New York, Buffalo, was "Shakespeare in China: A Comparative Study of Two Traditions."

MARIA DEL SAPIO GARBERO is professor of English literature at the University Roma Tre. She has written extensively, mostly in Italian, on a broad range of topics in her field. From 2003 to 2007 she was coeditor of *Textus: English Studies in Italy.*

SAYRE N. GREENFIELD is professor of English at the University of Pittsburgh at Greensburg. She wrote *The Ends of Allegory* (1998) and co-edited *Jane Austen in Hollywood* (second edition, 2001).

RICHARD LEVIN is professor emeritus of English at Stony Brook University. He wrote *The Multiple Plot in English Renaissance Drama* (1971), *New Readings vs. Old Plays: Recent Trends in the Reinterpretation of English Renaissance Drama* (1979), and *Looking for an Argument: Critical Encounters with the New Approaches to the Criticism of Shakespeare and His Contemporaries* (2003).

Bibliography

Allman, Eileen J. *Player-King and Adversary*. Baton Rouge & London: Louisiana State University Press, 1980.

Brown, John Russell, and Bernard Harris, eds. *Hamlet*. London: Edward Arnold (Publishers) Ltd., 1963.

Charney, Maurice. *Style in "Hamlet."* Princeton: Princeton University Press, 1969.

Cox, Lee Sheridan. *Figurative Design in "Hamlet": The Significance of the Dumb Show*. Columbus: Ohio State University Press, 1973.

Curran, John E., Jr., and James Nohrnberg, *Hamlet, Protestantism, and the Mourning of Contingency: Not to Be*. Aldershot, England: Ashgate, 2006.

De Grazia, Margreta. *Hamlet without Hamlet*. Cambridge, England: Cambridge University Press, 2007.

Dillon, Janette. *Shakespeare and the Solitary Man*. London & Basingstoke: Macmillan Press, 1981.

Edwards, Philip. *Hamlet, Prince of Denmark*. Cambridge, England: Cambridge University Press, 2003.

Eliot, T. S. *Selected Essays,* new edition. New York: Harcourt Brace, 1950.

Farley-Hills, David, John Manning, and Johanna Procter. *Critical Responses to Hamlet 1600–1900*. New York: AMS Press, 2006.

Fergusson, Francis. *The Idea of a Theater*. Princeton: Princeton University Press, 1965.

Fisch, Harold. *"Hamlet" and the Word*. New York: Frederick Ungar Publishing Co., 1971.

Flatter, Richard. *Hamlet's Father*. London: William Heinemann, Ltd., 1949.

Goodland, Katharine. *Female Mourning and Tragedy in Medieval and Renaissance English Drama: From the Raising of Lazarus to King Lear.* Aldershot, England: Ashgate, 2005.

Gottschalk, Paul. *The Meanings of "Hamlet."* Albuquerque: University of New Mexico Press, 1972.

Hiscock, Andrew. *The Uses of this World: Thinking Space in Shakespeare, Marlowe, Cary and Jonson.* Cardiff, Wales: University of Wales Press, 2004.

Holland, Norman N. *Psychoanalysis and Shakespeare.* New York: McGraw-Hill, 1966.

Jones, Ernest. *Hamlet and Oedipus.* New York: W. W. Norton & Company, Inc. 1949.

Joyce, James. *Ulysses.* New York: Random House, Inc., 1961.

King, Walter N. *Hamlet's Search for Meaning.* Athens: University of Georgia Press, 1982.

Knight, George Wilson. *The Wheel of Fire.* London: Methuen & Co., Ltd., 1949.

Knights, L. C. *An Approach to "Hamlet."* Stanford: Stanford University Press, 1961.

Kottman, Paul A. *A Politics of the Scene.* Stanford: Stanford University Press, 2008.

Lacan, Jacques. "Desire and the Interpretation of Desire in 'Hamlet.'" Translated by James Hulbert. *Yale French Studies* 55–56 (1977).

Lewis, C. S. "Hamlet: The Prince or the Poem?" *Proceedings of the British Academy* 28 (1942): 139–154.

Long, Michael. *The Unnatural Scene.* London: Methuen & Co., Ltd., 1976.

Mack, Maynard, Jr. *Killing the King: Three Studies in Shakespeare's Tragic Structure.* New Haven & London: Yale University Press, 1973.

Maher, Mary Z., and John F. Andrews. *Modern Hamlets and Their Soliloquies.* Iowa City: University of Iowa Press, 2003.

Nuttal, A. D. *A New Mimesis: Shakespeare and the Representation of Reality.* London: Methuen & Co., Ltd., 1983.

Prosser, Eleanor. *Hamlet and Revenge.* Stanford: Stanford University Press, 1971.

Robertson, J. M. *The Problem of "Hamlet."* London: George Allen & Unwin, Ltd., 1919.

Rose, Mark. *Shakespearean Design.* Cambridge: The Belknap Press, 1972.

Schwartz, Murray M., and Coppelia Kahn, eds. *Representing Shakespeare.* Baltimore & London: The Johns Hopkins University Press, 1980.

Semenenko, Aleksei. *Hamlet the Sign: Russian Translations of Hamlet and Literary Canon Formation.* Stockholm, Sweden: Stockholm University, 2007.

Siemon, James R. *Shakespearean Iconoclasm.* Berkeley & Los Angeles: University of California Press, 1985.

Waldock, A. J. A. *"Hamlet": A Study in Critical Method*. Cambridge: Cambridge University Press, 1931.

Watkins, Raymond Marion. *From Elsinore to Mexico City: The Pervasiveness of Shakespeare's Hamlet in Xavier Villaurrutia's Invitación a la Muerte*. Saarbrücken, Germany: VDM Verlag Dr. Müller, 2008.

Wilson, John Dover. *What Happens in "Hamlet."* Cambridge: Cambridge University Press, 1935.

Acknowledgments

Daryl W. Palmer. "Hamlet's Northern Lineage: Masculinity, Climate, and the Mechanician in Early Modern Britain," *Renaissance Drama*, Volume 35 (2006): pp. 3–25. Copyright ©2006 Northwestern University Press. Reprinted by permission of the publisher.

Carolyn Sale. "Eating Air, Feeling Smells: Hamlet's Theory of Performance," *Renaissance Drama*, Volume 35 (2006): pp. 145–168. Copyright ©2006 Northwestern University Press. Reprinted by permission of the publisher.

Amy Cook. "Staging Nothing: *Hamlet* and Cognitive Science." *SubStance: A Review of Theory and Literary Criticism*, Volume 35, Number 2 [110] (2006): pp. 83–99. Copyright © 2006 Amy Cook. Reprinted by permission of the author.

Lingui Yang. "Cognition and Recognition: Hamlet's Power of Knowledge," *Foreign Literature Studies/Wai Guo Wen Xue Yan Jiu*, Volume 28, Number 117 (February 2006): pp. 16–23. Copyright © 2006 *Foreign Literature Studies*.

Paul Menzer. "The Tragedians of the City? Q1 *Hamlet* and the Settlements of the 1590s," *Shakespeare Quarterly*, Volume 57, Number 2 (Summer 2006): pp. 162–182. Copyright © 2006 The Johns Hopkins University Press. Reprinted by permission of the publisher.

Bradley Greenburg. "T. S. Eliot's Impudence: *Hamlet*, Objective Correlative, and Formulation," *Criticism: A Quarterly for Literature and the Arts*, Volume

49, Number 2 (Spring 2007): pp. 215–239. Copyright © 2008 Wayne State University. Reprinted by permission of the publisher.

Maria Del Sapio Garbero. "Translating *Hamlet* / Botching Up Ophelia's Half Sense," *Textus: English Studies in Italy*, Volume 20, Number 3 (September–December 2007): pp. 519–538. Copyright ©2007 Maria Del Sapio Garbero.

Sayre N. Greenfield. "Quoting *Hamlet* in the Early Seventeenth Century," *Modern Philology: Critical and Historical Studies in Literature, Medieval Through Contemporary*, Volume 105, Number 3 (February 2008): pp. 510–534. Copyright © 2008 The University of Chicago Press. Reprinted by permission of the publisher.

Richard Levin. "Gertrude's Elusive Libido and Shakespeare's Unreliable Narrators," *SEL: Studies in English Literature, 1500–1900*, Volume 48, Number 2 (Spring 2008): pp. 305–326. Copyright © 2008 William Marsh Rice University. Reprinted by permission of The Johns Hopkins University Press.

Index